What People Are Saying About
Chicken Soup for the Nature Lover's Soul . . .

"I was introduced to rock climbing at age sixteen, three years after I'd gone blind. Feeling the texture of the granite, the patterns of hot and cold across the surface, and when I got up high, hearing the massive sound of open space all around me, I knew the adventurous life I'd thought was lost had instead only begun. Ever since then, as I've traveled the world climbing tall mountains, I've tried to breathe in as much joy and beauty from nature as humanly possible. That is why I'm so excited about the release of *Chicken Soup for the Nature Lover's Soul*. A book praising the life-giving powers of our open spaces is long overdue."

Erik Weihenmayer
world-class athlete and the first blind person
to reach the summit of Mt. Everest
author, *Touch the Top of the World: A Blind Man's Journey to Climb Farther than the Eye Can See*

"In this hectic, worry-filled world there are few places we can turn for peace, solitude and a soothing voice. *Chicken Soup for the Nature Lover's Soul* offers just such a refuge—an invaluable reconnection to the natural world that so many of us have lost, yet need so deeply."

Bill Thompson III
editor, *Bird Watcher's Digest*

"This is the book that you'll want to make room for in your backpack, or time for at the end of a hard day's work. These inspiring stories help you escape into nature and all of its magic, while weaving together words that will restore your faith in humankind."

Radha Marcum
editor, *Hooked On the Outdoors*

"I write about the outdoors for a living and, from time to time, I find myself so involved in the process of writing about nature that I forget why I'm writing. I started the book one night before I went to bed, thinking I could read a few stories each night and make the book last a couple of weeks. Instead, I stayed up until three in the morning and finished the entire book. The stories touched me deeply, and I found my mind wandering back to earlier days—fishing off the dock with my grandpa, backpacking on a grueling Colorado mountain trail with my daughter and nephews, eating my brother-in-law's lousy cooking on any of a hundred fishing trips. Like me, you might devour *Chicken Soup for the Nature Lover's Soul* in one sitting, or savor it at a slower pace. Either way, this powerful collection is sure to inspire you to cherish the great outdoors and all of its wisdom for a long time to come."

Mark D. Williams
outdoor writer and humble fishing expert

CHICKEN SOUP FOR THE NATURE LOVER'S SOUL

Inspiring Stories of Joy, Insight and Adventure in the Great Outdoors

Jack Canfield
Mark Victor Hansen
Steve Zikman

Health Communications, Inc.
Deerfield Beach, Florida

www.hcibooks.com
www.chickensoup.com

We would like to acknowledge the many publishers and individuals who granted us permission to reprint the cited material. (Note: The stories that were penned anonymously, that are in the public domain or that were written by Jack Canfield, Mark Victor Hansen or Steve Zikman are not included in this listing.)

Don Sheldon. [Our title for] "Regrets" from A LIFE ON THE ROAD by Charles Kuralt, copyright ©1990 by Charles Kuralt. Used by permission of G.P. Putnam's Sons, a division of Penguin Group (USA) Inc.

Manatee Meeting and *Jump, Mullet, Jump.* Reprinted by permission of Linda Ballou. ©1999, 1998 Linda Ballou.

Roaring River. Reprinted by permission of Suzanne English-Walker. ©1999 Suzanne English-Walker.

The Beech. Reprinted by permission of T. Edward Nickens. ©1999 T. Edward Nickens.

A Place Called Summer. Reprinted by permission of Douglas C. Rennie. ©1998 Douglas C. Rennie.

(Continued on page 355)

Library of Congress Cataloging-in-Publication Data

Chicken soup for the nature lover's soul : inspiring stories of joy, insight & adventure in the great outdoors / [compiled by] Jack Canfield, Mark Victor Hansen, Steve Zikman.
   p. cm.
ISBN 0-7573-0146-0
   1. Outdoor life—Anecdotes. 2. Nature—Anecdotes. I. Canfield, Jack, date.
II. Hansen, Mark Victor. III. Zikman, Steve.
GV191.24.C45 2004
796.5—dc22

2003068550

©2004 Jack Canfield and Mark Victor Hansen
ISBN 0-7573-0146-0 (trade paper)

Publisher: Health Communications, Inc.
         3201 S.W. 15th Street
         Deerfield Beach, FL 33442–8190

Cover design by Larissa Hise Henoch
Inside formatting by Dawn Von Strolley Grove

Every single story that nature tells is gorgeous.

Natalie Augier

We dedicate this book to all those
blessed by nature's wisdom and wonders.

Contents

3. OUR COMMON BOND

4. ON LOVE

5. THROUGH THE EYES OF A CHILD

6. A MATTER OF PERSPECTIVE

7. THE HEALING PATH

8. MAKING A DIFFERENCE

9. TO THE LIMIT

10. NATURE'S WISDOM

Foreword

My family ran a small dairy farm in Minnesota's prairie pothole country. The fields I knew as a child were dotted with isolated wetlands and bordered by wooded fence lines. Whenever I could, I roamed the countryside from pothole to fence line to woods in search of adventure. I built forts, trails and campfires, and discovered blackbirds, meadowlarks, ducks, foxes, snakes, gophers, bugs, deer, and yes, adventure.

One day when I was about eleven years old, I was working the cattle in the yard. Suddenly a long ribbon of big white birds appeared in the sky from the north, circling overhead then landing in a freshly plowed field behind the barn. Silhouetted against the stark landscape, they were the most spectacular creatures I had ever seen. And there were so many of them.

After a few minutes, something spooked them and they rose back up to the sky—eventually disappearing into the southern horizon and leaving me to wonder: What were they? Where did they come from? Where were they going? Why did they stop here? Why now?

I had seen a migration of snow geese—and a lifetime of curiosity about nature had begun. For the first time, I sensed that my own little piece of Earth was part of a much larger world; that, through the birds that graced us with their seasonal presence, all of us were connected as threads in a larger tapestry. Something changed in me, something that created a bond with nature that has lasted to this day. "Nature" was no longer just an intellectual concept: It had become personal.

Transforming experiences like this are common among people who love nature. I call them Wow! experiences; exhilarating moments that leave you speechless. There is one essential element common to all of the many Wow! experiences I've heard people talk about: They don't take place in front of a television, video game or computer screen—or even in a classroom. They happen out of doors, face-to-face with the real world, in the presence of birds and wildlife, amid the glorious unpredictability and spontaneity of nature.

Each of us is made up of the same particles as the rest of this Earth. There is something inside of us that longs to be connected back to nature. As a conservationist, I believe that I am a better person if I spend time outdoors enjoying nature. It is an essential part of my spiritual diet. And like other human instincts we don't fully understand, I believe this longing is connected to our survival.

That's why, for many people, enjoying nature leads them to want to learn more about it, and then to do something to protect it. I frequently ask people who are involved in conservation what got them hooked—what motivated them to become involved. The answer I hear most often points to direct experiences outdoors that created a personal bond with nature. It might have been summer camping trips with the family, biking, fishing, or just growing up in a rural area and roaming. They are emotional experiences, not intellectual experiences. Providing the opportunity for such experiences in nature is critical to inspiring people to value the natural world—and to protect it.

Conservationists tend to think big. We are drawn to great, expansive ecosystems. Places like the Arctic National Wildlife Refuge and the Everglades get our attention.

This is good, but there's another scale of conservation that's just as important to remember. Often, we need look no further than our homes, backyards and communities.

Whether you set up a feeder and watch birds, putter around the garden, or go for a walk in a local park, you're connecting with nature. We participate in these activities in staggering numbers. Gardening is one of the most popular outdoor activities. More than 70 million of us are birdwatching, up from only 18 million nearly twenty years ago, making birding the single fastest-growing outdoor recreation.

We do it because it's fun, but such things as gardening or feeding birds are simple ways each of us can start doing our part to save the planet, to give something back. There is much more we can all do, from participating in a local Christmas Bird Count to helping to protect local open space. You can begin right at home and in your yard, by planting less grass and more native species, using energy efficient appliances, buying certified wood, or even installing solar panels. Consider serving organic food or driving a hybrid car.

When you do these things, you're not just enjoying nature: you're also giving something back to it, helping protect it in a simple and direct way. Taken together, the actions by each of us in our own small, personal way means healthier habitats for people and animals.

The greatest untapped force for conservation is people like you and me, acting together, in the personal choices we make every day at home, at work and on vacation.

Most people want to do the right thing for the environment, if only they knew what to do. The answers need not be complicated, or even difficult. First, get out and enjoy nature. Experience it. Have fun. Then, learn more about it. Find a few simple ways you can do your part. Read books like this one. Check out the Audubon Web site, and the sites of many other organizations and agencies that make consumer information available. Then, act. Do your part.

It's our planet. Only we can save it.

John Flicker
President, National Audubon Society

Acknowledgments

The path to *Chicken Soup for the Nature Lover's Soul* has been made all the more beautiful by the many "companions" who have been there with us along the way. Our heartfelt gratitude to:

Our families, who have been chicken soup for our souls!

Inga, Christopher, Oran and Kyle Canfield, and Travis and Riley Mahoney for all their love and support.

Patty, Elisabeth and Melanie Hansen, for once again sharing and lovingly supporting us in creating another book.

Rob, for his sweet loving on each step of the trail. To Steve's parents, Thelma and Joel Zikman, for being there at every twist and turn with open hearts. To Steve's sisters, Janice Gritti and Susan Zikman, to Revo Gritti and Steven Wise, and to his nephews and nieces—Josh, Justin, Michael, Karissa, Meredith, Baylee and Rebecca—for all their joy and laughter.

Sandra and Desmond Fung, for their gentle support. To Lisa Carnio, for sharing the path with unconditional love, even from afar. And a special hug of loving thanks to Barbara Freeman and Lea Freeman, for their constant inspiration and wisdom.

Our publisher Peter Vegso, for his vision and commitment to bringing *Chicken Soup for the Soul* to the world.

Heather McNamara and Tasha Boucher, for producing our final manuscript with magnificent ease, finesse and care.

Thanks for making the final stages of production such a breeze!

Leslie Riskin, for her care and loving determination to secure our permissions and get everything just right.

Nancy Autio, Barbara Lomonaco and Gretchen Stadnik, for nourishing us with truly wonderful stories and cartoons.

D'ette Corona, for being there to answer any questions along the way.

Patty Aubery, for being there on every step of the journey, with love, laughter and endless creativity.

Maria Nickless, for her enthusiastic marketing and public-relations support and a brilliant sense of direction.

Patty Hansen, for her thorough and competent handling of the legal and licensing aspects of the *Chicken Soup for the Soul* books. You are magnificent at the challenge!

Laurie Hartman, for being a precious guardian of the *Chicken Soup* brand.

Veronica Romero, Teresa Esparza, Jesse Ianniello, Russ Kamalski, Robin Yerian, Stephanie Thatcher, Jody Emme, Trudy Marschall, Michelle Adams, Dee Dee Romanello, Shanna Vieyra, Lisa Williams, Gina Romanello, Brittany Shaw, Dena Jacobson, Tanya Jones, Mary McKay and David Coleman, who support Jack's and Mark's businesses with skill and love.

Bret Witter, Lisa Drucker, Allison Janse and Susan Heim, our editors at Health Communications, Inc., and their assistant Kathy Grant, for their devotion to excellence.

Terry Burke, Tom Sand, Lori Golden, Kelly Johnson Maragni, Randee Feldman, Patricia McConnell, Kim Weiss, Paola Fernandez-Rana, Elisabeth Rinaldi and Pat Holdsworth, the marketing, sales, administration and PR departments at Health Communications, Inc., for doing such an incredible job supporting our books.

Tom Sand, Claude Choquette and Luc Jutras, who manage year after year to get our books translated into thirty-nine languages around the world.

The art department at Health Communications, Inc., for

their talent, creativity and unrelenting patience in producing book covers and inside designs that capture the essence of *Chicken Soup:* Larissa Hise Henoch, Lawna Patterson Oldfield, Andrea Perrine Brower, Anthony Clausi and Dawn Von Strolley Grove.

Our tag team of associate editor interns for learning and for teaching, including Thuy Banh, Shari Barlia, Dena Bess, Jennifer Cecil, Cheryl Cheng, Carsten Cheung, Tabby Davoodi, Rebecca Elliott, Trina Enriquez, Michele Fitts, Emmy Gilliam, Cyndy Glucksman, Christine Guluzian, Jeanie Kim, Kim Kirkendall, Karen Lease, Eugene Lee, Marisha McGaffee, Melissa McKeown, Stephanie Neifing, Jung Park, Tammy Park, Jennifer Prakash, Sarah Pross, Krithana Ramisetti, Cindy Teruya, Lisa Turner, Chaniga Vorasarun, and Carrey Wong.

All the *Chicken Soup for the Soul* coauthors, who make it such a joy to be part of this *Chicken Soup* family.

Our glorious panel of readers who helped us make the final selections and made invaluable suggestions on how to improve the book: Fred Angelis, Madonna Auffant, Lisa Baker, Linda Beckwith, Dennis Berk, Cathy Calato, Lynette Charters, Nan and Jake Currie, Jack Dawson, Pim Dodge, Lorraine Drown, Julie Easton, Cory Fisher, Shirlee Fitleberg, Robert Fung, Donald Gurley, Le Anne Harper, Kitty Howe, Sylvia Hribar, Danny Kamen, Laurie Kinerk, Renee King, Dennis Lewis, Jean Marie Maxwell-Foote, Simone McGaffee, Carmen McKee, Kristie McLean, Ron Nielsen, Stasha Pozman, Mimi Richards, Kim Rosenthal, Donna Schilder, Gila Shapiro, and Susan Zikman. Your feedback was a gift!

Terry Moore, for his determined attitude and a renewed sense for the adventure, beauty and fragility of life. Terry was an avid outdoorsman and writer who was a great inspiration during the course of putting together this collection. He died of cancer at thirty-two, leaving behind his wife, Suzy, and their two young sons, Ben and Brett.

The many extraordinary organizations and publications that helped spread the good word about this book, including:

www.GORP.com, Jeff Beckham at *www.greatoutdoors.com*, Tim Hamill at *www.alloutdoors.com*, Jeff Blumenfeld at *Expedition News*, Irene Rawlings and Angela Keane at *Mountain Living* magazine, Walter Rivers at *Big Sky Journal*, Bill Thompson III at *Bird Watcher's Digest*, Dave Pegg and Alison Osius at *Climbing Magazine*, Tom Shealey and Jim Gorman at *Backpacker*, Steve Madden and Ellen Wagner Carpenter at *Outdoor Explorer*, Emma Kendell at *On Your Bike* magazine, Denise Damiano Mikics at *New Jersey Outdoors*, and Dennis C. Knickerbocker at *Michigan Out-of-Doors*.

South African Airways and Marcus Brewster Publicity, for helping us reach places afar.

Janice Lasko and Kay Peterson at *Escapees* magazine, Eugene Buchanan at *Paddler*, Jessica Riback at *Sports Afield*, Jim Seymour at the American Canoe Association, Michele Jin at *Passionfruit*, Tracy Puckett at *Outdoors Unlimited*, Tony Stucker at *Trips* magazine, Wendy Ballard at *Doggone*, Ann Wallace at *TravelScoop*, June Kikuchi at *WildBird*, Barbara Leonard at *Trailer Life*, Brenda Steiner at *Lively Times*, Corey Schlosser-Hall of Wilderness Inquiry, Deborah Weirick at Children Affected by AIDS Fund, Roger Brunt at the North American School of Outdoor Writing, Jody Newman of the League of American Bicyclists, and Page Crosland at Rails to Trails.

Andrea Lagomarsino at O.A.R.S., Peter Grubb at River Odysseys West, Brian Konradt at Freelancing for Money, Kathy Ptacek at *Gila Queen's Guide to Markets*, Marshall Whitfield at *www.writersmarketplace.com* and Nicole Bishop at *www.writerfind.com*.

Ryan Mucatel at Alan Taylor for T.E.A.M. Challenge, Blue Magruder at Earthwatch, Brett Harvey at the American Society of Journalists and Authors, Beverly Hurley at the Midwest Travel Writers Association, Joyce Banaszak at Minneapolis Writers Workshop, Bradley Kirkland at the Writers Club, Amber Vogel at the *Journal of African Travel Writing*, Ishbel Moore at the Canadian Authors Association, Eileen King at Outdoors Unlimited and the Outdoor Writers

Association of America, Cathy Kerr at the Society of American Travel Writers, Penny Porter of the Society of Southwestern Authors, and James Plouf at *www. Travelwriters.com.*

And, most of all, thanks to everyone who submitted their heartfelt stories, poems, quotes and cartoons for possible inclusion in this book. While we were not able to use everything you sent in, we know that each word came from a magical place flourishing within your outdoor soul. May the spirit of nature carry you gently toward peace.

Because of the size of this project, we may have left out the names of some people who contributed along the way. If so, we are sorry, but please know that we really do appreciate you very much. We are truly grateful and love you all.

Introduction

Everybody needs beauty as well as bread,
Places to play in and pray in,
Where nature may heal and
Give strength to body and soul alike.

John Muir

Nature has always been my sanctuary. A couple of summers ago, I was desperate for a break and decided to head up
to Canada where I grew up. I thought carefully about what I
wanted to do and came up with the perfect three-pronged
prescription.

First stop: Algonquin Park, three hours north of Toronto.
It's the quintessential Canadian experience—5,000 square
kilometers of remote lakes, linked by often-grueling
portages.

Rob and I picked up our gear at Algonquin Outfitters. Bill
Swift started the business in the early '70s, and the sign in his
office said it all: "If you are grouchy, irritable or just plain
mean, there will be a $10 charge for putting up with you." It
was actually an apt description of old Bill himself, who had
recently passed away and whose son Rich was now running
the shop along with his wife, his mom and a battalion of outdoor enthusiasts. They decked us out with everything we

would need for our five-day trip: food, tents, sleeping bags and, of course, a lightweight Kevlar canoe.

While I had been paddling since I was a boy, it was Rob's first canoe adventure. We put in at Canoe Lake and, with each stroke, forged a watery path into the wilderness, cutting our ties to the stresses of everyday life. At the far end of the lake, we carried the canoe and our packs on the first of many portages from one body of water to the next—ten lakes in all, plus myriad creeks and swamps with names like Otterslide Creek, Big Trout Lake and Grassy Bog. By day, we steered past blue heron, beaver dams and bullfrogs. At night, we slept under shooting stars and the Big Dipper. We endured rain, cold, mud and mosquitoes, but by the time we made it back to the shores of Canoe Lake, we were refreshed and revitalized. Nature does that.

Our next stop was Killarney Mountain Lodge on the uppermost tip of Georgian Bay in northern Ontario. Our hosts, Jennifer East and her parents, Maury and Annabelle, built this easygoing retreat in the 1960s and have managed to retain its rustic charm. We spent three days at Killarney, enjoying the surrounding natural beauty at a much more relaxed pace.

With Captain Bob and his wife Diane, we sailed on the forty-six-foot yacht, *Stormy Night,* taking in views of Killarney Ridge and the spectacular La Cloche Range of rugged, pink granite and shining, white quartzite. We were told that this is the only place on Earth where one can find striped maple trees.

We disembarked on Philip Edward Island in West Desjardins Bay where we hiked the Chickinishing Trail and painted watercolors of the windswept pine trees that grace the landscape. In the boat's guest book, I read an entry from a woman named Susan: "Ran from civilization and found true beauty here." Nature does that.

Our final stop was Toronto where we explored the city's wide array of green space: ravines replete with raccoons, birds and squirrels, a fresh herb garden on the roof of the seventy-five-year-old Fairmont Royal York Hotel, and the forty-acre waterfront Music Garden opened by Yo-Yo Ma and inspired by undulating riverscapes, wildflower meadows and forest groves of wandering trails. Nature does that.

Nature presents itself in a variety of forms, and we can connect with its many wonders in myriad ways. From the serene to the very extreme, each story in this book is about that essential connection. Whether you are scaling a summit, camping with friends, floating peacefully along the river's edge or resting in a hammock in your own backyard, nature offers incomparable moments of exhilaration and adventure, beauty and awe, serenity and healing.

As you read each story in this book, we hope that you too will be inspired to get out there and savor all that Mother Nature presents.

Steve Zikman

Share with Us

We would love to hear your reactions to the stories in this book. Please let us know what your favorite stories were and how they affected you.

We also invite you to send us stories you would like to see published in future editions of *Chicken Soup for the Soul.* Please send submissions to:

Chicken Soup for the Soul
P.O. Box 30880
Santa Barbara, CA 93130
fax: 805-563-2945

You can also visit or access e-mail at the *Chicken Soup for the Soul* site:

www.chickensoup.com

We hope you enjoy reading this book as much as we enjoyed compiling, editing and writing it.

1

POWERFUL PLACES

If we can somehow retain places where we can always sense the mystery of the unknown, our lives will be richer.

Sigurd F. Olson

Don Sheldon

*It is always worthwhile to sit or kneel at the face
of grandeur, to look up into the placid faces of
the earth gods and feel their power.*

John Burroughs

Of all the flyers into whose hands we have placed our
lives, Don Sheldon is the one I'll always be most thankful for.
We had heard of him before we met him. Everybody in south
central Alaska had heard of him.

Wandering around Alaska one spring, we thought we'd
take some pictures of Mount McKinley-Denali, the great
mountain of the continent. On clear days, the old giant can
be seen from a hundred miles or more away, but as usual, we
wanted close-ups. We drove to Talkeetna, the village that has
always served as headquarters for expeditions to McKinley
and was best known as the home of Don Sheldon, the fabled
mountain pilot.

He turned out to be a slender, unassuming man with
thinning hair. He wore a plaid shirt, army pants and work
boots. *Very modest-looking,* I thought, *for a legend.* He said he
was free for a couple of days, and we engaged him to fly us
up to the mountain. As we helped him roll his ski-equipped,

single-engine Cessna out of the hangar, he made gentle jokes
about the dangers of mountain flying.

"Never know what we'll run into up there," he said, shaking his head and smiling. "You sure you boys want to do
this? Well, let's fuel 'er up then."

I noticed he pumped his gas through a chamois strainer.

Light, fluffy cumulus clouds floated above the Alaska
range when we approached, Izzy riding beside Sheldon up
front, and a soundman named Stan Roginski strapped in
behind with me. Izzy thought it would make a wonderful
shot to fly through a cloud straight at the mountain with the
camera rolling, so that when we came out of the cloud, the
sunlit peak of McKinley would appear suddenly and
dramatically.

"Let's try that cloud over there," Izzy said, and the mountain scenery tilted dizzily as Don Sheldon banked one way,
then the other, to oblige. We flew toward the mountain
through one cloud after another. Izzy was never satisfied
that we had captured quite the desired spectacular effect.
There were a lot of clouds to try, and we tried most of them.
I found myself gripping the armrests and trying to keep my
breakfast down each time we broke through into the sunlight, steered straight for Mount McKinley and veered
sharply away at the last minute.

"Let's try that one over there," Izzy said, pointing to yet
another cloud close to the peak.

"If we try that one," Don Sheldon said, "it will ruin my
reputation."

"What do you mean?" Izzy asked.

Sheldon said calmly, "That one's got rocks in it."

"Look," I said, "is there someplace we can set this thing
down for a while? Maybe we need a rest."

"I know just the place," the pilot said, putting the plane
over on one wing again and tilting the nose sickeningly
downward. "I think I even brought along a Thermos of coffee
for you boys. We'll take a coffee break."

He set the plane's skis for landing, dropped the flaps and,

a few minutes later, brought us to a bumpy stop in the snow in a big curved bowl, an ice field of the Ruth Glacier.

When Sheldon shut down the engine and we stepped out into the sunlight, I was nearly blinded by the brilliance of the white world surrounding us. The glacier formed a vast, silent basin surrounded by massive slopes, a universe of ice and rock. Range upon range of mountains stretched before us into the measureless distance, and behind us, towering almost straight up from the ice field, rose Denali itself, with snow blowing from its summit thousands of feet overhead.

After a long silence, one of us said, "Good God!"

"Yep," Don Sheldon said, "I've always sort of liked this place myself."

We spent a long time just standing there before we remembered we were supposed to be taking pictures. Don Sheldon tramped about thoughtfully in the snow while we worked.

When it was time to go, he had a little news for us.

"Good news and bad news," he said. "The good news is that the sun hasn't gone down yet, and I can still get this plane out of here and back home before dark.

"The bad news is that the sun has made the snow so mushy that I can't take off with all of you on board."

I gulped, "You can't?"

"Nope," he said. "Too much weight. Best I can do now is take one of you back to Talkeetna, and maybe some of your gear. Two of you are going to have to spend the night up here, I'm afraid. I'll come back for you in the morning."

I looked around, imagining the nighttime temperature on the glacier. Also imagining wolves and polar bears.

"Nothing up here to hurt you," Don Sheldon said. "I'll dig a couple of sleeping bags out of the plane for you."

While he was doing so, he added, "Oh, and you won't have to be alone either." He nodded toward a rocky outcrop about a mile away at the edge of the ice field. "You can't see it from here, but there's a cozy one-room cabin on the other side of that rock. Some of the climbers use it for a base camp.

There's a Catholic priest in there now on some kind of a retreat. He's a nice guy. Father Ron is what I call him. He's been up here a while. He won't mind a little company."

I was still letting all this news sink in, about the necessity for two of us to spend the night in this wilderness, and then about there being a cabin in this unlikely place, and not only a cabin, but also a priest . . .

I heard Izzy say, "I'll stay." He shouldered his camera and the tape recorder and took one of the bedrolls. Then I heard myself say, "Sure, I'll stay, too." Don Sheldon handed me the other roll of bedding and a long length of rope.

"Better rope yourselves together when you walk over there," he said. "You know. Crevasses. See you tomorrow."

He climbed into the pilot's seat with Stan beside him, started the engine and began his takeoff run down the glacier. The plane lifted off and turned toward home. We watched until it vanished among the mountains.

Izzy tied one end of the rope around his waist and handed me the other end, regarding my 220-pound bulk doubtfully. "If one of us falls into a hole in the ice," he said, "it better be me, I guess." We started across the glacier with the setting sun casting our shadows a hundred yards ahead of us and creating imaginary hidden crevasses every few steps.

It must have taken us nearly an hour to make it off the ice and into the rocks of the mountain. When we started up, we could see a big, red-bearded man wearing a bright parka coming down toward us, carrying a coiled rope of his own over one shoulder, and in his hand, a staff. He looked like a Biblical prophet of the mountains.

"Good afternoon, Father," I said.

"Never mind the Father blather!" he boomed cheerily. "Sorry to be late in greeting you! The truth is, I wasn't expecting company! Haven't seen another soul since sometime last month! Here, let me carry some of that load for you."

He talked loudly all the way up the hill, not stopping even to ask where we had come from and what we were doing there. It had been weeks, I guess, since he had heard the sound of his own voice.

"I suppose Don Sheldon dropped you off," he said, "unless you took a wrong turn on a stroll in Anchorage and hoofed it up here. Don likes to show off his shelter. He built it himself, you know. He got tired of climbers freezing in the storms. Tough work, you know, having to fly their bodies back down and all, so he flew a few loads of lumber and nails up here—and here we are. Welcome to our humble abode!"

The cabin was small, six-sided and half-buried in snow. Inside, sleeping shelves were built up off the floor under a ring of windows. A wood stove squatted in the center of the room with a fire crackling inside. That's all there was to the place. It looked very good to me.

"I am pleased to offer you northern exposures with a view of the mountains," Father Ron said, dumping our bedrolls on the shelf. "All the exposures have a view of the mountains. The menu tonight is stew. That is the menu every night." He walked outside, dug around in the snow for a black iron pot full of beef and beans, came back in and set it on the stove.

"Dinner will be served shortly," he said, "but first the cocktail hour." From his duffel bag on the floor under the shelf, he produced a bottle of Christian Brothers brandy. "We like to support the brothers in their good work," he said. He unscrewed the cap and passed the bottle ceremoniously to Izzy to drink first.

Over tin bowls of stew, Father Ron told us that he had come to Alaska seeking solitude in the loneliest place he could find. Somebody in Talkeetna had told him about the Mount McKinley shelter, and he had talked Don Sheldon into flying him up there. He was escaping a critical bishop in Boston or someplace. He said this sojourn in the mountains was partly for religious reflection and partly for figuring out what to do with his life.

"Well," I said, "I guess it doesn't help your solitude much for a couple of strangers to show up at dinnertime and stay all night."

"I am very glad to have your company," Father Ron said solemnly. "I've never been alone for so long before. Let me tell you what I have discovered about being alone: It is a great gift, but it is damned lonely."

I laughed.

"But now," Father Ron said, "the after-dinner show! Look over your shoulder."

In the sky behind us, a faint white light was shimmering. It grew brighter, changed to a shade of purple, then pink and suddenly shot in a streak to the dome of the sky. Izzy and I stood up and stared through the window.

"*Aurora borealis*," Father Ron said. "It is Latin, meaning 'the northern dawn.'"

I had seen the northern lights before, glowing dimly on some northern horizon. This was different—a display of brilliant pastels that trembled over the silhouettes of the mountains, a big Wurlitzer jukebox in the sky. Ripples of color rose in layers from bottom to top and unexpectedly sent bright streamers flying so high that we had to draw close to the window to see where they ended above our heads.

"Charged particles from the sun entering the atmosphere of the Earth," Father Ron intoned. He was used to the show.

"If you gentlemen will excuse me, I am going to retire," he said, and soon he was snoring lightly in his sleeping bag. But Izzy and I sat there on the shelf through the short subarctic night watching those bright rivers of light transform the dark world. For one night only, we had the best seats on the planet for nature's most spectacular show. It faded away only with the rising of the sun. Both of us were left awed and exhausted. Neither of us has ever been able to describe that night adequately to others, though we did our best to tell Father Ron what he had missed as soon as he awakened.

"Very good, very good," he said, with a sort of pride of ownership. "We do our best to satisfy our guests in this inn. How do you take your coffee? Black, I hope."

We were just roping ourselves together at the edge of the ice field when Don Sheldon's silver Cessna appeared overhead, turned upwind and landed. Father Ron helped carry our gear out to the plane. He took off his mittens to shake hands. Izzy and I climbed aboard, waved once and left the big, bearded prophet standing there on the glacier, alone again with only God to talk to. I have not seen or heard of him since. I hope he worked it all out up there in the mountains, but I have no way of knowing.

"Pretty nice night?" Don Sheldon asked over the engine noise.

"It was okay," I said. "Not a very good place to sleep though, what with the lights coming in the window."

He chuckled. "I thought you might not mind it up there," he said. "I haven't seen every place, but it's the prettiest place I've ever seen."

"Well," I said, "me, too. How can I ever thank you, Don?"

He said, "Don't thank me. I wanted to take you home with me last night. Thank the soft snow on that glacier."

That's what he said, but I wonder. I wonder whether Don Sheldon sized us up as a couple of guys who thought we were in a bigger hurry than we really were and would benefit from a night to slow down and look around and think about this place where we were.

I can't ask him. Don Sheldon had cancer then, knew he had it and died less than a year later. You can find his name on the new Geological Survey map of Mount McKinley, printed in small letters on a white patch that represents the ice field where he landed us for coffee and wouldn't take us home until we'd spent the night, the place he said was the prettiest he'd ever seen. The beautiful, big white bowl of the Ruth Glacier where the northern lights put on their show every night is forever named the Don Sheldon Amphitheater.

Charles Kuralt

Manatee Meeting

Full to bursting, the sea accepts, widens our reception. We are overflowing and the sea contains us. And then when we are stretched, when we are broadened, opened up to a new life, the sea gives us back to ourselves.

Susan St. John Rheault

Walking alone on a remote beach in southwest Florida, I was startled to hear splashes and a deep sigh coming from the water just offshore.

As I squinted in the direction of the sounds, the rounded gray back of a sea creature rose amid a red froth, rolled turbulently at the surface, then sank back into the Gulf. Moments later a broad nose emerged and exhaled in a great snuffling breath. It was a manatee, and by the looks of the reddish-colored water and the way it was thrashing, it was in trouble.

I had often watched manatees in these warm coastal waters, but I'd never seen one act like this before. Usually just their big nostrils appear for a gulp of air as they forage on sea grasses or swim slowly to greener underwater pastures. But I also knew how common it was for these

lumbering giants to be gashed by boat propellers or en-
tangled in crab traps.

I wanted to help, but what could I do? There was no one
else on the beach, and the nearest phone to call the Marine
Patrol was miles away.

Tossing my beach bag onto the sand, I began wading
toward the animal, who continued to writhe as if in distress.
I was still only waist deep when I came close enough to make
out the bristly whiskers on the manatee's muzzle as it thrust
up out of the sea. Then, to my surprise, a second muzzle,
much smaller, poked up beside it.

I pushed on through the shoal water, but now the manatees were also moving toward me. Before I knew what was
happening, I was in chest-deep water encircled by not one or
two, but at least three blimplike bodies. I felt elated and
slightly dizzy like the kid who is "it" in a schoolyard game.

A bulbous snout emerged next to me. In the translucent
water, I could clearly see the rest of the huge mammal, and
there, nestled close behind her, a smaller version of her massive body.

Then, with incredible gentleness for such an enormous
creature, the larger manatee nudged the little one with her
paddle-shaped flipper and pushed it to the surface beside
me. I wanted to reach out and touch the pudgy sea baby, but
I hesitated, not knowing the rules of this interspecies
encounter.

As the two slipped back underwater, two other manatees
moved in from behind and slid by, one on either side, rubbing gently against my body as they swam past. They circled
and repeated the action, this time followed by the mother
and her calf. Emboldened by their overtures, I let my hand
graze the side of the small manatee, now clinging to the
mother's back, as they made their pass. Its skin felt rubbery
and firm like an old-fashioned hot-water bottle.

The group completed several more circuits. Since they
obviously enjoyed touching me, I began stroking each of
them as they sidled by. When one of them rolled over for

a scratch, I knew I had made the right move.

Eventually, my new friends made their way off toward deeper water. I stood anchored to the spot, not wishing to break the spell, until finally the rising tide forced me back to shore.

I suppose I will never know exactly what took place that morning. I like to think that the manatees included me in their celebration of a birth; that I was welcomed to meet the newest member of their tribe. But over time I have come to cherish the experience without questions.

During that unexpected rendezvous, I felt more in tune with the rhythms of life on this vast planet than I ever have. The memory has become a song I sing to myself when I have the blues, a dance I do to celebrate joy.

And each year, during the last week of May, I pack a lunch and head for that isolated stretch of beach for a quiet little birthday picnic on the shore. After all, you never know who might show up for the party.

Linda Ballou

Roaring River

If people concentrated on the really important thing in life, there'd be a shortage of fishing poles.

Doug Larson

During the summer of 1977, my husband Bill and I, along with our two sons, eight-year-old Ryan and five-year-old Jon, headed off for a week-long tour of the state parks in southern Missouri.

Being from the flat lands of Illinois, we had heard much about the beauty of the Ozarks' hills and valleys, and we were not disappointed.

The last park we visited was Roaring River State Park. The river was cold, clear and stocked with trout. It was here that my husband and sons discovered fly-fishing. As novices, they didn't bring many trout home that trip, but I did manage to take quite a few pictures.

When we got home, we vowed to go back to Roaring River as soon as we could, and over the next six years, we visited many times. Every March first we trekked out for the opening day of trout season, and it was a given that we would also spend our summer vacations there. With each trip, Bill

and the boys got more proficient at fly-fishing, and I
continued to take photos of their progress.

In 1983, Bill had a chance to transfer to the Ozarks region,
and six months later, we relocated to Springfield, only sixty
miles from Roaring River. Now every weekend could be
spent doing what we all loved. Many times I would receive a
call from the high school telling me that the boys had
skipped school again, and I always knew where to find them.
There they were, standing side by side on the banks of the
river, oblivious to anything or anyone around them. Life was
good.

Time went by, and the boys grew up. Ryan went into the
service and was stationed in Louisiana, where he did some
fly-fishing on Toledo Bend Lake. Jon got married, started college and had a beautiful baby girl named Kylee. Over the
next years, he also held a full-time job and his marriage came
to an end, but he still continued to go fishing with his dad
and brother.

Then, one cold morning in December of 1994, Jon woke us,
complaining of a deep and agonizing pain in his abdomen.
We rushed him to the hospital. The doctors ran many tests
and finally gave us the dreaded diagnosis: liver cancer. He
was only twenty-two.

Jon quit work and school and was put on a routine of
chemotherapy treatments. Between therapies, he set out to
do things he had wanted to do for a long time. He took several trips out west and spent a short time in Montana, where
he promised to return someday to fly-fish the blue-ribbon
trout streams.

Then one evening in 1996, Bill and I attended a movie
called *A River Runs Through It,* the story of a father and two
sons living in Montana who fly-fish every chance they get.
We walked out of the theater unable to control our emotions.
We looked at each other and immediately decided that,
somehow, we were going to get Jon to Montana that
summer.

I did some research on the Internet and found the best

places to fish. We scraped together the money we had and borrowed the rest. When we told Jon, he was thrilled. Ryan was expecting a baby at any time and regrettably was not able to join us.

We rented a cabin about fifty feet from the Madison River. Before we even had the car unloaded, Jon was at the river's edge.

Bill and I walked down to watch him. He was totally at peace and in his element. It was just Jon, his pole and the rushing river. It was as if time stood still. There was no cancer, no sadness. There was just Jon and a river full of trout.

We spent two wonderful weeks together. Although we had little money, we hired a guide to take Jon and Bill up to the high mountain lakes to fish for wild trout.

A year later, after his last round of chemo, Jon was tested again, and all signs of cancer were absent. He was in remission.

The next months were filled with happiness and plans for the future. Jon had met a wonderful young woman, Brandy, who had a two-year-old son, Isaac. He, Brandy, Isaac and Kylee went everywhere together. Kylee loved to fish beside her dad, and Jon was teaching Isaac how to fly-fish. He and Brandy made plans to get married in June of 1999.

Suddenly, in the late fall of 1998, Jon's cancer came back. He continued to lose weight, and in December we found out that the cancer had spread to his brain. He started radiation treatments, which caused him to have seizures. He was down to 120 pounds on his six-foot, one-inch frame.

Through all of this, he never lost his hope or his sense of humor. He was bald, and one of his friends sent him a clown wig. He sat up in his hospital bed, put the wig on and smiled from ear to ear for my camera.

He was able to leave the hospital for a brief period in the spring, and the wedding was moved up to May. Several days before the wedding, Jon rallied and seemed to be getting stronger. The wedding was held outdoors, in Brandy's parents' yard—a very simple ceremony with only family and close friends in attendance.

In June, we made our last trip with Jon to Roaring River. He couldn't fish for very long, but fish he did. He stood stock-still while waiting for that elusive trout to bite. Weakness didn't deter him from the rhythmic cast of his fly rod. A slight breeze rippled across the clear, deep stream as we watched him drink in the sights and sounds of this area that he loved so much. It was as if he knew this would be his last trip there.

On July 12, 1999, our son Jon passed away quietly with his family by his side. Services were held in an abandoned country church overlooking the Ozark hills, as he had wanted.

When you are raising children, you never know what you expose them to that may shape their entire lives. A chance trip to Roaring River introduced our boys to fly-fishing. It gave them a lifetime of camaraderie, brotherly love and communion with nature. As Jon once shared, "I never feel closer to God than when I'm in the middle of a trout stream."

This past March first, Ryan took Isaac to Roaring River for opening day of trout season just as he, Jon and their father had done so many times in the past. Isaac caught three trout; his dad would have been so proud of him.

The torch has been passed.

Suzanne English-Walker

The Beech

We do not remember days, we remember moments.

Cesare Pavese

I grew up in the woods behind the house of my childhood, a fifty-acre sprawl of wildness firmly situated within the city limits of High Point, North Carolina. Anyone could tell you where "the woods" were, for there the neighborhood kids converged each day after school and all day long in the summer. We built leaf forts and log forts, underground forts and tree forts. We caught snakes and frogs and terrible colds. We swore alliances and broke our trusts. We learned to love and to lie while we defended our allies, attacked our enemies, and wrought—or so we thought—pure havoc on the free world.

A creek trickled between our yard and the edge of the woods and formed a sort of border between a world of parents and grades and acne cream and a world we had all to our own. We lent it the same cartographical significance as we did the woods: "The creek," it was.

In our woods grew an ancient beech tree with a trunk squat and fat like the belly of an old man. Its once-smooth bark was gnarled and pocked and scarred with carved dates and slashed initials. The names of lovers and loners were there, the names of kids who walked to the elementary school up the hill or to the high schools on the other side of Lexington Avenue. There were the initials of little boys who prowled the woods before little girls and driver's licenses stole their attention, and—who knows—the initials of fugitives on the lam, the last wild Indians, a bogeyman or two, or any of the myriad creatures that populate the imaginations of young boys in the woods.

Some carvings are difficult to read, for the years have misshapen the knife blade's route, the trunk bulging and stretching and cracking with age. I remember, though, the oldest date we could discern: "1918," carved deep into the bark alongside indecipherable initials, a date that, to adolescent boys, seemed inconceivably long ago.

There are other initials on the old beech tree, signs and wonders whose import, like the very carving, is incomprehensible. And high on that trunk—or as high as we could reach—are the chiseled letters: "WW."

There are, we still are fond of saying, only two "Wolverine Warriors" in the world. From second grade through twelfth, Timmy Lassiter and I walked to school along the knobby, rooted paths of the woods—and the Wolverine Warriors knew those paths better than any of the other neighborhood kids. We knew which part of the woods held more rabbits and where most of the squirrels lived. We knew which trees to climb for the best view of enemy territory, which paths provided the best escape routes when under attack. We used birdcalls to communicate; we hid our love letters in hollow stumps. We knew where the best Christmas trees grew, and where a small Confederate camp was attacked by a band of marauding Yankees. Yankees, we thought, in our own backyard.

Timmy and I could hardly have known that those simple letters would brand us for life. They've given us a tangible symbol of commitment, one that we feel in the rough bark of memory now that years and miles keep us apart. We'd sworn to be blood brothers, but neither of us could bear to slash a palm or even prick a finger. Instead, we each dug a single "W" into the tree. Just as Timmy was finishing, the knife slipped and sliced through the tip of a finger. Blood poured from the gash, and he smeared it in the freshly carved initials, turning to solemn brown the fresh cream-colored cuts in the tree.

For years I told my friends that we bravely slit our fingers to seal our pact. This is the first time I've told anyone the truth.

It's a crazy sort of thing to remember, I suppose, and an unlikely symbol of one's childhood. But from that day to this, Tim Lassiter and I (only his mother calls him Timmy now) have never turned our backs on the friendship we swore to on the old beech tree.

And my love affair with woods has never faded.

Most of us remember the woodlots of our childhood, places of respite from a world that seemed too quick to cancel our dreams. Vacant lots where the robins nested, granddaddy's farm, the backyard treehouse, a corner in the attic—all these were woodlots of one sort or another. They were places of respite, of renewal, or of outright escape from Mama after you'd sassed her from across the street.

That old tree in my woodlot still stands, although the surrounding woods have largely been reduced to fake colonial homes and cul-de-sacs. There still are paths through the remaining trees, but you can see clear through the thickets now, from border to shrinking border. No longer could a little boy hide in those woods, press himself deep enough into the brambles that the world on the other side of the creek disappears. But the tree still stands. Some little boys might stare up at the letters "WW" and wonder what they mean, run their fingers across the date "1973" and think that seems inconceivably long ago.

As for Tim and me, fax machines and e-mail keep us posted. We have followed different paths from our common woodlot, trails at times rough with differences, trails that now lead much closer than ever before. We still use the lessons we learned from the woods. When crossing streams, we choose our steps carefully. When choosing sides, we look long across the stream. We love whenever we can, and we lie when we must. And we still wreak havoc on the world, or so we think.

I've found other woods now, larger woods, where the deer aren't imagined and the borders aren't near. It seems I've made a life of looking for woodlots—searching for places and people passed over by the rest of the world. I hunt for untold stories, tales like forests untouched by saw or backhoe, for lands and lives grown old with years and vision. Only in woods large enough to lose your way can you truly find it.

But in all my wanderings, there is only one ancient beech tree, trunk fat and squat, in the woods of reminiscence. I return to that stone-strewn ground on occasion, either to leave behind bits of my boyhood—another chunk of innocence lost, one more dream tarnished and bent—or to try to find the boyhood I left behind. The paths through the woods don't seem nearly as wide as they did when I was a child; the trees aren't as tall as I remember.

Except for the beech. It is still there, large as it is in my daydreams. Carved on its face are the initials of little boys, but from its roots spring the souls of men.

T. Edward Nickens

A Place Called Summer

My daughter is quiet beside me in the front seat, until at last she sighs and says, with a child's poetic logic, "This reminds me of the place I always like to think about."

Barbara Kingsolver

While re-reading Ray Bradbury's classic coming-of-age novel *Dandelion Wine,* I get to the part where the book's main character, twelve-year-old Douglas Spalding, wakes up to "a sound which was far more important than birds or the rustle of new leaves . . . the sound which meant that summer had officially begun . . ." It was the sound of the lawnmowers starting up.

I put the book down and let my mind meander through my own preteen summers long, long ago . . .

Summer days, when I was a boy, meant baseball. I'd get up early, work a few drops of Neat's Foot Oil into the smooth, black pocket of my Rawlings Duke Snider glove, load my bat into a hollow metal cylinder that I had jury-rigged to my bike frame, then pedal off to some sun-washed, freshly mowed grass field to punch out singles, steal bases and run down fly balls until the sky turned indigo.

The warmest mornings found me on the downtown pier, my wormed hook tempting jacksmelt and walleye as I sat, feet dangling over the side, reading *Tarzan* and the complete *Hardy Boys* series.

But the best part of my boyhood summers was the two weeks each August that I spent in the mountains with my sister, mother and new stepfather in a cabin he had built himself. In this summer world, the sun rose out of a ravine, passed languidly over the shaded cottage and slid down behind a forested ridge, leaving stars in full command of the ink-dark mountain sky.

Behind the cabin was a creek that I never found the end of. Wearing my P. F. Flyers, I walked on water by jumping along on partly submerged rocks. My favorite spot was a half-mile upstream where the water branched off into three deep, black, boulder-enclosed pools.

That's where the frogs lived—some green like leaves, others almost black, and all of them slippery and slick. I would catch them and giggle when they'd squirm and croak and pop their eyes out like they were plugged into something. Sometimes, I made faces back at them and moved them through the water while making speedboat sounds. Eventually, I'd toss them back in and set off again on my streamside odyssey, brushing aside images of looming September.

Summer was special then, as much a *place* as it was a season.

It was a place where you could do endless cannonballs and can-openers off the high board and slosh about aimlessly in the big "plunge" without obsessing about SPF factors. A place where your eyes could track that girl who sat next to you in class all year—and who now looked so different in a swimsuit—knifing through the big pool's opals and turquoises, her long hair streaming behind her. A place where you could grin at your mom through a watermelon mustache, sleep out in the backyard (in the days before air-conditioning made every season the same), and set off sparklers and night crawlers on the Fourth.

In summers past, almost everything of delight occurred outdoors.

One evening, as I lay outside in the cool mountain air looking up at the shooting stars that passed every night like fiery line drives, my mom would say, "Make a wish, honey."

I would try, of course, but it was tough to come up with one.

Everything I could think of to wish for was already there—all around me.

Doug Rennie

Alaska Time

My prayer is that Alaska will not lose the heart-nourishing friendliness of her youth—that her people will always care for one another . . . and that her great wild places will remain great and wild and free.

Margaret Murie

My husband Greg worked the Bristol Bay salmon season every summer. For years Greg had urged me to join him with the kids, and when our youngest turned three, I said, "Yes."

I imagined six weeks in a cozy cabin with a lush landscape outside our door, the perfect escape from the tedious deadlines, duties and responsibilities that had become our life. The kids and I watched the movie *The Wilderness Family* and saw a happy clan sawing logs and saving a baby cougar. Adventure beckoned! With anticipation we flew to King Salmon, Alaska.

Greg arrived at the airport in a battered truck. Wedged together in the cab, we bounced down a highway of potholes. The tundra stretched before us, flat and peculiar, the sky a vault of scattered clouds. There were no discernible features to orient ourselves. No rise of peaks or spine of hills to navigate with. My eyes slid uninterrupted to the wide horizon. I drew a breath and looked away.

We pulled into a rutted drive and lurched to a stop before a structure that vaguely resembled a trailer.

"Here it is!" Greg said. "Home! I have to get back to the boat. I'll see you in the morning."

He gave big hugs of encouragement and left us standing in the dust with our bags as we watched him drive off.

Home was a truck container. Someone had cut windows from the sides, called it a trailer and set it upon a scraped-off patch of tundra. We stepped gingerly on the plastic fish box that comprised the threshold to the door.

"This can't be it!" our nine-year-old daughter cried. "I could never, ever live here!"

It smelled like a swamp on a warm day. Greasy towels hung on a rack. The faded sofa was missing a leg. The water ran tea-colored from the faucet, and to our horror we discovered a strange trumpet-shaped lichen growing from the carpet of the bedroom. Home sweet home!

I rolled up my sleeves and went to work while the kids fled outdoors to dig rivers and channels in the dirt that was our yard.

The days unfolded endlessly; there was no darkness at this latitude. The light did strange things to our appetites, to our sleeping habits. Bedtime became a battle when the sun called my children out to play at midnight. Squalls blew in and, to the kids' delight, filled their river world with currents of water joining mud, skin, clothing and children in a happy marriage of mess. The mosquitoes drove us like cattle from tundra to trailer to car. In the evenings bears nosed around the margins of the trailer searching for garbage. We had twenty hours of available light to see what had become of my Wilderness Family.

One sun-filled night I hung clothes on a line strung between scrub alders, then sat down to watch the kids play baseball with neighboring children. They moved the bases around in the dirt at will. The three-year-old was allowed ten strikes. One girl declared that older boys could hit only within the base lines or they were out. She glanced over at me.

"You wanna play?" she asked.

I shrugged, thinking there was something else I should do.

"She's a good player!" my son cried.

I smiled. I hadn't played since high school, but I rose to the plate.

"Batter up!" the girls shouted.

I hefted the bat . . . pitch . . . and swung. A home run deep into the tundra.

I was in league with the big boys now. We played for hours under that midnight sun, laughing and shrieking, changing rules, shaking the dust from our bodies. Suddenly, I was a girl again, unfettered and breathless with the crazy fun of it all.

The next morning, I changed the rules. Our days would be governed by the urges and appetites of our bodies, not the clock. We began to rise at whatever time we woke, eat when we were hungry and sleep when we were tired, even if that meant dinner at ten and bedtime at two. Problems that seemed overwhelming a few days earlier suddenly fell away, and the weeks stretched long, empty of duties. We called it Alaska Time.

With Alaska Time I became a willing ear for listening to worries and dreams. My arms were idle for holding, for pouring plaster in bear tracks, for throwing a baseball. Once again, my newly opened eyes could see the treasures available to children: Mud. Boundless light. Midnight drives to watch caribou graze and eagles wheel in the sky.

Alaska Time is watching a radiant sunset at home and naming the stars that bloom in the heavens. Alaska Time is when the rules change, the dishes wait, the phone goes unanswered.

Alaska Time is in the words, "Yes, I want to play!"

Nancy Blakey

Goose Island

My children call it Goose Island, although "island" is an obvious exaggeration. A little rock pile with a half-dozen scraggly shrubs, it doesn't even appear on most charts. At high water it measures less than six feet by twenty.

The goose part is accurate, though. Every spring, for the past fifteen years, a pair of Canada geese has chosen the rock pile for its nesting site. But not just any spot on Goose Island will do. Each year they form their nest in exactly the same location, a little indentation between a couple of flat rocks on the highest point above the water line.

Mother Goose gathers small twigs and vegetation to frame the nest, then plucks down from her breast to create a soft lining. Two flowering dogwoods provide a little camouflage, and by maintaining her perfectly immobile stance, she is able to escape detection. Fishermen regularly pass within yards of her hiding place, unaware that she is there.

One spring, I decided to visit Mother Goose regularly, while she incubated her eggs. My early-morning, five-minute paddle to the island was a great way to start the day. I always brought a few crusts of bread on these visits, which the nest-bound mama would hungrily devour. While she was busy filling up on the bread, she would allow me to examine her nest and its contents—six large white eggs.

By the second Saturday in May, she had been sitting on the eggs for twenty-four days. She greeted me with less civility than usual and was especially protective of her nest area. As she reached for a piece of bread, I discovered the source of her newfound surliness—a number of grayish-yellow fluffballs peeked out from beneath their mother's breast.

Five adorable baby geese filled the nest, but it was the egg that caught my attention.

Normally, all the eggs in a clutch hatch within hours of each other. While Mama gave me suspicious glances, I slowly lifted the remaining egg from the nest and held it to my ear. No sounds came from within, so I gave the egg a gentle shake, expecting it to be empty. To my surprise, I could feel something inside. I realized that the gosling had not been strong enough to break from its shell and had probably exhausted itself in the effort.

Carefully, I cracked the egg on a rock, not knowing what to expect. Inside was a wet mess of down, with a bill at one end and two gangly grey feet at the other. There was no sign of life.

Using my shirt, I lightly patted the pathetic creature dry. The head hung limply. There was no response to my coaxings, so I placed the unfortunate bird in amongst its brothers and sisters and resigned to let nature take its course.

The next morning, I awoke early. It was Mother's Day.

As my daughters and I prepared a special breakfast for my wife, I couldn't help but think about the gosling that hadn't been strong enough to escape its shell. I decided to paddle over to the islet after breakfast and bring a Mother's Day breakfast for Mother Goose to help her celebrate the birth of her quints.

As I headed toward the canoe, bread in hand, I was greeted by a marvelous sight—Mama Goose and all *six* of her goslings lined up behind her.

She had come to show off her brood and, just maybe, to let me know my efforts had not been in vain.

Tom Lusk

Catfishing with Mama

And in the end, it's not the years in your life that count. It's the life in your years.

Abraham Lincoln

My mother was a fishing fanatic, despite her Charleston, South Carolina, blue-blood upbringing. When she was twenty she graduated magna cum laude from the College of Charleston and left that city of history and suffocating social rules forever. With the twenty-dollar gold piece she got for the Math Prize, she bought a railroad ticket for as far west as it would get her. Austin, Texas, was $19.02 away.

There she met my father and proceeded to have seven children—all girls. She also took up fishing, and by the time I was born, she had enough tackle, lawn chairs and fishing hats to fill a steamer trunk. To my father's horror, her favorite lure was blood bait. Bass and catfish were her prey.

Every summer it was my mother's custom to pack the seven of us girls into the DeSoto and drive from Austin to Charleston to visit our grandparents. We camped and fished the whole way.

Mama's preparations for the fifteen-hundred-mile trip consisted of packing the car with seven army cots, a basket of

Stonewall peaches and sixteen gallons of live bait, with her tackle box and assorted rods and reels thrown in. Her idea of successful traveling was to get us all in the car without one of us sitting on the blood bait or being left at a gas station. Once she'd done a head count and ascertained the security of the bait, she'd drive like A. J. Foyt until it was too dark to go any farther. This meant we were usually tired, hungry and lost on some back road in the middle of Louisiana or Mississippi when we stopped to camp.

"Stopping to camp" in our case meant suddenly swerving off the road when my mother spied a river or lake that stirred her sporting blood. She never once planned our stops like normal people do, timing themselves to arrive at a campsite or park around dusk. But this was the 1950s, when people still slept with the screen door unlocked and left the keys in the car. We felt perfectly safe at any roadside area, and we were.

The trip that brought us face to face with history was the one we took in the summer of 1958 when I was ten.

Three days into the journey found us somewhere in the mountains of Kentucky. I was never quite sure where we were at any given point on these trips, since I knew only one landmark—the tree-lined road to my grandparents' house— the finish line. But again, we had driven for hours into the night futilely looking for water. When we finally pulled off the road, the hills around us were black as midnight under a skillet. Then a slice of a quarter moon slid out from behind a cloud and delicately illuminated a rock gate in front of us.

"Oh, look," Mama cried, "a national park!"

There was an audible sigh of relief from the back seat. "Let's camp here, Mama!" we clamored urgently.

Since she had been slapping her cheeks for the last hour to stay awake, she agreed.

We cruised down a black dirt road into the parking area. Nestled nearby was the outline of a log cabin. Beyond that, the glint of water.

"See that!" Mama said excitedly. "A sleeping cabin. By some kind of lake. This is paradise."

We parked and unloaded the car, dragging our stuff into the log cabin.

It was open and empty. We could see it was very old and rudimentary, but it had a bathroom with running water. For us it was luxury quarters. We bathed and ate our dinner of kipper snacks and soda crackers, with Moon Pies for dessert. Then we snuggled into the cots that we'd fixed up in the one bare room.

Mama set off with long strides toward the water, gear in hand. The faint murmur of her voice as she conversed with her tackle box drifted through the open windows. With that and a cozy roof overhead, my sisters curled up and fell to sleep like a litter of puppies.

I picked up my rod and reel and, still in my pajamas, slipped quietly out the door. Across the damp grass I could see my mother's silhouette making casting motions. For a moment I felt the thrill of anticipation inherent in fishing: There was a fat catfish with my name on it waiting out there, I just knew it.

I joined my mother, and we fished together, just us—the water and the quarter moon. It was one of those moments that form a permanent part in the book of parent-child memories, although it was destined to be brief.

Mama could practically conjure up fish to her, and sure enough, within half an hour she got a strike and brought in a fourteen-pound cat.

Probably my Fat-Cat, I thought irritably.

"Look," she said, bending around me, her hands grasping mine as I held my rod. "Let me show you . . ."

She made a deft flicking motion, and suddenly my line shot across the water. The light of the moon made it look like the trail of a shooting star. It fell silently on the dark water and disappeared.

"Right there," she said lowly. "Hold tight to it."

She turned away and began cleaning her fish. I gripped

the rod until my knuckles were white. I had a feeling for what was coming. Suddenly, the line lurched tight, and my arms shot forward. I almost flew into the black water of the lake.

"It's a big one, Mama!" I yelled. "I don't think I can hold it." My feet were slipping down the bank, and the mud had oozed up to my ankles. "Mama, quick!"

She grasped me around the waist and yanked me back up the bank. The pull on the line lessened.

"Now! Bring it in now!" she shouted.

I reeled in as hard as I could. Suddenly, the fish was right there below me, lying in shallow water. It was a big one, all right. Almost as big as Mama's.

"Good work," she said, leaning over and carefully pulling the catfish onto the bank. It slapped the wet grass angrily. I was exhausted. We took our fish back to the cabin and fell into a deep sleep.

It seemed only minutes later that our sleep was penetrated by voices. Lots of voices. Suddenly, the door of the cabin burst open, and sunlight and a large group of people led by a woman in a uniform flowed into the room. The uniformed person was in the middle of a speech.

"And here we have the boyhood home of President Abraham Lincoln—aagghhhhh!"

We all screamed at once. My mother, protective in her own quixotic way, leapt off the cot, her chenille bathrobe flapping, and shouted at the intruders, "Who do you think you are, bursting in on a sleeping family like this?"

The guide was struck speechless. She gathered herself with visible effort. "Ma'am, I don't know who you are, but this is Abraham Lincoln's Birthplace National Historic Park," she reported tersely.

Her eyes quickly shifted sideways to take in two huge catfish lying on the floor. Although she tried to conceal it, her lips pursed with disgust. I knew right off she wasn't a fisherman.

"And his lost cabin," she continued, "is not an overnight

stopover for fishing expeditions. This is a restricted area with guided tours beginning at 7:00 A.M. and . . ."

"Oh my God, we overslept!" Mama shouted. "Pack the car, girls. We've got to get on the road!"

We lurched into a flurry of experienced cot-folding and were out the door in seconds.

"But ma'am," the guide called at my mother's disappearing back, "you weren't supposed to sleep in here. This is Lincoln's Log Cabin. It's a National Treasure!"

"We treasure our night here," my mother shouted back, as she gunned the car around. "Abe wouldn't have minded."

With that we roared off in the direction of South Carolina. I saw a sign as we left: "Leaving Hodgenville, Kentucky, Abraham Lincoln's Birthplace. Y'all Come Back."

"Not likely," my mother laughed. "A good fishing spot, but I hate to do anything twice, don't you?"

And that's how it happened that, during the summer I was ten, the course of history was changed. Unofficially, to be sure, but if there had been a historical marker by that lake, it would now have to read: "Abe Lincoln Fished Here . . . and So Did I."

Lin Sutherland

Burroville

It is not down on any map; true places never are.

Herman Melville

Back in 1974, when I was in my early twenties, I befriended a group of hikers who were mapping a desert trail from the Mexican to the Canadian border. Offering to try a few routes for them through Death Valley, I made the drive to a base camp near Ulida Flat, where I camped for the night.

At first light, I started my trek up an alluvial fan into an unnamed canyon in the Cottonwood Mountains. After about an hour of hiking through the rock-strewn wash, I made my way deeper into the shadows, and the bray of a burro told me I wasn't alone. With slow, careful steps, I rounded a bend and found myself in Burroville—population: 100. I looked around and saw that the majority stood in little groups along the slopes, while several others were perched atop the perpendicular cliff walls.

I continued walking and was soon met by an imposing welcoming committee—a dozen big Jacks with massive heads, standing shoulder to shoulder and daring me to approach. Although they stood a good thirty feet away, their resolute stance and effective blockade of the canyon ahead made me pause a while to consider my next move. I'd never heard of anyone being killed by a burro, but it was clear they had no plans to let me pass.

Several moments went by until one of the big Jacks pawed at the ground with his hooves and another looked behind him, as if to check the rear for a surprise attack. That's when I saw what the burro was actually looking at . . . a Jenny and nursing foal standing close beside the canyon wall about twenty feet back. Our eyes met, and the female's flanks shuddered as she watched me with a wariness that only a true wild thing can display.

When I lifted my gaze to scan the slopes behind her, I was surprised to see other females and their young, planted in groups of two and three all around me. Suddenly, I realized it was the time of year for foals to drop, and the big males were merely protecting their mates and babies. I must have let out a big sigh, because one of them pricked up his ears and raised his head as if waiting for me to speak.

"Don't worry, guys. I'm just passing through," I called gently.

No response, just a flutter of flanks and a few ear twitches. Clearly, the subtle approach wasn't working, so I picked up a rock and lobbed it near the biggest Jack. It fell at his feet, and he lowered his head to sniff it.

Clearly, the burro had no intention of moving, so I reluctantly turned and began to make my way back down the wash in defeat. That was when a loud bray made me about-face once more.

To my surprise, the big Jacks were lumbering out of the wash and making their way toward the northern walls of the canyon. Now, only the biggest of them remained at the edge of the bank, staring at me. Suddenly, the way was clear; I'd won the standoff. I started up the canyon, but was stopped by the look in the burro's great brown eyes. As we stood there staring at each other, a shudder passed through me.

In that instant the message he sent me became clear: He

was asking me to leave the canyon—politely, and with some measure of supplication, but plain as day. And I knew then I couldn't go on, couldn't violate his trust. So I turned and headed back down the canyon.

As I retreated, I considered my role in creating a desert trail that hundreds of hikers would traverse each year. Today's unknown route through a rugged canyon might well become a dotted red line on some future map. Was it so important that people knew about this place?

I began to think it wasn't.

Maybe what this Earth really needed was a few more unnamed canyons. Maybe there's some intrinsic value in knowing that some mountains will never be climbed, that a handful of jungles will remain unexplored. Must we really clamber up every alluvial fan, map every desert canyon, and slap a name on every dry lake and rocky outcropping?

Perhaps, in the end, it's enough just knowing they're out there—somewhere.

John Soennichsen

$\overline{\underline{2}}$

WILD AND FREE

*A*ll *good things are wild and free.*

Henry David Thoreau

River Baptism

You will do some foolish things, but do them with enthusiasm.

Colette

The summer I turned thirteen, my family's summer vacation was a visit to our relatives in the mountains of North Carolina. My cousin Jim, who was my age, took me down to his favorite swimming hole along the river. It was a deep pool under a high canopy of leaves. From the top of a twenty-five-foot cliff, we looked down into the shimmering water and across to a sandy beach.

Standing beside us on the edge of that cliff grew a big white oak tree, with its roots sunk deep down into the rock. And hanging from a limb that stretched out at just the right height and angle was a rope swing.

"Look here," said Jim. "This is the way you do it. You got to get a running start. Then you grab the rope and swing out and up as high as you can, and then you let go and fall to the water. Here, I'll show you."

Jim made it look easy, and when his head surfaced in the bubbling water, he hollered up, "Now it's your turn!"

I was certain I was going to die, but at thirteen dying is

better than looking bad. When I came up sputtering, Jim smiled approvingly, and we swam a few strokes to the beach, lay on the hot sand for a while, and then swam back across the pool to do it again.

Jim and all of his friends always wore the proper North Carolina swimming attire, because skinny-dipping was a time-honored tradition among boys throughout the mountain states. Sometimes I felt like I was a wild boy, or a beaver sliding through the water. Jim said he felt like an otter, since he loved to turn and twist in the deep pools and could swim underwater a long way.

Jim's family was Baptist. On Sunday, Jim's mom made us dress up in straight-jacket white shirts and stranglehold ties, marched us down the street and filed us into church.

"You must be baptized, by water and by the Spirit!" the preacher thundered. That water baptism sounded mighty good. I sat there dreaming of the river and waiting for the wonderful moment when the sermon would be over, and Jim and I could go running down the path to the river.

On the tails of the closing prayer, Jim and I flew out into the sunny day and home for a quick sandwich. Then we plunged down the trail into the woods alive with the hum of cicadas hanging thick in the branches of the burr oaks and hickories.

When we got within a hundred yards of the rope swing, Jim said, "I'll race you!"

"You got it!" I replied.

We dropped our clothes right there and tore down the trail to see who could get to the rope swing first. I was a fast runner, but Jim was faster. He pulled ahead of me and dove for the rope. With a shriek of victory, Jim swung out over the water and up, to the very top of the arc. In perfect form, Jim let go of the rope and looked down to see where he was going to land.

But there—not twenty yards away on the beach—stood the preacher and two dozen of the faithful, performing a baptism. I could see they were looking straight up at Jim with their mouths wide open.

As fervently as Jim prayed to fly, he quickly descended from the heavens. Jim abandoned his plans for a graceful swan dive and instinctively assumed the cannonball position—known for its magnificent splash.

The whole congregation got baptized that day, but Jim never saw it. He broke his record for underwater swimming and was around the bend and out of sight while the congregation stood stunned and speechless on the shore.

"Don't worry, Jim," I consoled him later. "I'm sure everybody thought you were an angel, and besides, it turned out fine. You got the river dunking you wanted, and those folks will *never* forget that baptism."

Thinking about it now, I don't think there's much difference, anyway, between wild boys and angels, or between heaven and a rope swing on the river.

Garth Gilchrist

Pumpkin

At first she wouldn't let me close, wouldn't let me see her tag. Every day she sat near me on the beach, her shiny buff coat blending in with the sand.

She used to be the neighbor's dog, until she was abandoned and left to fend for herself. And then, from her spot on the sand, she discovered me and my kayak.

Each day I would get into my boat and paddle off. The clear water goes from pale blue to deep bottle green, and I can see the kelp moving like a hula girl, waving through schools of small silver fish, reaching up to the reflection of clouds dancing on the glassy surface.

As I paddled above rocks covered with mussels and starfish, looking for dolphins, I would see her: an aging Golden Lab following me along the shoreline. Her huge webbed feet made it awkward for her on the sand.

Often, when I tired in the kayak, I would stretch out in the boat on my back. This day I bobbed around in the ocean just beyond the surf break, watching pelicans as they hovered above.

It was peaceful out there, listening to the water lap and the seagulls fight over a morsel on a rock. I was completely relaxed, drowsy from the sun and the lull of the waves, when I heard a distinct labored breathing.

Something bumped the boat, something heavy in the water next to me. Disorientated and suddenly fearing the worst in the form of a shark, I bolted upright, setting the boat rocking, looking for the oncoming fin.

It was Pumpkin.

She was just as wild-eyed until she saw me. I realized that she had come to find me. When I'd lain back in the boat, I disappeared from her view, and she came to the rescue, a wet, blonde Lassie. The clumsy gait that had made her so ungainly on shore was gone as she fluidly swam around the kayak, a serene look in her big brown eyes. From that moment on, she was my dog.

Years went by, and Pumpkin's health failed her on every level but one: She could still swim. It was heartbreaking to watch her navigate the stairs and sand, but I let her do it, knowing the freedom that the water brought to her.

One Saturday, Pumpkin was having a hard day, and I locked her behind the gate so she wouldn't overdo it. I headed out in the kayak, slicing through small green waves and bubbles of white foam, and came across a pod of dolphins relaxing just beyond the break.

I lay back in the boat as they drifted nearby, their delicate puffs of air meshing with the tranquil sounds of the beach.

Then I heard another creature's breath and the familiar bump on my yellow kayak. Pumpkin. She had broken through the gate and dragged herself across the sand the moment I reclined in my kayak.

She still watched over me, swimming out to the friend she had chosen. The dolphins didn't seem to mind. Like a beautiful surreal dream, three species gently floated together on top of another world.

Pumpkin died later that year. I sprinkled half of her ashes on the sand where we met, and then I paddled out, releasing the rest into the ocean that set her free.

Jewel Palovak

Camp Air

Those who contemplate the beauty of the Earth find reserves of strength that will endure as long as life lasts.

Rachel Carson

Last summer I found myself in the Santa Monica Mountains, hiking among chaparral, canyon sunflower and wild rabbits with Roberto, an eleven-year-old boy who has AIDS. In his hand he clutched a clear plastic jar, and together we were looking for something to put in it.

Every August, children affected by HIV and AIDS come to this summer camp in the majestic headlands of Malibu, California, and find a sanctuary. Camp Pacific Heartland is a typical summer camp, free from the social misunderstanding these kids face elsewhere. There they can enjoy the same opportunities that other children have for learning and playing in nature.

We had given each camper a clear plastic jar at the beginning of their visit and encouraged the kids to place mementos and souvenirs from their week at camp into their jar, creating a collection of memories to enjoy at home.

Roberto excitedly showed me what he had already

collected: a rock he found on a nature hike, a flower that was growing outside his cabin, and a Polaroid photo of him and some new friends on carnival night.

"What else would you like to put in the jar?" I asked.

He looked around at the brown and green hills, down to the dark blue sea where we had seen a pod of playful dolphins the day before, and took a deep breath. Then he paused, laughed a bit and said, "Camp air."

I knew what he meant. If Roberto could crack open that jar sometime during the long year ahead and take a deep breath of fun, love and support, then maybe the tough drug regimen he was on, the painful loss of his parents years ago and the ongoing struggle to live in a society that still cannot completely embrace him—well, maybe these obstacles would be a little easier to handle.

Camp air smells like the morning mist from the ocean and the afternoon sun on the mountains. It comes from the glee of children. It is part hilarity, part tears. It has the aroma of safety and freedom. It contains a brush of colored chalk on the sidewalk, a flash of disco lights on dance night, a taste of macaroni and cheese in the cafeteria, a few notes of a camp song.

I laughed with him, and together we screwed the lid on tight and held the jar up to our eyes. There was the rock, the flower and the picture—and, swirling around, I swear I could almost see inside Roberto's precious supply of magical air.

Lisa Cavanaugh

Last Outing

I looked out of my tent, and the snow was coming down so hard that I couldn't see a thing. It was blowing sideways and had already drifted up one side of my tent. It was cold, very cold. It must have been twenty or thirty degrees below zero. Why was I out there?

Snow in Michigan by the first of November is not unheard of, but this was a downright blizzard. I was sure this would be an all-time record. Thirty-two degrees and a foot of snow can be a beautiful, pleasant experience. This was not!

What is it about me that makes me do these things? Why do I take these chances? I love the outdoors, the sounds of the wild, the sunrises and sunsets, everything that you can only experience by getting outdoors and camping. I have all of the equipment to stay warm and dry in any weather, but this was ridiculous.

I was wishing that I had not ventured out that weekend, but there I was, and I was going to have to survive! The wind was making my tent snap and flap so hard and so loud that sleep was totally out of the question. My goosedown sleeping bag was supposed to be good to minus ten degrees, but I was already shivering quite a bit.

My last meal had been the night before, and it was going on 11 A.M. I hadn't eaten any breakfast, and I didn't have anything with me in the tent. My energy wouldn't last much longer.

My wife, Amy, was probably worried about me, too. She had warned me last night that it was going to be cold and windy. She is so loving that I know she would have joined me if I had asked her to. But I told her not to bother, that I just wanted to get this one last outing out of my system. She was probably snuggled up in front of the fireplace with a good book. I wished I were with her. I had carried a couple of my magazines along thinking I would read by flashlight, but I was too cold to enjoy reading about bass fishing.

With that thought, I knew I had to get out of there. My original plan was to try to wait out the blizzard, but I realized that wouldn't work. I was cold, and I was hungry. I would freeze or starve to death before this one was over. But how should I do it?

Should I try to take everything with me? I hated to abandon my equipment, but it would have taken too long to break down the tent, and the sleeping bag is too bulky if it isn't rolled up tight and stuffed in its bag. My hands were too cold to do that, and it's almost impossible to do with gloves on. I was sure my things would be all right here for a while. I would carry what I could and leave the rest behind.

I took another peek out the flap, and a blast of wind with tiny ice darts smacked me in the face. This wasn't going to be as easy as I thought. At thirty below your skin can freeze in a matter of minutes. Once that happens, well, I wasn't going to think about that . . .

I was ready to make a run for it. I wasn't in great shape, and I couldn't run far, but I was afraid that if I walked I would freeze before I got there. I looked around inside the tent one last time to make sure I wasn't forgetting anything critical. It took a couple of seconds to get my glove around the tent zipper, but when I did, it jerked straight up to the ceiling, and I bolted out into the frozen landscape.

The snow was deep, but light. I kicked my way through the snow. How far would I have to run? Could I make it all the way? I was almost out of breath when I hit the back door of the house and burst through.

"Hi, honey, how did you sleep?" asked Amy. "I thought that bit of snow and wind we had last night might have woken you up sooner. Are you going to bring the tent in from the backyard, or will you want to sleep out again?"

James Hert

Pepper

I think I could turn and live with the animals;
they are so placid and self-contained.

Walt Whitman

Rounded heaps of soft, white sand reflected the milky moonlight, making the large hyena den a bright stage instead of a deep, black pit. I parked the truck about fifteen yards from the den entrance, switched off the lights and stared at the empty hole, wondering if they were still alive.

Only a few nights before, their mother Star, whom we had known for many years, had been killed by two lions. The three brown hyena bundles—Pepper, Cocoa and Toffee— were now orphans, their bodies thin and their mouths dry. Time and the Kalahari were stealing the last of their strength.

Alone, without a phone or radio, I could make out the glow of our campfire flickering against the trees more than three miles away. Eventually, three small, dark and fuzzy heads peeped out of the center hole—little hyena periscopes scanning the surface for any sign of danger. Sensing nothing unusual, they crawled cautiously from the den and plodded slowly around the area, sniffing old, dried bones. At last, when their mother never arrived with food, they moved slowly back into the den.

The next night both Mark and I went reluctantly to observe what would surely be their last night. We sat quietly under the brilliant desert sky, observing the empty mounds of sand.

Suddenly, a soft rustle sounded in the bush, and into the clearing walked the cubs' aunt, carrying the remains of a large rodent. She walked to the entrance of the den and purred loudly until the weak and hungry cubs emerged. They circled her with excited squeals, grabbed the handout and ran inside to feed in the security of their den. We sat stunned. We had just witnessed "adoption" of brown hyena cubs, a behavior never previously observed by man.

During the following nights, their half-brother, aunts and female cousins brought them scraps and carrion, and they became strong and playful once more. Each afternoon, I would check them out, but after weeks of cub-watching from the truck, I felt too detached in my man-made vehicle. I wanted to feel the same sun and wind, experience the same smells, sounds and sights as my young companions.

So one day before the cubs made their appearance, I stepped quietly from the truck and sat on the ground in full view and waited. The cubs had seen us inside our vehicle plenty of times, but I wondered how they would react to my sharing their space. Would they be afraid, curious, defensive? Brown hyenas are usually not aggressive toward people, but still the cubs were seventy-five-pound carnivores, equipped with weapons strong enough to tear me to little bits.

Only a few minutes later, Pepper's head popped up from the entrance. Her dark brown eyes caught mine and held them captive. She was only about eight months old, but her face was already dry and cracked by the Kalahari sun. Numerous scars etched her cheek. Her hair was tangled and matted with grass seeds and burrs. In short, she was beautiful.

She bounded out of the hole in one single motion and walked directly toward me without hesitation. Her head and ears were held erect, her eyes wide, taking in all the details of this strange-looking primate sitting cross-legged at her den.

When she was two feet away, she stopped. Her face was at my eye level, and as she stretched her neck, her nose reached to within inches of mine. She sniffed in deeply; I did not breathe at all. We stared into each other's soul.

Her thirsty eyes searched, and I wondered what she could see of me. I sat exposed and vulnerable, unable to live in this harshness without my canteen and sun block. I must have looked rather puny, weak and short of jaw, but she did not hold this against me.

When she was old enough to leave the den, Pepper often came by our camp. She would poke her head in while we were bathing or walk up to our dining table by the fire. But occasionally she would just lie nearby, and I would sit beside her, no more than three feet away. In silence, we'd scan the moonlit desert together, and running my fingers through the sand, I knew that I was part of the earth.

Delia Owens

A World Transformed

I've been taking leaps of faith all my life, but as I ascended the bridge, a massive steel arch towering 750 feet above a bone-dry river bottom, I could find no metaphor for the sheer silliness of what I was about to do.

Already giddy from transpacific jet lag, not to mention the endless hairpin turns that finally brought me to this remote outpost on New Zealand's South Island, the height barely registered. Abandoning caution, I bounded up the metal rungs.

It was a crisp, clear afternoon in early spring. The rugged alpine terrain sported a fresh green coat broken by outcroppings of porous karst. That a river had once flowed here, I knew only from the gorge it had carved out. Not a drop of water moistened the black bedrock into which I was about to pitch headfirst. There had been a cold snap, forcing me to layer on nearly all the inappropriate clothing I had brought with me. I could see my breath as it collided with the gusting northerly wind. While I waited my turn, I swaggered along the bridge where the bungee crew rigged up the oversized rubber bands that would twang me back from certain suicide. Ominous formations of jagged rock leered up at me like open jaws.

Two young travelers queued up in front of me, returnees from the day before who hadn't gotten up the nerve to jump. Pale with panic, they clasped each other's hands, mumbled mantras and finally plunged into the abyss, thrashing and wriggling like caught fish on a line.

Then it was my turn. I mustered dignity. As two hulking Kiwis secured the bungee cord to my ankles, I forced myself to breathe deeply, aware suddenly of the pit of my stomach. The wind gained force, whistling through the bridge's steel ribcage. A rain of pine needles fell about me. I positioned myself at the edge of the plank and leveled my gaze on the horizon. Snowcapped peaks pierced the firmament, casting glare into my squinting eyes. I willed my body steady. Why I was about to hurl myself off a bridge I couldn't have said at that moment, having already gone mute from the lips inward. My fortieth birthday loomed a month off. Perhaps rites of passage defy chronology. Perhaps New Zealand's natural majesty had simply broken down the boundaries.

It occurred to me that I might not reach forty. The prospect unsettled me, but equally daunting was the inevitability of graying and bone loss should I survive. Not that I wanted to die—in truth, I had never been more eager to live—but I needed to spit in the eye of my mortality one last time before midlife caught up with me. Clench-jawed, I lined up my feet, took one more greedy breath and jumped.

My flight was brief, a split second letting-go of everything that bound me to Earth: gravity, mass, caution . . . tomorrow. I soared through a landscape of streaks and swirls. Unseen angels called my name.

Then—boing!—the cord snapped me back, straining every joint, whipping hair into my gaping mouth. Laughter—my own or someone else's? Scrubby expanses of wilderness, dribs and drabs of cloud a blur around me as I bobbed, spun and finally dangled upside-down by my ankles. Slowly, the riverbed came back into focus. Hands reached up to ease me into a world transformed: an arabesque of sculpted stone where the sky had once been, unending blue along the bottom. It was all new, all waiting, and I was swinging low on my elastic lifeline, eager to begin again.

Germaine W. Shames

The Tooth

When you reach the top, keep climbing.

Zen Proverb

"The Tooth" is a 5,605-foot fang of rock that thrusts up from the jawbone of a ridge in the Cascade Mountains of western Washington state. The east face of the rock rises nearly 1,000 feet above the ridge, the west side 300 feet, and the summit is a lovely smooth slab.

One sunny morning in 1943, when I was fourteen years old, my brothers Barney and Louie and I set out to climb The Tooth with our climbing teacher, Tom Campbell.

Tom was an experienced mountaineer who had lost an arm while serving in the U.S. Army's famous Tenth Mountain Division and now climbed with a hook screwed into his prosthetic arm. He had taught us the basics on Monitor Rock, a thirty-foot-high artificial wall of rock and cement in west Seattle, not far from our home. But this would be our first "real" climb.

That morning we hiked up a trail from Denny Creek through old-growth forest, crossing and re-crossing the snow-fed stream until, after about three miles, we reached a big rockslide. Leaping from one lichen-encrusted boulder to the next, we gradually picked our way up through the slide.

At the top, we followed game trails across scree and low brush, rising through open alpine forests to the west face of the ridge. Next, we followed a trail north through fragrant scrub cedar and, when the going turned really steep, roped up: Tom leading, then Barney, me, and finally Louie—the order in which we were born. We wormed up through stunted trees and between huge boulders, carrying the rope in coils between us, until we arrived at a notch in the north ridge.

Above us, The Tooth rose skyward, still in morning shadow. Directly ahead was a short but nearly vertical wall of rock—the first pitch of the climb. Along the rock face I could see good footholds and handholds. This would be easy.

Tom hopped over a three-foot gap to the rock face, climbed up a ways, found a good position where he could brace himself to support the next climber, took in the slack rope between himself and Barney, and then called down: "On belay. Climb!"

"Climbing!" Barney called back, as we'd been taught, and started smartly across the gap.

As he did, I saw him look to his left and hesitate for a split second. Then his movements became slow and deliberate, as if he were climbing in molasses. I watched his moves, as I had been taught to, so I could use the same holds he used, but I was impatient, wondering what was taking him so long. Finally, he reached Tom and got into belay position. It was my turn.

"On belay. Climb!" Barney shouted.

"Climbing!" I yelled back.

The gap lay in shadow. I stepped up to its edge, began to move out over it to the cliff a few feet away, glanced down past my left foot . . . and froze solid.

The cliff plunged straight down for what looked like a thousand feet. Everything below was so tiny, so far away. I was absolutely terrified.

More than a half-century later, I can still see clearly every detail of rock, lichen and shadow in that fearsome void. Scrambling around on a thirty-foot artificial wall in west Seattle had taught me a lot about climbing technique, but very little about what climbers call "exposure"—that heart-in-your-mouth surge of sheer terror when you first look down from a great height.

I willed myself across the gap, struggling to resist the palpable gravitational pull of the abyss below. From that point on up the rock face, every move I made was measured, focused, deliberate. Moving only one limb at a time, maintaining what climbers call a three-point suspension, I crept ever so slowly upward toward Barney. When I finally reached him, my mouth was dry as dust. It took me a moment to compose myself into a sitting hip belay. Then I called down to Louie: "On belay. Climb!" My voice was a croak.

"Climbing!" Louie signaled from below.

"Check out the view below your left foot," I added.

His eyes were as round as an owl's when he came up the rock wall to my belay spot.

That day, Barney, Louie and I all made the same vow: "Dear God, if you get me down off this mountain alive, I promise I'll never climb another mountain again." Barney, the older and wiser brother, kept his promise.

Louie and I have spent the rest of our lives breaking it.

Jim Whittaker

3

OUR COMMON BOND

A joy shared is a joy doubled.

Goethe

What Shade of Lipstick Goes with Dirt?

It is in the shelter of each other that the people live.

Irish Proverb

"There are only three things I'm worried about," my mom said over the phone. I could picture her standing in front of the kitchen bay window, the phone cradled against her neck as she chopped fresh oregano for dinner. "Getting attacked by bears, going to the bathroom . . . you know, number two . . . and looking ugly for the pictures."

I mustered my most confident, yet gently reassuring voice. "I'll beat the bears away with a stick if I have to, but we probably won't see any. Squatting in the woods is no big deal; you'll have to trust me on that one. And I promise we won't publish any ugly pictures in the magazine. If we do, we can always put one of those little black bars across your eyes, like they do for fashion don'ts in *Glamour*."

It was settled. I would take my fifty-one-year-old mother, Priscilla, and her twin sister, Linda, on a three-day backpacking trip—an assignment for *Backpacker* magazine. I was excited, but also nervous. Mom and Aunt Linda are not your average hairy-legged hiking gals. To them, spending a day in the Great Outdoors means eighteen holes of golf and steaks on the grill.

But they each have three outdoor-loving kids, and they were anxious to see what all the fuss was about.

"Can I at least bring some lipstick?" Mom pleaded as I checked her pack contents at the trailhead. We were at the doorstep of California's Desolation Wilderness. The weather was promising, our chosen route was challenging but not difficult, and with my friend Tracey to help ferry the load, Mom and Aunt Linda would have to carry only clothes, sleeping bags and a few essentials. And herein lay the great debate.

I'd already jettisoned mascara, an eight-inch hairbrush and two Victoria's Secret silk bras, all of which Mom thought were vital to her safety and well-being. My pack full of food and group gear weighed close to fifty pounds, and I'd sacrificed my fresh undies and spare T-shirt so I could carry a puffy pillow for her. But I allowed the lipstick, rationalizing that it was lip balm with color.

I cinched up her pack, checked the weight and watched Mom wait behind Aunt Linda for a final primp in the car sideview mirror. They were as nervous and giggly as schoolgirls getting ready for the senior prom.

The twins took off at a respectable clip, trekking poles shushing, blow-dried hair bobbing. The climb was gradual, and the views of Lake Tahoe were inspiring. When we stopped for lunch in a sunny boulder field, Mom dropped her pack and said proudly, "That was nothing compared to the StairMaster."

Even though we were only a few hours into our trip, I was relieved to see them both smiling—and not just their regular, "Hello, lovely day, isn't it?" smiles. These were ear-to-ear, round-eyed, "We are strong and healthy hiking machines and, wow, look at that view!" smiles. I felt what every Cub Scout leader must feel: nervous that trouble could happen at any moment, but happy to see "my kids" enjoying themselves.

"It's about three miles to camp," I told them. "Why don't you put on your fleece jackets so you don't get chilled while we break?" It suddenly occurred to me that the parental tables had turned. I sounded like my mother.

Mom, sitting on a rock next to her sister, said sweetly, "Okay."

I was never that obedient.

"Lunch is served," I said, plopping a communal bag of gorp at their feet and handing them each a whole-wheat bagel bulging with cheddar, salami and brown mustard. We ate in silence until Aunt Linda blurted out, "This tastes incredible!"

"It's absolutely gourmet!" gushed Mom, who's famous for her cooking skills and for her fancy sandwiches in particular.

"And this gorp," said Aunt Linda, who's equally talented in the kitchen, "did you make it yourself?"

Had it been anyone but these two I'd have assumed sarcasm, but this time I was genuinely touched.

At 8,000 feet, after an afternoon of amicable rambling, Aunt Linda rounded a corner, stopped and gasped. "Priscilla, look at this!"

Sprawling before us was Upper Thelma Lake, shimmering in the afternoon sun like a giant sapphire. And there was not a soul around.

We found an established campsite with perfect views. Mom and Aunt Linda soaked their pedicured feet in the cool lake while Tracey and I pitched camp.

When our four-person tent was set up, Mom crawled inside and collapsed. I poked my head in and discovered that she had arranged our beds neatly, with Tracey and me on the outsides—to protect her from the bears, she said. Mom was lying contentedly on her back, smiling up at the screened ceiling.

Soon we were sipping cups of Cabernet around the camp stove. Mom was reclining in her camp chair, watching intently as I chopped garlic and onion to add to the simmering lentils. I picked up a piece of onion that had fallen on the ground, blew the dirt off, then dropped it in. Her eyes widened. "Don't worry, Mom, a little dirt won't kill you," I said. When the lentil and rice burritos were finally served, they oohed and aahed, bestowed more exclamation points on my culinary talents, then gobbled down seconds.

With dusk upon us, conversation revolved around the prospect of getting ambushed by bears. During dinner, cleanup and pre-bed chores, they stayed well within the safe, yellow circle of lantern light, tensing with every rustle in the darkness. Once inside the tent they felt safe and were soon shuffling cards by candlelight.

The next morning was a glorious day: warm and sunny, with cotton-candy clouds drifting through a deep blue sky. Our plan was to take our time hiking without packs to a nearby lake, stop for lunch, then loop back.

Not twenty minutes down the trail, my mother and her sister had already ticked off the names of five types of wildflowers. They'd never before set foot in a high mountain meadow, but years of tending lush gardens back home had turned them into amateur botanists. By day's end they'd taught me to identify ten new wildflowers, which was ten more than I'd learned while lugging around a two-pound field guide on countless other trips.

After lunch, we slowly made our way back to camp, meandering through open meadows filled with flowers, then along a gurgling creek. Mom lingered, and when I turned around to check on her, she was doubled over, yanking on the tongue of her boot. "I think I might be getting a blister," she said sheepishly.

I removed her boot, saw that she was blister-free, then changed the lacing to relieve the pressure. Kneeling in the dirt, as I double-knotted her laces, I wondered how many hundreds of bowknots she had tied for me over the years. She stood up and took a few steps.

"Much better," she said. "Thank you, honey."

"You're welcome. I figure I probably owe you a few."

One of my earliest memories is of my mom taking care of me when I was sick. I must have been four or five, and I woke up in the middle of the night wheezing and gasping and hacking like my lungs were filled with sawdust. Mom turned on the shower as hot as it would go, sat me next to the bath-tub, and rubbed my back and talked gently until my lungs cleared.

On our final night in the mountains, it was my turn to take care of Mom. She has a chronic ear problem that can feel "like someone's shoving a skewer into the side of my head," as she once described it. It had started bothering her that afternoon, and as we ate dinner I could see it was getting worse. Every few minutes, she'd wince and tilt her head to the side. As soon as dinner was over, she took four pain relievers and went into the tent to lie down.

I tried to stay calm. She wasn't in danger, but to see her in agony made me feel ill. Then Aunt Linda remembered their mother's home remedy, which I improvised by soaking some cotton with olive oil. I gently packed her ear with the cotton, then placed a hot-water bottle next to her head. She was asleep within minutes.

I stayed awake most of the night, listening to the wind howl and the snow crystals bounce off the tent. At 3:00 A.M. I found Mom wide-eyed with pain. I felt the hot-water bottle next to her head: lukewarm.

"I'll get up and heat some more water," I whispered.

"No, don't be silly," she murmured back to me. "There's a storm out there. You stay right in your sleeping bag. I'm fine."

Fifteen minutes later, with a fresh hot-water bottle against her ear, she was sleeping peacefully. Lying there next to my mother, listening to her breathe, I thought, *This must be what it's like when your child gets sick or hurt. I'll be a basket case.*

We rose the following morning to dark gray clouds, strong winds and an inch of fresh snow. The weather may have been dismal, but Mom's ear was better.

On the way down the mountain, snow pelted us from all directions, wind tore at our faces, and the trail became more slippery by the minute. The twins couldn't get over it. Mom poked her nose out from her hood and watched a pine tree sway like a blade of grass.

"It seems like we should be miserable out here in this storm," she said, and Aunt Linda finished her thought, "but we're completely comfortable!"

By now, Mom and Aunt Linda were pros with their trekking poles. With great satisfaction, I watched them maneuver down the slick mountainside with the grace of veteran Nordic skiers. But what amazed me most was that they seemed in no great hurry to get back to civilization. Such rough weather would have prevented them from walking to the end of the driveway a week before, but now they were happily strolling along in it, even stopping from time to time to gape at the wind-lashed lodgepoles.

As we approached the end of our hike, I realized that our adventure had been one of my most satisfying ever. My mom, who had slept under a roof every night of her life, was, if only temporarily, a true outdoorswoman.

That night we met my father, uncle, brother and cousin at a fancy restaurant. Mom and Aunt Linda—freshly showered, blown-dry and rouged—looked healthy and younger than ever. They babbled excitedly, rehashing trip details for the eager audience.

As the coffee was served, Mom turned to my dad and said, "Danny, you should have seen Kristin. She took such good care of us. I was so proud of her."

"Funny you should say that, Mom," I said. "I was just thinking the same thing about you."

Kristin Hostetter

"If this is a simple hike, why the rope?"

Jump, Mullet, Jump

For words, like nature, half reveal and half conceal the soul within.

Alfred, Lord Tennyson

I moved to Florida's panhandle from Providence, Rhode Island, when I was seven, and I came home in tears after my first day in my new second-grade class.

"The teacher made me be a mullet," I wailed to my mother. "Some of the other kids got to be kingfish or snapper or blue-fish, but I have to be a mullet," I sobbed.

I had no idea what a mullet was. I guessed it must be some kind of fish, but I sure didn't like the sound of it, and I absolutely did not want to be called one. My mother, a newly transplanted Yankee herself, was wise in the ways of cod and haddock, but could offer nothing in the way of mullet advocacy.

The problem was passed on to my stepfather, a Gulf Coast native and the reason we had moved to Florida.

"A mullet!" Dad exclaimed, upon hearing the story. "Why, that's just about the very best thing you could be 'cept maybe a porpoise."

I must have looked dubious, because he continued, "Tell

you what, we'll go out to the bayou, just you and me, and I'll introduce you to some."

We drove out of town in the new mustard-colored Chevy, then took a winding sand-and-shell road to a tiny beach at the edge of a shallow bay. The late afternoon sun reflected pinky-orange on the surface of the water. The air smelled like a heady combination of my mother's cedar chest and old Easter eggs. My stepfather squatted by the edge of the water and motioned for me to join him.

"Sometimes you have to give them a little encouragement," he said. He cupped his hands around his mouth like a cheerleader and called, "Jump, mullet, jump."

The response came so quickly that I almost jumped myself. Just a few feet away from us a plump snub-nosed fish leaped straight up into the air, then fell back into the water with a smack.

Wonder-struck and wide-eyed, I mimicked my stepfather, and we chanted in unison, "Jump, mullet, jump!" We must have kept those fish hopping for nearly an hour before the sun got so low that we had to leave and head home.

I could barely wait to tell my mother about the acrobatic fish and how we made them leap right out of the water. The next morning, I was eager to get to school so I could join the other members of the mullet group.

It's been nearly half a century since that memorable afternoon on the bayou, and I now live on an island just off the coast of Florida. During certain months of the year, scores of mullet swim into the saltwater canal behind my house.

Sometimes, on quiet nights, I am roused from my sleep by the splashes of their timeless leaping ritual. And, even though it's been many years since I found out that the mullet were going to jump whether I gave them orders or not, I still smile and repeat the words my stepfather taught me so long ago.

"Jump," I whisper, "jump, mullet, jump."

Linda Ballou

A Different Kind of Mother's Day

Holy earth mother, the trees and all nature are witness of your thoughts and deeds.

Winnebago Indians

Most people thought I was crazy. I was a forty-seven-year-old housewife, mother of four children, had never really considered myself an athlete, and I was attempting to hike the 2,000-mile Appalachian Trail from Georgia to Maine by myself.

I had plenty of good days and my share of bad days, yet nothing compared to Mother's Day, 1989. Back at home, it was a time for me to be pampered. The girls cooked, I received lots of wonderful presents, and everyone tried to make it a perfect day. But this Sunday, I was by myself and missing my husband and kids very much.

There I was, thousands of miles from home—tired and dirty, walking in a spring rainstorm and really feeling sorry for myself. I decided to call it a day, get out of the rain at the nearest shelter and fix myself something hot to drink and eat. I searched the pages of my guidebook for the nearest shelter and started looking out for it.

When I arrived at the trail leading to the shelter, I was

faced with a wild, rushing creek and no way to cross. I didn't know how to swim and, even if I could, I don't think it would have been wise to enter the swift flowing water with a heavy pack on my back.

I gazed at the high water for a minute and then started back down the trail when, suddenly, two teenage boys yelled out. There was a fallen tree further along the creek, and I could cross on that. When I got to the spot, I realized there was no way I could make it over. The tree was slick and not very big, my pack was wet and heavy with gear, and I was afraid of heights and water!

I motioned to them that I couldn't do it.

"Come on, we'll help you!" they shouted back and crossed over the log to my side of the creek. The sixteen-year-old took my pack and carried it across; the nineteen-year-old took my hand and led me across. Nervously, I followed along, being careful with each tenuous step.

When we finally got safely to the other side, I was so grateful I hugged them both.

Together, we headed to the nearby shelter. As it turned out, John and Patrick were brothers from Atlanta, Georgia, and had been hiking parts of the trail with their dad each of the past ten years. The boys loved Pop-Tarts and, because it was Mother's Day, they gave me their last one at dinner and said with a smile, "We're adopting you as our mother today, since our mom is back at home."

Eleven years and two attempts later, on September 9, 2000, at the age of fifty-seven, I finally finished the Appalachian Trail. My hike of a lifetime strengthened my faith in God, renewed my confidence in my own abilities and confirmed the fact that there are some really wonderful people in the world. John and Patrick were two of those, but then again, I'm biased—after all, I am their "mother."

Joyce Johnson

Daddy's Garden

To create a little flower is the labor of ages.

William Blake

When I was little, I used to think my dad raked the maple leaves into a big pile so that we kids could dive into it and play. In those days, I thought the wheelbarrow that accompanied him to the back garden was meant for the rides he gave us back to the house. His flower garden at the side of the house was his special place of refuge—and it was there that his soul brushed mine to forever bond.

Daddy's garden was full of surprises. Rock paths led to gold-fish ponds and little rooms made of evergreens and furnished with stone benches. Birdbaths stood in odd places, and a fountain surrounded by red geraniums and blue lobelia sent water music throughout the garden from an off-center mound in the lawn. As Daddy tended his garden, his gentleness and love radiated to the plants, which responded with luxuriant growth and color. Pulling weeds with him was never tedious, because his love radiated to me as well.

After I grew up and got married, I still spent many Sundays side by side with my dad—pruning, weeding,

fertilizing, laughing, basking in the warmth of his unconditional caring. But as the years went by, I did more while he
gradually did less.

Daddy's spirit stayed strong, but the feebleness of his
eighties drove him to sell his property and move to a retirement community.

Before the new owner could bulldoze the garden, my dad
helped me take samples of everything: the roses, the various
perennials, the dahlias, the peonies, and even some of the
rocks from the pathways. We took these—along with a birdbath, the fountain and a stone bench—and put them in my
backyard where I made a miniature garden to echo my
father's.

As I watched Daddy walk with his cane through *our* garden, I knew that every step was precious, every handful of
earth he moved a gift, every rose he pruned a blessing.

At the retirement community, I tended my dad as he had
tended his flowers. Every day, I had morning coffee with
him, and in the afternoon I took him shopping. I organized
his medicines and took him to piano concerts. In the spring,
I drove him through the suburbs to look at other people's
flower gardens or to my house to hear his own fountain
singing with birds.

Two years into his new life, I held his hand as he passed away
of pancreatic cancer. I felt his young, strong spirit with me, as if
he was worried what his leaving would do. But his death could
not break the bond between our souls, and I walked barefoot in
the grass to receive comfort from the earth.

Now, years later, I still sense my dad beside me as I walk
in my garden—the child of his garden. I can feel his enjoy-
ment at the hummingbirds splashing in the birdbath. His
laughter still echoes in my mind as I pull weeds from around
the rosebushes. I carry his spirit in my heart, and with each
flower that blooms, I know that he is with me.

Linda Swartz Bakkar

What Best Friends Do

One touch of nature makes the whole world kin.

William Shakespeare

As children growing up in the countryside of New Brunswick, Canada, in the late 1950s, my seven siblings and I created our own entertainment. Fortunately, we had parents who introduced us to the joys of nature.

Every season was special to my mother, and hardly a day passed that she didn't remind us how lucky we were to live beside a beautiful river at the foot of a hill lined with maple trees. Dad taught us how to tap those maple trees and gather the sap, and Mum boiled it down to produce delicious maple syrup.

In early spring we were all ushered out to the back porch to listen to the Spring Peepers, the first songs of the frogs in the nearby creek. Mum called them her "boyfriends," and it became a contest to see who would hear them first and alert Mum. My older brothers showed me how to gather polly-wogs, the eggs of frogs, and we visited the pond regularly to observe their development. We'd also report back to our parents on the purple and white trilliums and violets. Summer nights were spent lying on our backs in the apple orchard, watching the sky for shooting stars. And we'd listen to the call of the loon off in the distance.

When my son Greg was six, we were fortunate to move back to this special place my dad called "God's Little Acre." Dad helped Greg and me plant our first vegetable garden.

The year my father died was also the year my marriage ended. Greg was now a young man in college and lived away from home. Bruised and hurt, I moved away from the land I loved so much to the city of Toronto, where I could lose myself.

Fate stepped in, however, and I met my soul mate, my kindred spirit. Ross is a man much like me, a lover of nature and the simple things. One of the first gifts he bought me was a yellow canoe.

When it came time for me to meet his seven-year-old daughter Morgan, I was determined just to be myself. Thanksgiving was our first weekend together. I love children and I have a wonderful relationship with my son, but I always wanted a daughter to round out our family. I knew Morgan couldn't be my daughter, since she already had a loving mother, but I felt I could be a significant part of her life.

The weather was unseasonably warm in Toronto, so the three of us went for a walk along the river, just minutes from our small house. We gathered leaves while exploring the riverbank. This was one of my favorite ways to spend an autumn day. Morgan liked it, too. Her dad took pictures of us feeding the ducks and playing in the fallen leaves. Once home, I showed her how to press the leaves between the pages of large books. My dog, Bandit, joined us regularly on our walks through the nearby woods and along the streams.

All four of us climbed into my yellow canoe to explore more of the river. We saw lazy turtles sleeping on logs, well camouflaged except to Morgan's keen, young eyes. We took our bird guide with us so we could keep a record of the number of songbirds and waterfowl we spotted. Ross often commented that she seemed more excited about coming for her weekend visits and seeing me than seeing her poor old dad.

When Morgan was eight, I took her and Bandit to New Brunswick. I was anxious to show her my childhood home. On that trip, she saw her first fireflies, and as we did when we were young, she collected several in a bottle to see if she could light up the tent we had pitched on the beach by the river. Satisfied she could, she let them fly back into the night. Later we lay on our backs in the apple orchard, watching the shooting stars and identifying the constellations.

The next spring back in Toronto, we planted a vegetable garden in the backyard. Morgan was wide-eyed when I suggested she take off her shoes and socks and join me in our bare feet in the warm, soft soil. Together, we planted potatoes, carrots, beans and peas. Morgan drew signs for each vegetable. When the planting was complete, she and I hosed off our feet. Ross and Greg joined us, and suddenly the washing turned into a water fight as we screamed and ran for cover. Morgan was thrilled when she pulled the first carrot from our garden, wiped off the excess dirt and crunched the fresh, garden treat.

The year Morgan turned thirteen, we spent a quiet moment together looking at the photo album of our six years as a family, at the pictures of us that first autumn feeding the ducks and playing in the leaves. Then, as I turned the page, she looked at me and said, "You're not like my mother. You're more like my best friend."

There had been no trips to Disneyland and no extravagant gifts—just a simple time with our dog, enjoying nature in all its seasons, and doing the things that best friends do.

Willa Mavis

The Perfect Lake

A lake is the landscape's most beautiful and expressive feature. It is the Earth's eye, looking into which the beholder measures the depth of his own nature.

Henry David Thoreau

As our minivan turned off Highway 71 and began rumbling down yet another rutted gravel road, Dad started in again.

"Remember back in '45 when we had that whopper of a snowstorm?" he began as he maneuvered us around a corner and through another cloud of dust.

"What a doozy," Uncle Bob said, as stones pinged against the metal running boards like hail on a tin roof.

I had endured already thirty minutes of "remember when" stories as Dad and Uncle Bob drove us to Dad's "perfect" lake.

Dad had called the week before, begging me to come home to see Bob and a newfound lake. *Sure*, I thought, *some godforsaken no-man's-land.*

Growing up, Dad and I sort of steered clear of one another. I did my thing, and he did his. He didn't tell me what to do, and I didn't ask. Once in a while he'd ask me to go fishing or hiking with him. I always declined, begging tennis practice or better things to do. Other than that, he just didn't seem interested.

Looking back now, I always thought of Dad as a little too reserved, perhaps even weak. He never shouted. He never argued. He simply stated his ideas and let the rest of the world decide.

Now, with Dad in his seventies, I figured it was time to get to know him a little better.

So here I was, bumping down a deserted Minnesota road with nothing but silos, cornfields and the minivan's spreading dust storm for as far as I could see. When Dad launched another assault beginning with "back in '53," I tuned out. I dropped my head back onto the headrest and let my mind drift off to my apartment in Minneapolis.

A stack of unopened mail waited on my marble coffee table, piles of unread research articles were growing like mold next to my wrought-iron bed, and e-mails were multiplying in cyberspace, just waiting to engulf me with the click of a mouse.

I don't have time for a trip to Nowhereville, I thought. *What was I thinking? With three assignments due next week and a meeting with my editor to prepare for, this is the last place I should be. Besides, what can I really learn about Dad? He's the same as always—quiet, patient, simple. I can visit dear old Dad anytime.*

A boulder-sized bump jolted me back to po-dunk reality, and as I consciously unclenched my jaw, I made a decision. *I'm going back tomorrow,* I concluded. *I need to get back to the* real *world. I've got important things to do!*

Suddenly, Dad slammed on the brakes as I spotted the back end of a white-tailed deer disappearing into yet another cornfield.

"Good God!" I cried, bolting upright.

"Wow, wasn't she pretty?" Dad cooed as he eased off the brake and made a cautious right turn into a farmer's tree-lined driveway.

Continuing toward the barn, Dad whispered, "There she is . . . isn't she a beaut?"

Straight ahead of us, through an ocean of waist-deep grass, I could just make out a path leading to a tiny launching area. *Great, Dad's gonna mess around and get the van stuck,* I thought, as images of *Deliverance* flashed through my head.

The gravel made a final crunch as Dad rolled to a stop. Bob slid out to deposit a two-dollar launching fee into the rusted red Folger's can carelessly duct-taped to the weathered, paint-bare barn door.

We proceeded down the barely visible trail toward the lake, where two enormous jet-black, sweat-covered horses were tethered to a tree. They switched their tails and snorted a frothy "hello" as we bumped along past them toward the dockless "landing."

Bob and I got out to wait in the waist-high grass while Dad launched the boat. I immediately began scratching, wondering if my HMO covered Lyme disease.

The Crestliner splashed down, sending a widening ripple across the water. The three of us eased into the boat, and Dad pushed off, sending us on a silent glide toward the middle of the lake.

Eventually, I leaned back, propped my elbows on the metal sides and exhaled. The lake began to work its magic as the sun warmed my pale face and the breeze lifted the hair off my moist neck.

Tilting my head back, I looked skyward. Somewhere between me and the blinding orb overhead, an eagle soared, periodically casting a shadow over my face. The purr of the motor and the whoosh of the gently swaying poplar trees began to blur my mental image of important city business.

I glanced back at Dad and Bob huddled together over the tackle box. Weathered hands effortlessly tied knots and baited lines. Living a thousand miles apart and drawn together only once every ten years or so, they still chattered on like schoolboys. I turned away but kept an ear tuned to their conversation.

"Yup," Dad said, "I'm sure proud of her. As a kid she was such an independent thing—really didn't want me around much. A good athlete, talented musician, great student. I've still got all her clippings from the newspaper."

He paused as he attached another worm to the hook. "And now, she's a beautiful young woman and a talented writer. Still very independent, though. I'm really surprised she came," he said as he looked over at his brother. "Say, she's been published you know!" he beamed.

"Ya don't say," Bob offered.

"Yup, couple a magazines, some stories—technical stuff, too. I've got a copy of her stuff in a scrapbook back home."

I couldn't believe it. *My God*, I thought, *he has been interested all these years. He's hoarded the pieces of my life in bits of paper. Why didn't he tell me? Why didn't he ask to be included?*

I sat up, suddenly jarred by my realization. Before my eyes, dear old, uninterested Dad had come into full view. He *had* been interested in my life all those years, and even now he wanted to be a part of it. But in his reserved way, he had waited for my invitation.

In that moment, I saw for the first time that Dad wasn't weak. He had a quiet, yet incredible strength that didn't force or push. It didn't interrupt or interfere. It was patient, it waited, it endured, knowing I would eventually come to him.

Suddenly, in the Eden that surrounded me, I saw the man who was my father. *But how could we have been so different?* I wondered. *Where did he get this inner resolve, and why don't I have it?*

Dad and Bob chattered on while I leaned into my seat, trying to reorganize my memories. Soon, the hum of the motor replaced their banter. I turned to find the brothers staring out at the wilderness as a red fox scampered up a steep hill and disappeared into a burrow. Dad's pale blue eyes shone with a joy that I had never seen in his well-worn face.

This is it, I realized. *This is the source of his strength and patience. Nature, the outdoors, this place. He's always wanted to share it with me, but I was never ready.*

Shifting his gaze toward me, his face reflected a thousand folds of time and too many Minnesota winters. His Adam's apple bobbed as he swallowed, drawing in a deep breath. "I'm glad you finally came," he said. "It's only truly perfect when you're here."

"Me, too," I whispered, as a smile crept up from my heart to the corners of my mouth.

Then Dad's strong, rough hand took mine, and together we shifted our gaze to the water. My father had given me his "perfect" lake. In this one fishing trip, my father had shown me his strength and his world—only I could barely see them through my tears.

Linda Armstrong

The Two Old Fishermen

I sat on the high dune as I had done so many other mornings. The sun was just peeking over the eastern horizon, painting the low wisps of clouds with ever-brightening shades of orange and purple. I watched the old fisherman as I sipped my hot coffee from a large ceramic mug.

Even from the distance I could see the furrows etched into his deeply tanned skin—furrows earned over years of hard work on the tugboats. His chafed and callused hands displayed a strength that belied his eighty-five years of life. This was my dad.

Every Saturday in spring, he would arrive at the beach before sunrise, carrying his rod, a small tackle box, a sand spike and a plastic bag with his bait. As he reached the water's edge, he placed the tackle box, spike and bait on the sand and ran his line from the reel through the guides. He deftly attached a hook and weight on the end of the line and laid the rod down on the sand with his other gear.

From the plastic bag he retrieved a large whole bunker. Using the knife he carried in a sheath on his wader belt, he cut the bunker into several large chunks. Then, lifting his rod, he hooked one of the chunks securely to the end of the line. He walked chest-deep into the lightly pounding surf to begin his ritualistic ballet.

As I watched my father, I was aware that I wasn't the only

observer. The old seagull was there, too, as he always was. Scarred and with patches devoid of feathers caused by long-ago battles for food, he watched the old fisherman raise his rod above his head and bring it back behind him, baited line following. The bird's eyes remained steady as the man brought the rod forward with a powerful thrust, throwing the offering far out toward where the big stripers swam. Its gaze alternated between the angler and his plastic bait bag.

The old man now backed out of the surf, paying line as he went. He walked to the sand spike and placed the rod into it and set the drag on his reel. Only then did he indicate he was aware of the bird's presence.

The two old fishermen looked at each other, and I sensed a mutual respect. A moment later, the old man bent and retrieved another of his bunker chunks. He held it up for the gull to see and threw it far out into the water. Immediately, the bird screeched and took to the air, flying directly to the spot where the offering splashed, swooped down and snatched it from the waves. He flew back to the same spot on the sand to devour his prize. This, too, was part of the ritual.

The old man laughed at the display he had witnessed so many mornings before. His laughter stopped abruptly as he saw the tip of his rod bend over in a deep arc. A fish had taken his offering. Quickly, he pulled the rod from the spike and reset the drag, holding the tip high. It pulled down violently. He walked steadily into the surf, holding pressure on the fish, reeling slowly as he walked.

The battle lasted a full ten minutes, my father alternating between giving and taking line. All the while, the gull watched stoically, never moving an inch from his spot. In the end, the fight went to the old man, a magnificent striper lying at his feet.

Carefully, he removed the hook from the tired fish's mouth and carried it to the water. Gently, he lowered it into the surf and moved it back and forth, forcing water through its gills, reviving the noble bass. After a few moments, the great fish gave a quick flick of its tail and disappeared back into the dark depths, perhaps to fight another day.

The old angler had a look of tired satisfaction on his face as he began to gather up his gear. As he walked slowly back toward the house, he exchanged glances with the gull. He stopped and pulled the remainder of his bunker from the plastic bag. He tossed it in the direction of the bird and continued on home as the gull walked slowly toward the feast.

I returned to the house a short time after Dad did and asked how his fishing went. He replied with the same words he used every time I asked that question, no matter if he caught a fish or not: "Fine. Mighty fine."

But there was something else this time—an extra sense of satisfaction in his words. For some reason that fish was more important than any fish he'd ever caught. I smiled at the content look in his face.

That night, Dad died in his sleep. Quietly, peacefully. No words could convey my sense of emptiness over losing him. I felt so alone and afraid. The man who could never die was gone.

The day after the funeral, I returned to my perch on the dunes to watch the sunrise and say a final good-bye to my father. It was more beautiful than any I had ever seen—blazing colors announcing the arrival of a new day.

As the beach became clearer in the light, I saw the old gull in the same place he had always stood. He stared silently out to the sea. I watched with him.

Then, suddenly, the old bird broke the silence with a long series of screeches. I was startled momentarily, but quickly regained my composure. The gull then spread its wings and took flight over the waves. A short distance out it dove straight down to the water and retrieved a fish. Then it banked and flew toward me. As it passed overhead, it hovered for what seemed an eternity, looking down at me. I could see then that it was not a whole fish in its mouth, but a bunker chunk.

I knew then that my dad's spirit would always live on this beach that he loved so dearly. As I rose to walk back to the house, I smiled and watched as the gull flew off to enjoy this one last fish.

Stan R. Kid

My Canoeing Exam

Friendship is a sheltering tree.

Samuel Taylor Coleridge

One year at summer camp, I had been working hard preparing for a canoeing exam. I put in hours and hours trying to build up my strength and learn new soloing skills.

Rising each day at six, I persevered, practicing bow-cut landings and paddling miles back and forth across the lake on windy white-capped waves until the sun set. Weeks slipped by, and I knew I had given everything I could to reach my goal and pass the exam. I had completed the strokes, landings and a three-mile solo trip. All that lay ahead was a solo portage on hilly terrain, and I would get my badge. Deep down I knew how proud my parents would be to see me succeed at something I had tried so hard to achieve. This badge was for them. I would make them proud.

On the last day for testing, the weather suddenly turned bad. All swimmers and boaters were grounded because of the oncoming storm. As the wind picked up, I felt a knot growing in my stomach. Although my arms had strengthened considerably over the weeks at camp, my legs were still weak by comparison. While I could lift the canoe by myself and even run on flat ground, my knees buckled under the strain of going uphill. Now with the wind whipping in circles, I began to wonder if all my hard work had been in vain.

My best friend Ali was thinking the same thing. Each day at dawn, she and I would run down to the lake, paddles in hand, to practice our landings. Together, we'd shout out words of encouragement as we soloed in our separate canoes across the lake. Together, we'd flop down in our bunks after a day of straining our muscles, with smiles and giggles, reminiscing about our adventures.

Now the final test lay before us.

In order to pass, we were required to lift a canoe up onto our shoulders, run down a hill, turn around and head back up, without the canoe touching the ground. It was a one-shot deal—if the canoe touched the ground, we'd fail.

My name came first, and I took off down the rocky hill. As I ran, the wind tore at the bow, and I had to fight to keep from plunging forward. My ankles burned and my arms throbbed, but my knees held out.

Finally, I reached the turnaround point and took a moment to peer at the hill ahead. As I started up, I felt my knees buckle. I stumbled in the mud and fell on some rocks. My knees were bruised and bleeding badly, but the canoe was still perched on my shoulders. Then I realized I didn't have the strength to stand up again. A stab of fear gripped my heart. I couldn't fail now—not after all this work!

All of a sudden I saw Ali peering under the bow of the canoe, smiling. She told me that the examiner said there had been nothing in the books saying that we had to go both ways—up and down the hill. If we did two trips with the same canoe, as long as the canoe didn't touch the ground, she would be willing to go uphill both trips, and I could go down.

I hesitated. If I fell on the second trip down and dropped the canoe, both of us would fail the exam. We both knew Ali was the stronger and better canoeist and could easily pass the exam without me.

But before I could answer, Ali had hoisted the canoe onto her shoulders.

"The canoeing badge means nothing to me compared to our friendship," she screamed over the wind. "With all our hours of practice and hard work, we are closer than sisters— and that's reward enough for me."

As the rain splashed down on my face, tears began to trickle down as well. It may have been cool and blustery outside, but my heart has never felt warmer than it did at that moment, standing face to face with Ali.

"See ya later, Ali-gator!" I sputtered.

With that she scooted up the hill, and I followed quickly behind.

Two days later Ali and I sat at the awards banquet, all dressed up and beaming with joy. We both clutched the master's badges we had worked so hard for. And this time, as I turned toward Ali, I noticed I wasn't the only one with tears of gratitude.

Brenda Timpson

"This thing weighs a ton, Bubba! . . . I think
we're trying to pack in too many supplies!"

Tanya's Kite

*Ah, but a man's reach should exceed his grasp,
or what's a heaven for?*

Robert Browning

When I think of springtime, I think of renewal. The countryside thaws, flowers and trees bud, and the cold winds yield to the warm breezes of a new summer in that inexorable reaffirmation of life. This is the time, when conditions are just right, for flying kites.

Many springtimes ago, my little sister Tanya saved her allowance and bought a kit for building one of these aeronautical wonders. She was only about eight or nine at the time, but she methodically assembled it without assistance or advice, then set it aside, anxiously monitoring the weather, waiting for the perfect day.

It arrived one afternoon when a patch of rain clouds drifted beyond the horizon to reveal azure sky, the sunshine bathing our neighborhood in its warm glow and a steady breeze stirring from the south.

Tanya gathered every spare roll of string and twine she could find, then carried her prized pink diamond-flyer out to the driveway and launched it to the winds. Navigating between treetops, avoiding the hazards of power lines and utility poles, she carefully played out the string in her quest to watch it float higher and farther than any kite had ever flown before. She watched proudly as it continued to lift effortlessly into the air, tugging gently at its reins, begging for freedom to sail where it may.

I was loitering nearby, nearly a teenager by then. I was certainly too old for such childish games. But when the first roll of string had played out, I was pleased to help her tie on another, lingering for a while in case she might succeed in needing a third.

And still the kite climbed. By the time she added a fourth roll, an audience of neighborhood kids had begun to gather, some contributing more string to the cause, all cheering Tanya's remarkable feat.

Mom came out to assess the commotion, pausing to study the swaying, rag-tailed dot in the distance. She pulled me aside and quietly cautioned that soon the stress would be too much, that the string was sure to break, and Tanya would be heartbroken. Her warning was to no avail because our little aeronaut had decided to see just how high she could fly. For Tanya, testing the limits of the sky was more important than any certainty of retrieval.

I can't say how many rolls of string were used that day, but I do know the kite faded so far into the distance that it was virtually impossible to see. One boy set out on his bicycle, pedaling furiously northward, following what was by then a mere fleck in the sky. He returned some time later heralding that Tanya's kite stretched all the way past Ford Road, that it was hovering over the big cemetery with manicured lawns and a chapel and turtle pond, where geese gather to stand sentry over loved ones lost.

Eventually, it began to grow dark, and the audience drifted away for suppers, television and bedtime. It took quite a while, but Tanya, determined as ever, did eventually bring her great pink kite back home, unscarred and intact.

I don't know whatever happened to that kite. Kites

usually don't last very long; most are put away and forgotten, others broken or lost to those hazards of flight that lurk on the fringes of life. Some kites simply break free and float away on the winds, never to be seen again, hopefully to complete their journeys on their own terms, in their own time.

As the years passed, we learned to mark the coming of spring when Tanya launched a new kite. Sunny days with brisk breezes were sure to find her clutching a roll of twine, her eyes to the sky, a rag-tailed pink flyer dancing in the blue.

But even little girls who love the outdoors must grow up, so Tanya learned to fit canoe treks and campouts and kite-flying jaunts between the demands of a busy career, and to cherish those rare trips to visit our parents at their home on a lake in the mountains.

We'd go boating with Dad, and she'd lean out the bow, eyes closed, her arms catching the wind. We'd feed geese by the water with Mom, and Tanya would gaze wistfully whenever they flew off to disappear in the clouds.

And she would cajole me into hiking with her to a natural bridge, climbing the rocks for hours until we towered above the valley, pausing to watch as cascading waterfalls crashed into stair-step pools below. She always stood at the precipice and tilted her face up to the sun, and at those moments I knew that if I could give my sister anything in the world, it would be a magnificent pair of wings.

But like all seasons, springtimes must pass, and when Tanya was twenty-eight years old, on a cold winter night, her car slid across a patch of ice.

The string broke that night, and I lost my little sister, the beautiful young woman who loved animals and people, the little girl who was never afraid to play out a little more string, forever reaching for the sky.

Her funeral was attended by hundreds, a solemn assembly for those lucky enough to have loved her, all coming together to honor her life. I don't think that warm spring day when she'd decided to fly her pretty pink kite was even mentioned; so much had happened in the years since, too many poignant moments to recall.

We understood that her tethers to this world now would be the memories twined among those whose hearts she touched, each contributing another roll, so she could stretch toward the stars.

Tanya was buried just north of Ford Road, in the cemetery with the manicured lawns, close to the chapel and turtle pond, where geese gather to stand sentry over loved ones lost—under the timeless blue sky where prized pink kites dare to soar.

Stephen Geez

What Makes Grace Run

There is no other door to knowledge than the door nature opens; and there is no truth except the truths we discover in nature.

Luther Burbank

I suppose the more accurate question is, What *made* Grace run? I mean, after all, she is dead, has been dead for ten years now. But accuracy is hard to come by. This is an emotional issue for me, not one that's easily sorted out with facts. The fact is, I never knew Grace. So why do I feel so close to her?

Grace Andrews was killed by a hit-and-run driver shortly before Christmas of 1985. She was sixty-eight. He was drunk. She was out with her dog, going for her nightly loop around the lake that is the heart of this mountaintop community we call home. One of her daughters tells me that she tried to persuade Grace not to run that evening. "Let me go get the paper for you, Mom." Part of the daily ritual in Eagles Mere, Pennsylvania (population 123), is to walk or, in Grace's case, run over to Enza Laurenson's to pick up a copy of the local paper. Grace wouldn't hear of letting her daughter take over this errand.

"Oh no, I need to run."

Grace's last statement was an affirmation of something I already knew. I understand what it's like to need to run. This is something Grace and I have discussed, mostly when I'm out running when I shouldn't be, when I have cracked ribs or a swollen knee, or have just had a chemotherapy treatment.

I started running in the late '70s, about the same time Grace did. I didn't live in Eagles Mere then, but was a New Jersey graduate student going through an unhappy divorce. I was almost forty. Grace was sixty when she started to run.

What makes Grace run? She had no history of athleticism, except in her words, "years of chasing after my fourteen children." When pushed as to her reasons, she gave the answer that is word for word the same explanation I've provided curious friends: "It's just something I always wanted to do."

Many of Grace's sons and daughters and grandchildren are also runners. The year following her death, they held a race in Eagles Mere in her memory and honor: Grace's Run. It has been held every year since and has become a race associated with the triumph of spirit. Because Grace started running late in life, it is a race that puts special emphasis on the athletic ability of women over fifty. Although there are prizes in all gender and age groups, the large Grace Andrews Memorial Trophy is awarded to the first woman over the age of fifty to cross the finish line.

I had just turned fifty when my second husband and I moved to Eagles Mere. That year I amazed myself by winning the Grace Andrews Trophy. Her progeny rejoiced with me. I felt they were all really happy to see someone from Grace's hometown capture the honor. It was around that time that I began talking to Grace.

What makes Grace run? That year I told myself it was her competitive spirit. After all, Grace, like me, had not been content simply to run, but started entering races shortly after she'd developed the conditioning to run more than just a mile or two. It was the same with me. The first race I entered was a 10K. Within six months, I'd completed a marathon.

Anyone lucky enough to run in Eagles Mere soon comes to understand the profound beauty sketched by the natural world. A runner's high takes on a whole new meaning when the transcendence occurs beside a mountain lake surrounded by deep woods.

Like Grace, I run with my dog. Two laps around the lake, five mornings a week for almost eight years now, and each run has been different from all the others.

I've never seen the same sunrise twice. Every silvered shade of peach is lifted from a slightly different palette than the one from the day before. I really mean it when I call out, "Oh, look! I've never seen that deep a red in the morning sky." Sometimes deer will cross in front of me, drawing the dog quickly to attention, but he is a good boy and won't give chase. In the spring, tiny spotted fawns teeter on their spindly, little, bent-kneed legs. Once I had to stop and wait while a huge black bear finished calmly scratching behind his ear and finally cleared the road so I could continue on.

I thrill to piliated woodpeckers and great blue herons flapping slowly over my head, their long legs stretched out behind them. Every season brings a migration of a different sort.

I run in rain. I run in snow. I run with cleats strapped over my running shoes on those mornings when ice storms transform my world into a glittering, crystal wonderland. I run in fog so thick that only the memory of the road embedded in my feet guides me confidently on my way. I see the stars and moon fade. I watch night turn into day. I glory in blue-sky mornings. I see wind send branches crashing down. I run in cold so fierce my breath crystallizes and coats my hair with frost. I watch the lake freeze. I hear it thaw, tiny little shards of ice rubbing against each other and filling the air with tinkling melodies. I run when I am tired. I run when I am sick. But I always run.

What makes Grace run? Beauty has a lot to do with it.

The year I was doing battle with an advanced stage of ovarian cancer, I ran because I was still alive. Grace understood that. She was a frequent companion that year.

I didn't think I'd be able to enter Grace's Run that year. The hospital had me scheduled for some heavy-duty chemotherapy the week before the race. I knew from experience that my blood counts would be so low as to rule out any hope of racing. But, for a change, a low white-count worked in my favor. It was too low for me to receive the promised chemo, and I lined up at the start with visions of being once again the first-place woman over fifty.

My husband Gene, worried about my trying to race, insisted on running with me. I agreed but was secretly certain I would leave him and all the other old gray heads before the first mile was over. My prediction was partly right. By the time we passed the mile mark, I couldn't see another older woman anywhere. In fact, I couldn't see another competitor of any description, not because they were all behind me, but because they were all far ahead of me!

It wasn't until we hit the wooded, far side of the lake that I finally quit fighting the inevitability of my dismal showing in the event and relaxed and found the grace, so to speak, to just enjoy the experience. I finally listened to what it was that Grace had been trying to tell me.

"Beauty," she whispered, yet again, in my ear. And, of course, she was right. We ran through falling swirls of golden beech leaves. The sugar maple burned red and orange against the midnight-green banks of hemlock. Dancing water, mirrored light; the surface of the lake was too brilliant for the unshielded eye. My lungs were washed with air so clean, I felt I could drink it. The rest of the race was as glorious as any I have ever run.

Gene and I finished hand in hand, a deliberate tie for last, far behind the rest of the pack. I chilled easily in that cancer year, and so I hurried past the crowds that cheered us on and dashed home to take a shower.

As I was pulling on dry clothes, I heard Gene banging on the bathroom door.

"Hurry up," he told me. "You won the Grace Andrews

Memorial Trophy." Unlikely though it seemed, I had been the only woman over fifty in that year's race.

As I stood there accepting my award, I was certain I heard Grace giggle. *You imp,* I thought to myself and to her. *How in the world did you ever manage to persuade all those other older women to stay home this year?*

What makes Grace run? The answer has been there all along, so plain I couldn't see it. What makes Grace run?

It is joy, and nothing more.

Heather Trexler Remoff

4

ON LOVE

To love and be loved is to feel the sun from both sides.

David Viscott

One More Cast

Love is the river of life in the world.

Henry Ward Beecher

My daughter Chelsea stood knee-deep in the water, silhouetted in the sunset's waning glow. It was so dark she could no longer see her fly on the water. But still she cast, gracefully and confidently, hopeful for one last trout.

Kneeling on the nearby bank, I watched silently, proud yet a little sad. I willed a trout to take the fly, to provide sweet icing for this last outing before our lives would change forever.

But it was not to be.

"Time to go," I said.

"Just one more cast," she replied. "Just one more cast."

I smiled and recalled the first time she uttered those words. It was on our first fishing trip together, fifteen years ago.

Chelsea was just two and a half years old when we were invited to fish a stocked farm dugout. She helped me dig the worms in the garden, then eagerly pitched in to pack the gear. Bubbling with excitement as the rods were rigged up, Chelsea insisted on casting her own after I showed her how.

She shrieked with joy when the first trout hit her bait, almost wrenching the rod from her tiny hands. Her first fish.

An angler was born; I had a new fishing partner and a fresh outlook on a sport I had loved since childhood. The circle was complete.

When it came time to leave the dugout, Chelsea said—for the first of many times to come—those four magical words that are music to a father who fishes: "Just one more cast."

I packed up and still she sat, big brown eyes transfixed on the bobber floating on the pond's surface. When Chelsea finally, and reluctantly, got in the car, she recounted the outing all the way home, then provided her mom with a detailed narrative about each fish.

Over the next years, we fished together regularly, sharing conversations about fish and life, spectacular terrain, wildlife encounters, cold dunkings, sunsets, and other rich experiences that malls and video arcades can't provide. Mostly, we shared memories like the trio of swimming moose at that high alpine lake or the time we went flyfishing and Chelsea caught and released three trout—before I even made my first cast.

When Chelsea's younger sister Sarah was old enough to join us on outings, Chelsea eagerly helped teach her how to fish. Together, they'd catch night crawlers by flashlight in the backyard the night before a walleye-fishing trip. They delighted in holding up writhing double handfuls of the slimy critters, then knocking on the window to get the attention of their mom, who hates anything that crawls.

Chelsea developed a deep concern for clean water, healthy habitats and fishing ethics. Her commitment to catch-and-release became so absolute she'd gently rebuke me for keeping the odd brook trout for lunch.

Three years and many trips to lakes, ponds and small creeks after her farm pond initiation, I thought that Chelsea was ready for a larger river. After setting up my five-year-old partner on the riverbank overlooking a deep hole full of promise, I started casting my own line a few yards away.

"Daddy," she said sweetly but firmly, "you're going to have to move. This is *my* spot."

While my daughter's skills and confidence grew, many of her questions tested my knowledge of fishing and the outdoors. I answered them as best I could, but knew many responses fell short.

Once, we reluctantly agreed not to bring fishing tackle on a group hike to a pretty set of waterfalls on a clear mountain stream. But the plan changed when we got there. Several brookies were rising to eat hatching insects. Chelsea insisted on breaking out flies, split shot and fishing line from the survival kit, then promptly landed a trout with the emergency tackle tied to a willow branch.

One spring, she caught a twenty-inch bull trout, the biggest I had seen. Chelsea gently cradled the fish in the water, reassuring it of its safety with soft, soothing words, until it regained enough strength to swim away.

A few years ago, I noticed Chelsea was changing. A little girl no more, she started fishing apart from me, politely but firmly declining advice about fly selection, where to cast and just about everything else.

This sense of independence grew stronger in everything she did, from schoolwork to social life and all things in between. A confident, self-motivated young woman had emerged, seemingly overnight.

When darkness finally chased Chelsea off the river the night of our final outing, she insisted on driving me home—the first time ever after a fishing trip. Silently, I wrestled with feelings of sadness, joy and pride.

As we travel this morning to the University of Lethbridge, where the biological sciences program should provide many answers I couldn't, I'll face similar emotions.

And I'll wish we'd shared just one more cast before she left.

Bruce Masterman

Ah-nuld the Monkey

For the last ten years, I have led wildlife eco-tours in Costa Rica. Although I've had many exhilarating encounters with monkeys, sloth, jaguar and other exotic rainforest animals, there is one trip that stands out for me—when our tour group was privileged to witness a most extraordinary event.

On that particular trip, our band of wildlife enthusiasts included Jim and his teenage son, Andy. This father and son were not our typical clients. Jim was a stern-mannered former military man in his late fifties, who didn't say much, but often seemed to butt heads with his son. I felt sorry for Andy, whose enthusiasm throughout the adventure was at odds with Jim's hard edge and controlling manner. Once Jim even got a little rough with Andy, yanking him harshly by his arm when Andy lagged behind trying to catch a red and blue poison arrow frog. No one said anything, but most of the group gave Jim a wide berth after that.

I tried to spend a little extra time with Andy. He told me he was dying to see a jaguar. So we stole away late at night, after everyone else had gone to bed, to look for glass frogs and other nocturnal animals. It was our little secret.

Midway through the trip, in a remote area of Corcovado National Park, our group found a troop of twenty white-faced capuchin monkeys, which we stopped to observe.

White-faced capuchins are often used in movies because they are extremely smart and behave much like humans. While these monkeys are normally quite friendly and social, this troop had one alpha male that was unusually aggressive. He was very territorial, and by noon we had already witnessed several violent skirmishes. When any of the other monkeys got too close, he raced toward them, baring his teeth and sometimes even taking a swipe at them. We nicknamed him "Ah-nuld" after Arnold Schwarzenegger.

We followed the monkey troop, keeping a respectful distance from them as they foraged through the forest and occasionally stopped to feast on ripe figs hanging on the trees. Bringing up the rear of the troop was a very young monkey, not more than ten inches tall, whose mother was already teaching him how to climb branches and follow the others. Every so often the mother reached around the trunk of a wide tree to a branch on the far side. This was the hardest thing for the little monkey to do. He would stop, whimper, and go back and forth examining every other option before he'd finally make a leap around the trunk. Our group clapped excitedly each time he succeeded.

After a while, the young monkey grew tired and began falling behind. The farther behind he got, the louder he whimpered and wailed to get his mother's attention. His mother stopped and waited for him, but she never went back. Finally, the infant came to a large tree that was just too wide for him to get around. His crying grew louder and louder until at last his mother retraced her steps and allowed him to use her back as a bridge. Once safely around, she continued at the rear of the troop with the tired little fellow now clinging tightly onto her back, still crying.

His crying got louder and more annoying until it drew the attention of the alpha male leading the troop—the terrifying Ah-nuld. Baring his teeth and hissing angrily, the big male made his way over to the mother and child with fire in his eyes. The mother assumed a protective posture and let out a loud snarl. We all held our breaths, not sure what Ah-nuld would do, but expecting the worst.

When Ah-nuld reached the mother and child, his face suddenly softened. He looked directly at the baby monkey as if seeing him for the first time. Then Ah-nuld reached for the terrified infant, cupped the baby's tiny face gently in his hands and planted a kiss right on his forehead. The baby stopped crying immediately. Ah-nuld stayed there, gently cradling the baby's head and lovingly grooming his fur with his teeth.

Our group let out a collective sigh of relief. We were so struck by the tenderness of the moment that we barely noticed Jim, our own Ah-nuld, quietly sobbing. No one said anything, perhaps out of politeness, but I suspect inwardly everyone was glad to see Jim soften up a little.

Buzzing with excitement, we made our way back to the lodge. After dinner, I sat with Jim and several others on the veranda, swaying in hammocks and listening to the sounds of the rainforest, as beautiful and varied as a symphony.

The peace was broken when Andy walked out on the porch and Jim reached out, grabbing the boy's arm roughly. Andy tensed. My heart sank as I expected yet another power struggle between the two. All eyes were anxiously on the father and son.

Then Jim drew Andy to him, gave him a hug and said, "I'm so glad we're doing this trip together. I've always wanted you to have an experience like this. Andy, I know you don't always feel it, but I love you." Andy looked at his Dad in shock as if it were the first time he had heard him say "I love you."

Later, we found out it was.

Josh Cohen

The Promise

I looked up from our base camp on Mt. Shasta and saw that the heavens were almost white, so filled with stars. Our party was alone except for a single tent perched on the snow nearby. Its occupant was a young man about twenty-two years old.

Occasionally, I glanced over and saw him packing his day-pack for the next morning's climb. First he put in a small box, then two bottles and a lunch. He saw me staring and waved. I returned the greeting and got busy with my own preparations.

The next morning, the sun greeted the crisp dawn. After breakfast, my companions and I eagerly started our ascent. I went into my slow, steady trudge, trailing the others.

After a little while, the young man from base camp drew beside me and asked if it was okay to hike along. I hesitated. I really didn't want any company. Besides, I noticed that he limped; and I wasn't certain whether he could reach the top. I didn't want to abort my attempt at the summit to aid him.

"I'm glad for the company," I replied, in spite of my misgivings.

His name was Walt, and he told me that it was his third attempt to reach the top.

"When I was about twelve," he explained, "my father

brought me here and we started up, but the weather got bad, and we were forced to turn back."

Pausing, he smiled proudly. "Dad was a great outdoorsman and a wonderful climber."

We traversed for a short way in silence before Walt continued.

"I was born with a problem with my left leg, so I've always had trouble walking and running. But Dad refused to let that keep me back. When I was just a tiny kid, he used to take me into the Sierra to teach me to fish. I remember the first time I baited my own hook and hauled in a trout. He insisted that I clean it myself. It was the best fish I ever tasted."

We stopped by the side of the trail to put on our crampons. As we moved higher, he carried on with his story.

"When I got to be about nine, Dad started taking me into the mountains. Gradually, my leg became stronger, and eventually I could keep up with him. Last summer he called and asked if I would like to try for the summit again. We hadn't seen much of each other since my parents' divorce, and I jumped at the chance to be with him."

Walt looked down toward our base camp.

"We camped where you saw my tent. Neither of us was really in a hurry to climb. We just wanted to be together and catch up on the years we had missed. He told me that all he ever wanted was to live with his family and grow old among his children and grandchildren. Dad had long silent spells, and there was a sad aura about him."

I spoke little. I was trying to save my breath for the steeper incline. As we climbed higher, Walt kicked the steps, making my work easier. We came to a steep chute, narrow and icy, and it seemed to me that his limp was hardly noticeable.

"Why don't you lead?" he asked. "I remember that rocks tend to break away here, and I'd hate to knock one loose and have it hit you."

Ten minutes later, we stopped for a rest. By then I knew he was all of twenty-one, married and had a three-month-old son.

"My father and I got this far last time when I became ill from the altitude and my leg buckled under me. The pain got so bad, I couldn't go on. Dad hoisted me onto his back and, somehow, he brought us both into camp before getting help. The search and rescue team carried me to the hospital. Dad and I promised each other that we would try again."

Then Walt looked down and squeezed back a tear. "But we never got to do it. He died last month."

After a solemn moment, we trekked onward, and just below the summit, we rested again on a small rock outcropping. The sky blazed blue, and I could see at least 180 degrees to eternity. The sun was high, and its rays warmed me as I ate some trail food.

A few feet away, Walt sat on a boulder holding in both hands the box he had packed the night before. He whispered, "We're going to make it this time. You carried me last time, and now it's my turn to carry you."

At that point, Walt rose abruptly, and with no further word he headed to the peak. I stared into his face as he strode past me. He seemed to be in a trance with an almost beatific smile lighting his face. I followed.

Finally, we reached the top. I was only a few steps behind.

Carefully, Walt knelt on the snow, reached into his pack and reverently removed the box. Then, after digging a hole about fifteen inches deep and attentively pouring some of his father's ashes into it, he covered the hole and built a small stone cairn over it.

When he stood up, he faced north, then east, south and west. Turning his body toward each direction once again, he reached into the box and gently sprinkled some ashes to each compass point.

Walt's face was painted with joy and triumph behind a rush of tears. He flung the last of the remains into the wind and shouted, "We made it, Dad, we made it! Rest on our mountaintop. I promise I'll be back when your grandson can meet you here."

Mel Lees

Sonar

What a grand thing, to be loved! What a grander thing still, to love!

Victor Hugo

High up in an oak tree, the five hairless, newborn squirrels nursed, curled tightly against their mother for warmth. Using her bushy tail like a blanket, she draped it over her latest family. When the time came for her to feed, she covered the babies with the leaves and bits of bark that made up her nest. Eyes still tightly closed, barely two ounces at birth, the little ones were completely helpless.

By the time the squirrels were three weeks old, soft, distinctive gray fur covered their bodies. Somewhere between five and six weeks of age, their eyes opened, giving them their first glimpse of their new world. Already agile and swift, with sharp curved nails, they played tag up and down the oak tree's trunk, experimenting with jumps from branch to swaying branch. All but one.

At eight weeks, four of the young were foraging for acorns, hickory nuts, pinecones and other seeds. The littlest one was still eating from the stored supplies.

By the time they were four months old, the babies moved

out of the nest, and mother squirrel was having her second litter of the year.

The smallest female from the first litter half crawled and fell out of the oak tree onto the forest floor. Her siblings had already scattered. She could hear her mother chattering nearby. Carefully, nose sniffing, whiskers twitching, she groped her way toward the fading voice. Her hunched, shuffling gait prevented quick movement. Turning her head side to side, she listened intently. By now, her family had departed, leaving her behind. It was survival of the fittest in the woods.

Soft paws scraped over rocks and roots as the squirrel hauled herself over the obstacles. Her tail twitched with anxiety as she shrilly shrieked her distress. Nothing answered her calls for help. Heart pounding rapidly in her narrow chest, the squirrel continued her journey.

Within a short time, the little female panted her panic. Her body trembled with exhaustion. Curling into a tight ball, tail wrapped around and over herself, she waited.

Suddenly, a strange vibration rumbled the forest floor. Twigs crackled. Closer. Closer. The cadence pulsated throughout her body. Unfamiliar sounds made the squirrel tremble.

"Mom!" Johnny's keen eyesight had spotted the frightened baby. As the son of a licensed wildlife rehabilitator, he had helped raise many wild babies and knew that one lying so still on the ground was unusual. With gentle hands, he scooped the gray ball of fur off the forest floor.

"What is it?" I walked up alongside my son to find him petting the squirrel baby. The little one snuggled into the warmth of his cupped hands, relaxing as a finger delicately stroked her. His soothing voice calmed her as it murmured assurances of safety and comfort.

"Look, Mom," Johnny held her out for my inspection. Dark slits with tiny eyelashes showed where her eyes should have been. "She has no eyes. She's blind. I guess this one's a keeper, huh?"

Carefully cradling his precious find, Johnny and I took the little girl home. It was love, with or without first sight.

We set up a cage, and Johnny christened the newest arrival to our household "Sonar."

"Sonar. Sonar Squirrel, because of how well she hears," he explained.

Soon water, peanut butter, sunflower seeds and corn on the cob satisfied her thirst and hunger. Tentatively, she explored the safe confinement, a miniature forest complete with branches, stones and leaves. She discovered a bed of something soft and warm. Satiated and content, she cuddled into her new nest.

The blind squirrel had a name, a home and Johnny.

Sonar adored Johnny above the rest of the family. She eagerly responded to his voice, dashing into his arms as soon as he opened her cage door. "You're my squirrel-girl," he'd whisper as she would nibble his ears and run her soft paws through his hair.

Each morning, Sonar would search Johnny's shirt pocket, squeaking in delight when she discovered the treat he'd carefully hidden there. After school, she'd curl around his neck as he did his homework. He'd tenderly brush her tail out of his eyes so he could see his books. Occasionally, Sonar ventured down his arm to help him, nibbling at his pencil or papers.

Evenings would find her sleeping contentedly on his chest while Johnny watched TV in the living room, stroking her soft fur. Before heading off to his own bed, he'd carefully tuck Sonar into her nest, wishing her sweet dreams.

Two years and one day after Johnny found her, Sonar passed away nestled in my son's arms. Wrapping his little friend in his shirt, Johnny gently held Sonar one last time before burying her among our other departed critters.

At sixteen, my son was not too old to cry.

Linda Mihatov

The Okay Signal

Blessed is the influence of one true, loving human soul on another.

George Eliot

I was only fifteen when my father suggested I get my scuba-diving certification—fifteen years old and right in the middle of that stage when you can't relate to anyone, let alone your father.

My dad started diving when he was also in his teens, but fell away from it with the responsibilities and costs of raising three children. However, he never let his lack of any recent experience prevent him from telling stories of the "bathwater warm, crystal blue water" of the Caribbean and his days of adventure below it.

When he offered me the chance to visit a world I knew only from his stories and the pictures I'd seen in magazines, I welcomed the opportunity, but thought little more of it than a new activity that might prove to be fun.

Over the next months he drove me into the city and took the certification classes with me. He bought me my first mask and fins, and he was there when I received my dive license after my test in the frigid and murk-filled waters of upstate New York.

Soon afterwards, Dad planned a trip for the family, and we made our way to Key Largo, Florida. We would experience our first dive together, and I could finally see for myself all the wonders he had described.

As the dive boat moved away from shore, my stomach became nervous with the expectation of what I was about to do. At this point I noticed that I was the only younger person on the boat, which added to my insecurity and made me feel like I was somewhere I didn't belong. My eyes traveled from one face to another until I settled on my dad's reassuring eyes. He gave me a small smile.

I wanted to do this for him. I *had* to do this!

A short while later, the boat dropped anchor. My father and I entered the ocean together. As I got over the initial shock of the water, I took a deep breath and saw my dad next to me, sending me the okay signal. It was just what I needed to see.

With that we began our descent, and an unbounded spectrum of colors quickly opened up around us. No picture or television image could capture the beauty of what we saw.

A school of yellow jacks flitted gracefully above, swaying gently with the current. Countless parrot fish danced around, totally unfazed by our presence, while the angel fish and purple trumpet fish kept a slightly more reverent distance. I looked over at my dad gazing at me, savoring my joy.

Below us, a myriad of sponges and purple sea fans waved hypnotically, framed by red fire coral and the eerie-looking yellow and green brain coral. Darting in and out of the nooks in the coral, blue chromis and neon goby played hide and seek, while black grouper, barracuda and even a green moray eel looked on suspiciously.

I glanced over at Dad, and again he flashed the okay signal.

We swam around a bit more but before we knew it, our oxygen tanks were low and we had to head up. We surfaced and carefully made our way back to the boat. I gave my dad a big smile as I reached out to help him on board.

I left the water that day with a greater love and respect for nature. I took with me the knowledge that as confusing as life may get, there will always be a place where I can be at peace and feel at home. Most importantly, my Dad gave me a tangible connection that I desperately needed as an awkward fifteen-year-old. Learning to scuba dive provided us with a link that said he'd always be there for me.

Through the years, I haven't always been that great at expressing my feelings. Thankfully, Dad knows me well enough to realize that every time we slip underneath that bath-water warm, crystal blue water of the Caribbean and I give him the okay signal, I'm saying much more than "I'm ready to descend on our next adventure together."

I'm saying, "I love you."

Zach Wahl

The Tale of the Goose

We love because it is the only true adventure.

Nikki Giovanni

More than a decade ago, my wife Barbara and I bought a wonderful five-acre property on a small mountain. We feel incredibly lucky to live where we do. Every day we marvel at the beauty of our land, and we like sharing it with the fish, ducks and deer, as well as the horde of birds that grace it all year 'round.

The geese are a different story entirely. I must confess that for the most part I have never liked geese. They tend to travel in large flocks, make an awful din, are unpleasantly aggressive, and above all, they make a terrible mess. When they come in waves each spring and fall, it's a war of attrition. I want them to go; they are determined to stay. They settle at the edge of the pond and I run at them, flapping my arms and shouting.

The idea is to make them so edgy and uncomfortable they will decide to leave. For years I won; each gaggle would stay a few hours, or at most a day or two. Then they would decide it just was too unfriendly a place and off they would go.

Six years ago they came again, but something was

different. Two of the geese, clearly a pair, stayed away from the others, both on land and in the water. It was as if they were saying, "We're different. Don't include us with our brethren." When the others finally left, honking in anger, the pair left with them, but I knew something was up. I was sure they would be back. Two days later, they came back, quietly, in the evening, alighting in the pond.

They watched with concern as I walked to its edge. I knew they were waiting to see what I would do. As I looked at them, trying to figure what approach to take, Barbara joined me. "They are a pair. You know they mate for life. They won't bother us. Let them stay."

And so I did.

The ducks continued to come for their regular feedings. At first, the geese watched from a distance as the ducks ate. A few days later, I could see them watching from the far side of the pond and then, suddenly, with a huge flourish of honking, they charged over to join the ducks.

For six years they held sway on the pond. Each year the female nested, but only once did that result in goslings. When they were gone for any period, you could hear them coming from miles away; it sounded like an entire gaggle. And when they landed in the pond with great fanfare, they would talk to each other, honking loudly for a few minutes before settling down.

They were clearly devoted to each other, and gradually we found ourselves becoming quite attached to them. They had decided this was their pond: Ducks were okay, but not other geese.

At first they left it up to me to get rid of the other geese. Finally, after one particularly difficult time persuading some unwanted geese to leave, I turned to Mr. Goose whom we had named George and said, "Some help you are. It's your pond; you get them to leave."

Now I know geese do not understand English, and I knew it was pure coincidence, but after that George and Mrs. George took a very active role in flying at the intruders. Most of the time they succeeded, but when they couldn't make the invaders fly off, I would help out.

Our geese, like most geese, were very smart. Often they would join the intruders, and when I rushed them, they would squawk loudly and fly off. Invariably the whole gaggle would follow. Then the next morning or later that night, George and Mrs. George would return, boisterous as ever.

Almost always when we arrived home, as our car passed a small bridge at the bottom of the pond, the two of them would start a huge din, necks out straight, honking at the top of their voices.

"Our watch-geese," said Barbara. And so they were.

After any event on the pond that aroused their attention, they would face each other and talk. Their conversations were a marvel to watch. They communicated more in a given day than most human couples do in a week.

Their devotion was extraordinary. They were paired for life, together twenty-four hours a day, never far apart either in the confines of the pond or on the adjacent rolling lawns. It was easy to tell they enjoyed each other's company.

Gradually, they began to trust us. At first, they would stand on the edge as I fed the ducks, waiting impatiently until I went off a distance, then they would rush in, pushing the ducks aside to grab their share. It took several years before they led the run (or more properly, the waddle) for the food. George always came first, hissing if he felt I was too close.

They spent the day in the pond or at its edge. Sometimes George would stand on one leg, his neck and head buried in his wing, but at our approach, even fifty or a hundred yards away, he would stretch his neck and keep one eye riveted on us, suspiciously watching our every move.

As he became more trusting, George would stay with his head buried, but I could still see that eye fixed on me. It took a year before he would completely ignore me, letting me come within ten feet of them as I removed algae or leaves from the pond.

Then one day as I threw the corn, he came running up ahead of the ducks, stopping seven or eight feet away and talking softly without any hissing. And when I threw the corn on the ground, George eagerly pecked at it, eating and talking at the same time. I marveled at this feat—I couldn't figure out how he could eat and talk all at once.

And so it went. They became our friends; we were captivated by their devotion. We never spoke about it, but I think we both wondered if it could be that their bond to each other was greater than ours, even though we had been married for decades.

In early April they made a nest, but it was in a different site. Every other time it had been on the far side of the pond, behind a willow tree. This time it was close to us, in a wooded, protected area at the edge of the pond. I could see Mrs. George sitting on that nest—awake, watching, protecting. Perhaps they thought that a change of scenery, of nesting site, would change their luck and produce a gaggle of goslings.

At the same time George's personality changed dramatically; he would not permit the deer on the front lawn. He would honk loudly and angrily, then charge, running or flying just above the ground, wings fully spread, making an enormous din.

His behavior was clearly purposeful. He wanted a full pail of corn on the ground, and he saw to it that the marauding deer did not gobble it up. He tolerated the few ducks, but he knew they would not eat much of it. He wanted it there for the infrequent occasions when Mrs. George would leave the nest, eat and drink hurriedly, and then return to her maternal labors.

Sometimes when Barbara was gardening, he would come close to her and stand there until she got up and filled the pail with corn and threw it on the ground near the pond. Then Mrs. George would appear and feed while George, eating nothing, would stand guard.

And so it went for weeks. Then one day early in May, I

arose as usual, dressed and ambled to the garage to get the pail of corn. George was in the pond, but unlike every other day he seemed uninterested in my activities. I walked to the area at the edge of the pond where I ordinarily threw the corn. He remained in the pond, still uninterested. I threw the corn on the ground as usual. Thirty minutes later when I left for work, eight deer were there, and George didn't chase them. *That's strange*, I thought.

The next day George was sitting at the edge of the pond, not far from the nest. Again I threw a pail of corn. Again he paid no attention. I had a very queasy feeling. Something was wrong. I tried to locate Mrs. George, but she wasn't visible; perhaps she was behind the tree.

On the morning of the third day, George was sitting in the same place. I threw the corn down. Still no response. I looked at him. Something was very wrong. I walked to within a few feet of him and asked, "What's wrong, old man?"

With that he turned to me, and as I looked at him, I gasped, for in that eye there was an unmistakable look of terrible despair, of sadness, of overwhelming sorrow. And in that moment of communication between goose and man, I blurted out, "I'm so sorry."

Then, shaken by that look, I walked around to the nest. It was empty, but undisturbed. There were no eggs, no sign of a struggle.

I was to learn later that a coyote had killed Mrs. George in the middle of the night. Not knowing that his beloved partner was dead and puzzled by the benign appearance around the nest, I walked back to where George had been sitting, but he had left.

Later, after we knew the full story, Barbara said, "Maybe he has not gone forever. Maybe he'll be back. Sometimes they find new partners."

She was giving voice to that wellspring of inner hope that helps us all deal with tragic events. But we knew it was not to be. George, heartbroken, was not coming back.

That look of overwhelming sorrow in his eye has haunted me ever since.

Of course, life goes on. The flocks of geese returned almost immediately. There was no goose couple to tell them the pond was already taken and to drive them off. I still didn't want the pond overrun with geese, and, as in the past, I made it clear they were not welcome. They were tenacious, but so was I, and I harassed them until, protesting loudly, they flew off.

This went on for several weeks, and then I noticed that a pair stayed apart from the rest. One day after the larger gaggle had gone, they came back and stayed a few hours. They watched me closely, obviously testing whether I would let an isolated pair stay. When I left them undisturbed that first evening, they got the message. The next afternoon they were back, and the day after that. They haven't adopted the pond as their own just yet, but we think they will.

I hug my wife a lot more now. Whenever we walk, she has always been the one to take my hand. Now I seek her hand as often as she takes mine. She thinks it's my mellowing with age.

There is some truth in that, but for the most part it's George and his wife. Mostly, it is the tale of the goose.

Donald Louria

5

THROUGH THE EYES OF A CHILD

If a child is to keep alive his inborn sense of wonder, he needs the companionship of at least one adult who can share it, rediscovering the joy, excitement and mystery of the world we live in.

Rachel Carson

Swimming with Dolphins

Love is one of the answers humankind invented to stare death in the face, when time ceases to be a measure, and we can briefly know paradise.

Octavio Paz

"It's not easy to die when you are only fifteen."

Those were the words that began the story I heard from Robert White, a North Carolina factory worker. He and his wife were visiting their daughter Lee in the hospital as they did every evening, but Lee had already accepted her fate.

She knew she had an illness that would not spare her. She knew that, in spite of their finest efforts, the doctors couldn't save her. She suffered a lot, but never complained.

This particular evening, she seemed tranquil and composed, but suddenly she said, "Mama, daddy—I think I'm going to die soon, and I'm afraid. I know I'm going to a better world than this one, and I'm longing for some peace at last, but it's hard to accept the idea that I'm going to die at only fifteen."

They could have lied, telling her of course she wasn't going to die, but they didn't have the heart. Somehow, her courage was worth more than their pretense. They just cuddled her and cried together.

Then she said, "I always dreamed of falling in love, getting married, having kids . . . but above all I would have liked to work in a big marine park with dolphins. I've loved them and wanted to know more about them since I was little. I still dream of swimming with them, free and happy in the open sea."

She'd never asked for anything, but now she said with all the strength she could muster, "Daddy, I want to swim in the open sea among the dolphins just once. Maybe then I wouldn't be so scared of dying."

It seemed like an absurd, impossible dream, but she, who had given up just about everything else, hung on to it.

Robert and his family talked it over and decided to do everything they could. They had heard of a research center in the Florida Keys, and they phoned them.

"Come at once," they said. But that was easier said than done.

Lee's illness had used up all their savings, and they had no idea how they would be able to afford air tickets to Florida. Then their six-year-old, Emily, mentioned that she'd seen something on television about a foundation that grants the wishes of very sick children. She'd actually written down the telephone number in her diary because it seemed like magic to her.

Robert didn't want to listen. He thought it sounded like a fairy tale or a very sick joke, and he gave in only when Emily started crying and accusing him of not really wanting to help Lee. So he phoned the number and, sure enough, three days later they were all on an airplane and on their way. Emily felt a bit like a fairy godmother who had solved all their problems with a wave of her magic wand.

When they arrived at Grass Key, Lee was pale and terribly thin. The chemotherapy she'd been having had made all her hair fall out, and she looked ghastly, but she didn't want to rest for a minute and begged her parents to take her straightaway to the dolphins. It was an unforgettable scene. When she got into the water, Lee was already so weak she hardly had the strength to move. They had put her in a wet suit so she wouldn't get cold and a life preserver to keep her afloat.

Robert towed her out toward the dolphins, Nat and Tursi, who were frolicking about thirty feet away from them. At first they seemed distracted and uninterested, but when Lee called them softly by name, they responded without hesitation. Nat came over first, raised his head and gave her a kiss on the end of her nose. Then Tursi came over and greeted her with a flurry of little high-pitched squeaks of joy. A second later they picked her up with their mighty fins and carried her out to sea with them.

"It feels like I'm flying!" cried Lee, laughing with delight.

Lee's family hadn't heard her laugh like that since before she became ill. They could hardly believe it was true, but there she was, gripping Nat's fin and challenging the wind and the immensity of the ocean. The dolphins stayed with Lee for more than an hour, always tender, always attentive, never using any unnecessary force, always responsive to her wishes.

Maybe it's true that they are more intelligent and sensitive creatures than man. What was certain was that those marvelous dolphins understood that Lee was dying and wanted to console her as she faced her great journey into the unknown. From the moment they took her in hand, they never left her alone for a second. They got her to play and obeyed her commands with a sweetness that was magical. In their company, Lee found for one last time the enthusiasm and the will to live. She was strong and happy like she used to be. At one point she shouted, "The dolphins have healed me, Daddy!"

There are no words to describe the effect that swim had on her. When she got out of the water, it was as if she had been reborn.

The next day she was too weak to get out of bed. She didn't even want to talk, but when Robert took her hand she squeezed it and whispered, "Daddy, don't be sad for me. I'll never be afraid again. The dolphins have made me understand that I have nothing to fear." Then she said, "I know I'm going to die tonight. Promise me that you'll cremate my body and scatter my ashes in the sea where all dolphins swim. They gave me the most beautiful moments of my life. They have left me with a great feeling of peace in my heart, and I know they will be with me on the long journey that lies ahead."

Just before dawn, Robert's little girl woke and whispered, "Hold me, Daddy, I'm so cold." And she died like that in his arms a few minutes later—passing from sleep to death without a ripple. They only realized her suffering was over because her body became colder and heavier.

They cremated her as she wanted and went out the next day to scatter her ashes in the ocean amongst the dolphins. They were all crying—not only Lee's family, but also the sailors on the boat who had taken them out into the bay. And then, suddenly, through their tears, they saw the great arching silver shapes of Nat and Tursi leaping out of the water ahead.

As Robert recounted, "They had come to take our daughter home."

Allegra Taylor

Kristi and Holly

One of the deepest secrets of life is that all that is really worth doing is what we do for others.

Lewis Carroll

From the time our daughters could walk more than fifty yards carrying a small backpack, we took them hiking in the mountains. When our youngest, Kristi, was six, and her older sister Holly was ten, Russ and I decided the girls were proficient enough to go on a major hike to the top of a real mountain. We live on Vancouver Island in British Columbia, and one of our favorite hikes is the trek up Mt. Albert Edward.

In order to make the ascent, we first had to hike six and a half miles to our base camp at Circlet Lake. We took our time getting to base camp, stopping overnight en route and, on our arrival, setting up camp on the shores of the lake. After two cloudy, rainy days of huddling in our tent, we were ecstatic to wake up to a clear blue sky on the day of our ascent. The climb includes an ascent about 500 feet straight up a slippery slope to the ridge. We tied a rope around Kristi's waist for this part of the hike, and we were pleased with both girls' perseverance and energy.

Once on the ridge, it's a long, gradual hike to the final

slope up to the top. The peak is visible from a long way off, which is fortunate because like the proverbial carrot at the end of a stick, that perfect pyramid loomed enticingly in front of us almost as soon as we mounted the ridge. To be truthful, Russ and I had decided we would make it at least to the ridge, so we could all get a look at the top of a mountain. Then we would decide if our little team had the strength to go further. We stopped for a lunch break a short way along the ridge and suggested, "We could turn back anytime, you know," looking closely at Holly and Kristi for their reactions.

Holly urged us all onward, convinced we could and should do it. Kristi agreed, so on we went. As we slowly made our way along the ridge, we came to a rise where we saw a group of about a dozen teenage boys, all with heavily laden backpacks beside them, accompanied by a man with a big dog, a huge backpack, and believe it or not, a guitar. The boys all looked exhausted and unhappy, like they weren't going anywhere anytime soon.

When we passed by, there seemed to be a stirring in the group, like a breeze had suddenly revived them. As we trudged on, we were aware that the teenagers behind us were suddenly on their feet, backpacks hurriedly slipped on and their hike urgently resumed.

As we started up the final slope to the peak, the boys began to overtake us with a speed I would have thought impossible when I first laid eyes on them minutes before. As two hiked past us, we heard one murmur to the other, "No little kid's going to pass me!" We smiled to ourselves and continued our slow two-steps-up, one-step-back march up the loose scree.

Soon, along came the leader with his backbreaking back-pack, his guitar slung across it. I couldn't help thinking that if I were in his position, I would have settled for a harmonica. Even his large Labrador retriever had saddlebags slung across his back. "He carries his own food, like everybody else," the leader told us.

"I have to thank you guys," he went on. "This is a group of

young offenders who have been ordered to be part of an Outward Bound program, hiking in the mountains for thirteen days. They were grumbling and carrying on like they were climbing Mt. Everest without oxygen until they saw you. They couldn't believe that a family with little kids was doing this for fun, and they were determined to make it to the top before you guys did. So thanks."

We all laughed, and I could see Holly and Kristi grow right in front of me. That day, I think those young offenders gave our daughters a gift, the kind of gift that parents spend a lifetime trying to give to their children—the gift of self-confidence, of pride, of knowing you can do something that others think you can't. And our two daughters had the satisfaction of knowing that they had singlehandedly motivated other people to push themselves that much harder.

As we lingered at the summit, one of the teens approached us, desperate to ask a question, "Do you do this often?"

In the years since, we've hiked back up Albert Edward several times, but that was our first attempt. So I guess I could answer him now, "Yes, my friend. We do."

Star Weiss

Walking with Jenni

Love is a great beautifier.

Louisa May Alcott

Snow has returned to the Rockies. Outside my window, all the Douglas firs are sugared by a night spent in falling snow and frosting cloud. In the bare aspens, a Steller's jay cocks a white eyebrow and peers in the windows to see if we'll put out more peanuts. Mountain chickadees chuckle. Nuthatches beep and giggle. Two mule deer bucks stand grazing beside the gravel drive. The mist moving through the forest gives the magical impression of an elfin fairyland.

This morning, I'm wishing my five-year-old niece Jenni were here. She loved to go on nature walks. "Uncle Chuck, can we go botanizing?" was her frequent request, and out and away we'd go—in rain or shine.

Her brother Paul also loves "botanizing," but for different reasons. For him, it's an exercise in reading the landscape, a great adventure of identification and discovery. By the time he was three, he could identify a dozen trees by their English and German common names.

But for Jenni, a nature walk was about meeting new creatures that might need to be loved.

Squatting beside a tiny chickweed blossom, she would look up to me and say, "I love this chickweed. May I touch it?" She would stroke it with a finger and smile, and sometimes she'd bend down and touch it to her lips.

Walking with Jenni in the woods wasn't about cataloging, but about encounters—each one a possible new friend. Loblolly pinecone, sweetgum ball, fox squirrel, shamrock oxalis, spider web and snail—each one a possible source of delight, each receiving a nod or a variation of a hug.

Jaded adult that I am, I know nature to be a battlefield of endless struggles, a hard place where life and death trade places in a merry-go-round of unlamented losses and uncelebrated births. But walking with Jenni would restore my sense of wonder. With one wave of Jenni's small hand or the sound of her little voice singing its happiness, a dandelion seedhead became a crystal ball of fairy ballerinas waiting to be pirouetted out and through the summer air.

Even though it's been over five years since she was taken from us in a car accident, I try to keep walking with Jenni. Although the woods seem darker and more chilly than ever, she wouldn't have it so. Walking with Jenni, these woods are a wonderland, icicles are candy canes, and pine squirrels are glancing over their shoulder at me with glee.

Walking with Jenni, the world is here to be loved.

Charles Doersch

On Top of the World

The snow glistened like sparkling diamonds in the sun as Blain came zipping around the moguls at the base of lower Treasure. His bright yellow ski parka was easy to spot among the children coming down the same run. This was Blain's second year of skiing, and like many other twelve-year-olds in his sixth-grade class, he had taken to it like a duck to water.

As my husband Judd and I ran up the gentle slope calling out to our son, the snow crunched under our footsteps. Hearing his name and turning around, Blain was delighted to see us and to think we had seen him skiing down the mountain so expertly that cold, crisp morning. His expression changed to one of concern as he realized that something must be wrong.

It had been only twenty-four hours since the hospital conducted the tests and only a couple of weeks since his teacher noticed him putting his head on his desk when his work was completed. Then we spotted his enlarged spleen. When the doctors wanted to keep him overnight, Blain got teary-eyed and was very upset. He really wanted to be with his buddies from school on their special ski day. And then the doctor called: If we didn't get him off the mountain, our son might fall, rupture his spleen and die. They didn't tell us about the leukemia until later.

On the way down from the mountain, Blain slept with his head in my lap. He knew we were headed to the hospital, but he was exhausted. In his present condition, he was operating on pure guts, refusing to give up anything, even if he really didn't feel up to it.

Ever the outdoorsman, at ten years of age, Blain had become the youngest member of an exclusive group known as "The Circle of the Gobbler," after he called in and brought home his own spring turkey. He had nearly driven us out of the house with his endless clucks and gobbles as he spent all of his spare time practicing, trying to get just the right sound.

When he was only six, he and Judd went on a pack-in fishing trip with some friends, including a boy around Blain's age. They all rode into the high country on horseback, and Blain and his little buddy were flying high as they bounced along the mountain trail, astride their respective mounts. After setting up camp, they took out their fishing gear and headed down to the picturesque lake. It wasn't long before Blain and his dad had a stringer full of pan-perfect trout. They had caught their supper, and I'm certain that fish never tasted better to the two little novices. Alongside his day's catch, Blain looked like Huckleberry Finn as he posed for his proud father on the other side of the camera.

One weekend after Blain's radiation treatments were completed, some friends invited us to a picnic extravaganza. After eating our lunch, our fifteen-year-old daughter Lisa and a couple of other teenagers decided to climb the peak that was looming before us like a giant challenge. It wasn't long before others decided that it would be a great way to work off the delicious meal we had all just devoured.

I made sure Blain was busy throwing a Frisbee with someone and told him where I was going. Then I began my ascent along with some other hardy souls. It was a beautiful climb and not particularly easy. Along the way, we all had to stop periodically to catch our breath. As we reached the top, there was a great sense of accomplishment in having made the climb. The view from the summit was spectacular! The vehicles and those people remaining at the picnic site were as tiny as toys moving around below us. I looked for Blain, but couldn't see him anywhere. Then I spotted Judd making the climb; he was already about halfway up.

Suddenly, I recognized Blain's colorful shirt. He had decided he wasn't going to be left behind. If the rest of us had made the climb, so would he.

I prayed that he wouldn't fall and hurt himself. He was wearing western boots, hardly the best thing for climbing. Everyone began to cheer Blain on as he headed closer and closer. He crossed over a rockslide area, and I held my breath as he eased his feet over those slippery rocks. Slowly and confidently, he took his next step, one by one, with the same determination that had always marked his spirit. We were so proud of him.

No matter how demanding the challenge was or how badly he felt, our precious Blain had been through fourteen months of treatment, but he wouldn't give up. And slowly but surely, he made his way up the mountain—to be with his family and friends.

When our courageous son passed away eight days short of his thirteenth birthday, he was still on top of the world! And we're still right there with him.

Diane Graff Cooney

The Emily Tree

Children will not remember you for the material things you provided, but for the feeling that you cherished them.

Gail Sweet

The day started out as many others before. I was always in a rush, always trying to accomplish too much in a day's time, not giving my full attention to anything or anyone. It seemed as though the kids were always underfoot, and at four years and eighteen months, I guess they were—that's where they're supposed to be.

Many times I heard that these were the best days, that the kids would grow up too soon, that I should cherish the moments when they were young and actually wanted my attention. I couldn't see it, though. I was blinded by the overflowing work on my desk, the pile of bills in the mail and the long list of things to do.

It was a warm morning, so I took the kids outside and started weeding the flower beds as Emily and Logan played nearby. I was glad to have a moment to myself while the kids were occupied.

It wasn't long before I realized that the two of them were

sitting beneath a small tree in the backyard, looking up into the branches and singing a song. We had dubbed it "The Emily Tree" simply because it had been planted when Emily was a baby.

That very first summer, we sat our baby in her play pool beside the newly planted pin oak, a species chosen because of its ability to grow quickly. And now, here we were—days and months had passed, and Emily had grown quickly as well. She had turned into a bright and curious child who was always eager to learn and explore and help her little brother Logan do the same.

Curiosity got the best of me, and I headed over to ask why they were sitting there, apparently singing to the tiny tree.

Logan only smiled, but Emily told me softly in her matter-of-fact little voice, "You have to spend time with something if you want it to grow up nice and strong." She turned to finish her song.

Well, the weeds didn't get pulled that day. Instead, I went into the house, gathered a blanket and a picnic lunch, and joined my daughter and son under the Emily Tree.

Carol Troesch

Paddling Down North

Adventure must be held in delicate fingers. It should be handled, not embraced. It should be sipped, not swallowed in a gulp.

Ashley Dukes

It's only our second day paddling down the Yukon River. Already we're having fun bouncing off ripples on the outside bends. But this is not white water. The so-called "Thirty Mile" section that drains Lake Laberge holds little threat even for me, a novice in fast water. My son Ross is instructing from the stern of the canoe, having taken a course in "moving water." Yet I'm still worried about rapids that could upset us, or dumping gear that we need to get us through the next ten days.

I hear it first as a hissing, then glance ahead at the roughened surface. Is it wind or shallow water? I glance back to Brian and Roger. Their red canoe is tight to the right shore. "Let's go to the right," I decide. We dig hard across the current, toward the channel near the bank. As we approach, the water is getting faster. Ross, realizing that we should be pointing downstream, hollers to turn, but we're out of time; it's obvious that we'll hit the bar sideways.

"Hang on, we're into it!" I scream.

Wham! The keel hits bottom, and the water pushes us off.

"Lean downstream!" hollers Ross.

We hit again, but stay upright. We're clear of the bar, out into the channel, still dry and still upright.

When the adrenaline subsides, we check the canoe's shell under our cargo. No damage there. We contemplate the disaster that could have been, agree next time to keep better watch and accept that we have to point downstream in emergencies.

As the city boy, I wanted to canoe the Yukon River from Whitehorse to Dawson City, the goldrush route of the original "Klondike Stampeders" in the late 1800s. Ross had asked to come along. We'd hiked together before, on a long trek in Nepal when Ross was only sixteen, but now he was twice that age. In those days, he insisted on calling me "Gil," thinking that somehow using my first name would make him more mature and not just father and son.

We watch the river and whatever we can spot in the forest. At every historical marker on our charts, we pull out, dragging the canoes up the bank. Today, we're at the junction of the Teslin River and the Yukon. We tour the few log structures left standing from the days of the gold rush, trying to imagine the hardship of living through winter here. Then, back into the boats for the next stretch, I inspect the maps, while Ross and Roger search for caves along the river's edge.

I'm delighted that Brian and Roger are with us. Our meeting in Whitehorse was coincidental. The experience of these two brothers on long, white-water trips is invaluable. What surprises me is that Ross fits their mold so well, fishing for Northern Pike, panning for gold flecks at the creek mouths and inspecting the ancient remains of river boats wrecked on the sand bars.

The days slip past like the settlements on the banks. We paddle for several hours, then drift a straight run of the river, keeping an eye out for dead-end channels and shallow bars.

I follow the charts religiously, trying not to miss any navigation obstacle or an abandoned way station of the original "Stampeders."

We still have to face the Five Fingers rapids. Will the water level be high enough to get past the rocks? Will we be able to string the same course that our experienced partners run? A few morning hours of paddling, and I can make out the huge cliffs that mark the rapids and slice the river into fingers. I slow my strokes and do everything to avoid entering the suction line that will pull us in. Ross isn't worried. "Just follow the course the boys take, and we'll be through before you know it."

There's no place to beach here, and the current's speeding up. Roger goes into the gap on the right, so we follow. We're committed. Ross keeps paddling, faster now. The vortices off the pillars force us into the middle. We drop about three feet as we shoot through the gap, then we're into flat water again.

Brian hails us from our left; they've cut into a back eddy behind one pillar and sit almost motionless. We brace hard and swing in behind. While my heart slowly returns to a normal rate, everyone else shares the exhilaration of the fast passage. But it's not enough for Roger. He swings his bow around, and they head out into the current again, searching for standing waves to the left of the main channel. Ross wants to follow them. I pick up on their enthusiasm, enjoying the rush as we bounce over the waves. The canoe has more buoyancy than I expected. If there had been an easy way, we'd have gone back and run through it again.

Out of the fast water we relax into a lazy drift. This guy in the back of my canoe is a different person from the teenager I had hiked with those months in Nepal, different from the kid I had taught all of my outdoor skills. I can't remember doing anything like this with my dad.

Past the Five Fingers the days seem to compress. At the mouth of the White River we take a break. Ross unpacks his fishing rod and in five minutes catches a Northern Pike. Soon another, then a third.

A day later, we sight a scar on a hillside that marks the slide above Dawson City. We pass the mouth of Klondike Creek where all the big discoveries were made. I'm sorry the journey is ending, but it's been a great one for Ross and me— like Nepal of years ago, but better. A conversation between equals, not father and son. I've even learned how to run some white water.

As we haul out, Ross puts an arm around my shoulders. "That was a great trip. Thanks, Dad!"

I return the hug. The key word for me is "Dad."

Gil Parker

Mosquitoes

While on a campout at Cumberland Falls State Park several years ago, my son Tim and I spent the night sleeping in the back of our van.

In the middle of the night, Tim awoke scratching one of many mosquito bites and whispered, "Daddy, why did God put mosquitoes on Earth?"

I didn't have an answer, so I countered with a question, "Why do you think he did, Tim?"

He didn't respond and quickly fell back asleep.

The next morning, as we headed home, Tim suddenly exclaimed, "Daddy, I know why God put mosquitoes on Earth!"

I looked over and couldn't wait for the answer from his proud face.

"Because he didn't want them in heaven, that's why!"

Guy Lustig

Cassie

This was the simple happiness of complete harmony with her surroundings, the happiness that asks for nothing, that just accepts, just breathes, just is.

Countess Van Arnim

I knew a little girl with copper hair.

She loved her family, her cat, red-tailed hawks and watching squirrels from her grandmother's kitchen window. Most of all, she loved horses.

Cassie was a redheaded ball of fire. Even as a child, she would spend endless hours in the kitchen jumping broom handles and chairs as "Cassie the Wonder Horse."

My route to and from my office takes me by the stable where Cassie started her riding. The morning always seemed to be a quick rush with little time to reminisce. But as I drive past, I can hear echoes of days spent in a dusty arena watching Cassie practicing yet another jump. "Just one more, Dad, and then I'll stop!" I recall the hours it took to get her to leave the barn to head home. Every horse had to be touched, stroked, talked to, fed, stared at, admired, loved.

She had an awesome rapport with her animals. Her most

beloved horse, Elmo, would follow her around the arena right by her side as if being led, when in fact there wasn't a lead attached to his halter. She wanted him to do it that way, and so he did.

Her eighth-grade graduation in June 1995 was an exciting time for all of us. She was sad at having to leave Whitchurch Highlands, but welcomed her next years in high school.

Two months later, in August, Cassie was preparing for her riding lesson, and as usual she planned to spend the afternoon at the barn doing all the horsey things she loved to do. After unloading a large bag of horse feed, she complained that her shoulder was sore. During her lesson, Cassie rode over to her mom to tell her that her shoulder was worse, and she was feeling very tired. Sandra suggested that maybe she should end the lesson early.

Undeterred, Cassie finished the lesson, put her horse away and then agreed to see a doctor about the pain.

After many tests, we found out that Cassie's sore shoulder was in fact a collapsed lung caused by malignant tumors. Before we knew what hit us, we were swept up into a cruel surreal fog of chemotherapy, surgery and fear.

To make matters worse, we had to put Elmo down that Christmas of 1995 because of medical problems. Cassie, just home from three days of chemotherapy, wept for her friend and thanked him for the wonderful times they had shared.

Cassie fought the disease with every bit of strength she had, but the cancer did not retreat. The next months were filled with endless radiation treatments, major surgery and, finally, high-dose chemotherapy followed by a bone-marrow transplant. Sandra and I were devastated to watch our daughter, once so fit and strong, who could maneuver an 1,100-pound animal four feet into the air over a jump, become unable to pick up even a cup because the chemotherapy had left her fingers completely numb.

In August the following year, we brought Cassie home from isolation after her transplant, a frail shadow of the hair-flying, "no time to talk, gotta get to the barn, don't touch that phone it's for me!" teenager she was just twelve months before.

Holding her cat again, her joy returned. Soon, she was heading down the lane to have a heart-to-heart with Red, our family quarter horse.

Cass started back to high school that fall—just for one or two periods a week—taking the rest of her classes at home with a tutor. Her hair was growing back, not as much as she had before, but it was that same beautiful copper red. Cassie started to plan again for the life ahead of her.

In October, a woman named Laura from a local wish-granting organization offered Cassie the chance to have any-thing she wanted for the hardship she had gone through.

Cassie turned to her. "I don't think I should have a wish," she said. "They should save it for a child who isn't going to make it. They need it more than I do."

But Laura convinced Cass that she also deserved a wish.

Within a few weeks Cassie had picked her wish—to go to the Master's Cup at Spruce Meadows as a VIP. We had just missed the competition for that year, so the date was set for September 1997.

She was very excited and started planning her trip—who she would meet, who would be there, where she would like to go . . . a wish is a wonderful thing.

But by January our world was rocked again. The tumors had returned with a vengeance and, because of the amount of chemotherapy Cassie had already received, our options had run out.

Cassie's health was failing fast, and she was placed on morphine to reduce the pain. She celebrated her sixteenth birthday on February 19, and a couple of weeks later I took her to get her driver's permit. She was so proud of herself. We laughed at the thought of Cassie being pulled over for speeding and having to explain the morphine pack attached to her arm!

As the days passed, we realized it was becoming more unlikely that Cass would be able to make it to Spruce

Meadows in September. Laura made it clear that the Spruce Meadows trip would not be canceled and, in the meantime, she offered Cass the chance to meet Rosie O'Donnell, the second choice on her wish list. It was a wish that could be organized fairly quickly.

Meeting Rosie in New York was wonderful for Cassie. After all the turmoil and fear and pain of the past months, reality was in some far-off place. There were no doctors to see, no blood tests to wait for, no radiation, no reminders of situations and conditions. The city was lit that weekend by the glow of a sixteen-year-old girl's smile.

Despite the tenacity of her disease, our daughter remained in charge right to the very end of her life. One morning a few months later, Cassie sat up in her bed, took off her oxygen mask and very quietly lay back down in her mother's arms, finally free of the pain she had lived with for so long. Her favorite horse was waiting for her in her new life, and she had some riding to catch up on. We understood.

Cassie will not be sitting under the maple tree this winter holding out her hand to feed the birds, and never again will she stroke that soft spot at the end of a horse's nose. But the Cassie we knew, loved and still love is with us every day. She's with us in the whispered memories of the rockers on our front porch, the smell of a well-worn saddle and the snicker of a contented horse roaming in our front pasture.

Blaine Bonnar

Picking Marshmallows

Light tomorrow with today.

Elizabeth Barrett Browning

Sweet, wild berries plucked from roadside patches are a delightful side benefit of camping. Each summer, my husband Bob and I would send the kids off with their little metal buckets, and the next day we would all enjoy the fruits of their labor: raspberry pancakes turned on the grill, or firm blackberries to dot a hot cooked-on-the-campfire, peanut-butter sandwich.

The children looked forward to picking. We could usually find just about anything, from blueberries in early summer to raspberries and blackberries in August. Every year—except one.

"There's nothing around here to pick!" five-year-old Julie complained, poking a stick into the dying fire one late summer evening.

The season had been too dry; what few blackberries were left on the bushes were hard as marbles.

"Yeah, I looked all over," added four-year-old Brian. "Wish there was something."

That night, after the kids were zipped into their sleeping

sacks and I was sure they weren't awake, I handed Bob a bag of large marshmallows and I grabbed a bag of the miniatures.

"Get the lantern and follow me," I said. "We're going to make a memory."

"What?" He looked puzzled.

I told him about the kids' campfire conversation and Bob grinned, "Let's go!"

The next morning over pancakes, I said, "Kids, I think you're going to have something to pick today."

"Really!" Julie's eyes shone. "What?"

"What?" echoed Brian.

"Marshmallows," I said, as though I'd said it every summer. "Last night Daddy and I walked down toward the lake, and it looks as though they're just about ready to pick. It's a good thing we're here now. They only come out one day a year."

Julie looked skeptical, and Brian giggled. "You're silly, Mom! Marshmallows come in bags from the store."

I shrugged. "So do blackberries, but you've picked those, haven't you? Somebody just puts them in bags."

"Daddy, is that true?" he demanded.

Bob was very busy turning pancakes. "Guess you'll just have to go find out for yourself," he answered.

"Okay!"

They were off in a flurry, little metal buckets reflecting the morning sun.

"You nut," Bob said to me, laughing. "It won't work."

"Be a believer," I answered.

Minutes later our two excited children rushed into the clearing.

"Look! I got some that were just babies!" Julie held up a miniature.

"I picked the big ones!" said Brian. "Boy, I want to cook one! Light the fire, Daddy, quick!"

"All right, all right, settle down." Bob winked at me. "They won't spoil." He lit some small sticks while the kids ran for their hot-dog forks.

"Mine will be better because they're so little," predicted Julie. Brian shrugged, mashing two large ones on his fork.

We waited for the culinary verdict.

"Wow!" Brian's eyes rounded with surprise. "These are sure better than those old ones in the bags!" He reached for another. "These are *so* good!"

"Of course," I said. "These are really fresh!"

Julie looked puzzled. "How come all those marshmallow bushes don't have the same kinds of leaves?"

"Just different kinds, that's all," I replied quickly. "Like flowers."

"Oh." She licked her fingers, seemingly satisfied with my answer. Then, studying the next marshmallow before she popped it into her mouth, she looked up with the sweetest smile and said softly, "We're so lucky that they bloomed today!"

Nancy Sweetland

6

A MATTER OF PERSPECTIVE

So we shall come and look at the world with new eyes.

Ralph Waldo Emerson

Climbing with the Kennedys

"Have you ever climbed a mountain before?" I asked the senator.

"No," said Bobby Kennedy, on the phone from Washington, D.C.

"What are you doing to get into shape for the climb?" I asked.

"Running up and down the stairs and practicing hollering 'help!'" he replied.

Great, I thought to myself.

A year after John F. Kennedy was assassinated, the Canadian government named their nation's highest unclimbed mountain after the slain president. The peak rises in the glacier-clad St. Elias Mountains that form the border between the southwestern corner of the Yukon Territory and the panhandle of Alaska. The National Geographic Society and the Boston Museum of Science, along with the Canadian government, were cosponsoring a surveying expedition.

Because I had summited Everest less than two years earlier, the Society asked me to lead the climb. Then they told me I would be leading the former president's brother, Senator Robert F. Kennedy, to the top.

I first met the senator on March 21, 1965, when he arrived in Seattle from Washington, D.C. I was relieved. Although he had slept on the flight and looked rumpled and weary, he also looked—at a wiry five-foot-ten and about 165 pounds—to be in good physical condition. The next morning, we flew to Juneau, Alaska, and from there chartered a plane to Whitehorse, in the Yukon.

On the flights to Juneau and Whitehorse, Bobby and I sat together and talked. I found him somewhat shy, but warm and personable, and intensely curious about everything: me, our team, the mountain and mountain-climbing in general.

The next morning I showed Bobby how to walk in the snowshoes we'd be using for the first day's climb and tied him in as the middle man on our rope.

At 10:00 A.M. we started up the snow-covered glacier. He seemed content to be guided rather than instructed; I got the feeling he was a "learn by doing" person. But his curiosity about mountaineering and everything we had done as climbers was insatiable. Each time we stopped for a rest break, he'd pepper me with questions about climbs I'd made, problems I'd encountered and, especially, the details of the Everest expedition. (He became so interested in the Sherpa and their problems that he sent the check he received for writing a *Life* magazine article on his climb to a fund to improve living conditions for them in Nepal.)

Despite the fact that he'd never worn snowshoes before, and that we were climbing a pretty steep slope, he had no trouble keeping up—in fact, he kept asking me to go faster. I was setting my normal "guide pace," learned from many years of experience with clients on Mount Rainier. Typically, novices climb too fast and burn themselves out before they ever reach High Camp. I told him to slow down.

Before long, however, I felt the rope between us go slack and heard him moving close behind me again. I stopped and explained that if I fell through a snow bridge into a crevasse and too much slack had developed, it would mean a long fall for me and one hell of a jerk for him. He might even follow me into an icy tomb.

"Okay, Jim," he said, agreeably. "But could you pick up the pace a little?"

It had been a brilliant morning with the temperature rising to twenty-five degrees above, but now it was beginning to snow. I began to move faster, convinced that any minute now I would feel the rope tighten as he began to poop out. He never did. I felt great knowing he was in such good shape—by now I was certain that if we got a break in the weather, he would get to the summit.

Five hours later, having gained 3,000 vertical feet in deepening snow, a cardboard sign loomed ahead in the gathering twilight: "High Camp—Three Miles." Mountain humor—in fact, it was just over the rise. The advance team had already set up two tents and dug a beautiful snow cave with "Senate–Chamber–Members Only" spray-painted on the ice walls.

All through dinner, Bobby kept asking the other members of our team questions about their climbing experiences—where had they gone, what had happened, what had they done? Finally, we headed off to the tents to sleep.

During the night, however, the snowstorm turned into a raging blizzard, and our tent shuddered and flapped badly. I tossed and turned, worried that I'd have to call off the climb. Restless and uncomfortable, I yanked on the parka I was using as a pillow and tried to stuff the hood—with its wolverine fur ruff—further under my head.

"Ouch!"

I had grabbed Bobby's hair instead.

The wind howled on, and my old nighttime companions, my demons of doubt, cramponed into my consciousness. What a night.

By morning the wind still raged, and the temperature was close to zero. But when I peered through the tent flap, the sky was clear! Though windy, it was a good summit day, and at 8:30 A.M. we were roped up and ready to go.

At one point I stepped over a fragile snow bridge and warned Bobby that there was a crevasse and to stay in my footprints. He did exactly as I'd told him. Suddenly my rope jerked, and Bobby yelled "Whoa!" as he dropped chest-deep into the crevasse, his feet dangling below in empty space. Pulling himself out, he looked down the hole and shook his head—he couldn't see the bottom.

On we went up the mountain until we reached the most difficult section, the sixty-five-degree ridge of the summit pyramid. To my left was a drop of 6,000 feet; to the right, a somewhat gentler 1,000-foot slope. Ice crystals sparkled in the sunlight, and the wind had stopped. We stood there, breathing hard in the thin, cold air, staring up.

"Can that be climbed?" Bobby asked skeptically.

"I think so," I said, and got ready to tackle the last obstacle. I plunged my ax into the face and kick-stepped sixty feet up the ridge to where it began to slope off to the summit. I drove the ax into the snow, looped the rope around it and shouted to Bobby, "On belay! Climb!"

"Climbing!" he shouted back, and started up.

I expected him to fall. The slope was very steep—loose snow on top of hard-pack—and exposed. Beginning climbers tend to lean into a steep slope, to cling to it. It's a mistake; the force of gravity pushes their feet out from under them, and down they go. I knew this is what Bobby would do; I was positive he would fall. But he didn't. I had forgotten Bobby was a good skier and knew about snow. He didn't lean into the slope. He just kick-stepped up to me, hauled himself over the lip of the ridge and sat down, breathing hard.

We were now only a few hundred feet from the summit. I broke trail through soft snow and then stopped about a hundred feet from our destination. I coiled rope again, and Bobby came up.

"It's all yours, Bobby," I said.

"Can I go the rest of the way now?" he asked.

"Yes," I answered.

I stood quietly while he trudged up the ridge, laying the first human tracks on the virgin summit. When the rope was fully uncoiled and he was sixty feet ahead, I followed. He stopped for a minute catching his breath, and then walked to the highest point of Mount Kennedy, becoming the first human being to stand on the summit of the mountain named after his brother.

He stood alone, head bowed, and made the sign of the cross. Tears rolled down my cheeks and froze on my parka. From his pack he pulled out a pole and flag with the Kennedy crest, knelt down and drove it into the snow. After a few moments, I joined him, knelt on one knee, put my arm around his shoulder and congratulated him.

"This can never be taken away," I said. "There'll never be another who will be first on Mount Kennedy."

"Yes," he said quietly.

It was March 24, 1965. As the rest of the team reached the summit, we added the flags of the United States, Canada and the National Geographic Society, along with an eight-foot-high surveying marker, and took pictures. The Canadian Yukon shone white and silent below us. For Bobby, it was the top of the world. He dug a little depression in the summit ice and left behind a copy of J.F.K.'s inaugural address, an inauguration medallion and a couple of PT-109 tie clasps. Then we headed down.

Later Bobby would write in *National Geographic* magazine:

> *President Kennedy loved the outdoors. He loved adventure. He admired courage more than any other human quality, and he was President of the United States, which is frequently and accurately called the loneliest job in the world. So I am sure he would be pleased that this lonely, beautiful mountain in the Yukon bears his name, and that in this way, at least, he has joined the fraternity of those who live outdoors, battle the elements and climb mountains.*

It was also in this article that I learned for the first time that Bobby Kennedy was afraid of heights.

Jim Whittaker

The Big Tree

I was eight when I fell in love with trees. Our family had just moved from Missouri into a brick house in the Sammamish River valley, east of Seattle. Dad and I walked our land, gazing up at cone-shaped red cedars like giant tipis, western hemlocks as graceful as dancers and sky-climbing Douglas firs.

Up on the back hill grew a huge tree, a 700-year-old Douglas fir whose width proved broader than my father's outspread arms. Dad said he was sure it was the biggest tree for twenty miles around. The deep furrows in its bark flowed upwards like great canyons.

My father was an adventurer and a long-time lover of trees, so we weren't surprised when he decided one day to climb the big fir. But standing on the top rung of our long extension ladder and stretching his arms as high as he could, Dad couldn't reach even the lowest limbs.

"Thank goodness," sighed my mother.

Dad winked at me as he climbed down. "Maybe you can figure out a way to get up it in a few years."

I looked up at him, then up farther at the tree. The idea seemed impossible. It rose grandly into the blue northern sky, more of a god than a tree. I wasn't sure when, or how, but I knew right then I would climb it someday.

"You'll see the whole world from up there," Dad said.

I set right in to practice, and scrambled up first smaller and then bigger trees with growing agility. Fifty feet up in the hemlock that grew beside our garage, I was amazed at how our house looked so much smaller and the world so much bigger.

"The higher the tree," Dad said, "the more you'll see. And the more you see, the wiser you'll be."

"Don't encourage him so," my mom complained. "He's already more squirrel than boy. And what happens if he falls?"

"He won't fall. He's a good climber." Dad knew the value of tree climbing, and not just in the sense of boyhood fun and freedom. He wanted me to see the world from a broader perspective.

At twelve, I finally shimmied up between two close-standing trunks and got into the smooth-barked branches of a 125-foot-tall cedar. From the top I looked over the rooftops of the whole neighborhood! I could see the Thorsons having dinner on their porch, Mr. and Mrs. Fluharty talking as they picked beans in their garden, and Mr. Reed trimming the laurel hedge in his driveway, stopping to shoo a dog away.

I felt an omniscience being up there. I could see everything all at once—human things, the wonderful flow of trees and wind and birds and squirrels, and the clouds drifting across the sky.

When I was fourteen, a heart attack took Dad away from us. I climbed even more because it reminded me of Dad; somehow I could feel his strong, gentle presence in the branches.

I hadn't climbed the big tree, though. And I felt bad about that. Dad had wanted me to, and I wanted to. But it was just so huge and the branches so far up.

Years passed, and then in my first year of college, I went mountain climbing with friends and learned something about the use of ropes. My first day back home, I walked up the hill in our backyard with a purpose. I threw a stone attached to some rope over the lowest stub of the big tree.

When the rope was secure, I pulled myself up the side of the tree and stood on the broken-off branch. My heart pounding and my body plastered against the rough bark of the fir's trunk, I stretched my arms wide. Carefully, I reached for the next stub and hauled myself up. Before long I was in the limbs and climbing.

The strong, limber branches appeared to welcome me. "Here you are, at last," the tree seemed to say. The views opened up, wider and wider, and I could hear Dad's voice in my mind: "The higher the tree, the more you'll see . . . the more you see, the wiser you'll be."

I saw the houses along our lane, then the streets of the whole neighborhood, and then the town on the other side of the river. Thousands of cars and people, all living their lives. As I climbed into the higher branches, my view crested the nearby hills, and I could see out over Lake Sammamish to the Cascade Mountains still capped with snow, and I felt the expanse and lift of the land.

When I gained the top of the tree at last, I caught my breath. Puget Sound shimmered in the west, and across it the peaks of the Olympic range rose into the evening sky. Mt. Rainier, a huge and tranquil presence, rested in the distance. The sun was spinning into the burnished shades of evening when Mom came out the back door and hollered up into the yard, "Ga-arth, dinnertime!"

"I'm up here, Mom!"

Mom glanced up and around, then craned her neck back and finally caught sight of me waving from atop the big tree. She shrieked.

"Don't worry," I yelled. "I'm as safe as I'll ever be anywhere, and I can see the whole world, just like Dad said!"

I ate dinner like usual that night, but no food had ever tasted better. My father was there, too, beside us at the table. I could hear Dad's laugh and see his smile of approval, because I had made it to the top of the tree and seen the whole world—for both of us.

Garth Gilchrist

In the Hills of Africa

*Great spirit, help me never judge another until
I have walked in his moccasins.*

Sioux Indian Prayer

John and I rode out of the desert into Kenya's central high-lands and turned westward across the Rift Valley. As we climbed, thorny acacias and the rocky moonscape gave way to rioting vegetation and misty pine forests. Instead of the traditionally dressed, blood-drinking Turkana, we met Nandi people who favor shirts and slacks, Coca-Cola and French fries.

The Turkana people, who barely scrape a living out of the desert, had great needs. It seemed that every time I stopped to rest, they ambushed me with requests. They'd ask for money, food, sunglasses, even my bike.

In one village alone, I handed out money to the school, a leper with an erupting chest, a mother with a dying baby and a teenager who needed school fees. I couldn't keep this up. When two hungry kids approached me, I sent them away. I biked away from the village feeling terrible. How could I not help those kids?

As we cycled into the highlands, I hoped things would change. The cycling certainly did!

Rivers and streams marbled the landscape like fat on a good steak, creating the cycling equivalent of a roller coaster. From the bottom of each gorge we pedaled slowly, creeping up impossibly steep hills, only to fly down the other side with squealing brakes and rattling vertebrae.

Then it rained. Clouds from the east gathered at midday and dropped mothball-sized raindrops on us. The dirt road dissolved into mud that looked and felt like melted chocolate. It stuck to our tires and gathered into sticky globs at our brakes, clogging our wheels to a halt. Cycling became impossible. We had to push our bikes both up and down the hills. After ten hours on the road, we had covered only thirty-eight miles.

As we approached the town of Kapcherop, we started pedaling up a lung-wrenching hill. Three kids ran to the side of the road and yelled out, "Give me money, wazungu!"

I was tired and frustrated from the ride and sick of handing out money. It bothered me that these kids looked at me not as a visitor but as a charity. I angrily waved them out of my way, sending them skittering into the bush.

A few minutes later, another boy started running alongside my bike. I was still mad and ignored him. He ran and ran, for perhaps forty-five minutes as I cycled. Occasionally, I glanced over at him. He looked back at me and flashed a smile, but I just kept cycling, figuring he'd ask for money, too. I was amazed that he could keep up.

I reached Kapcherop before John. A crowd gathered, but I didn't feel like talking. Although they only asked about my journey, I figured they would soon ask for a handout. I looked at all of these people with their dirty bare feet and threadbare clothes and had to fight off the notion that I was somehow better than they were.

One young guy, however, wore a slick, red warm-up jacket and pants. I asked him where he got his outfit, and he just shrugged.

Someone in the crowd yelled out, "He's Joseph Chebet, the famous runner. He took second in the Boston Marathon."

Yeah, right, I thought. *In this tiny African village?*

"And *he* won the Honolulu Marathon!" the man in the crowd shouted, pointing to another man wearing dirty blue jeans.

"And *he* won the Chicago Marathon," exclaimed the villager, pointing to yet another young man.

I laughed, not believing a word of it, when John pulled up on his bike. He looked at the man in the red warm-up suit and recognized him immediately.

"I don't believe it," he whispered to me. "That's Joseph Chebet. He took second in the Boston Marathon!"

The other two men were Fred Kiprot and Moses Kiptanui. Indeed, they had also won marathons.

I suddenly felt ashamed. These were the fastest distance runners on the planet.

I angled my way over to Joseph Chebet, a shy, soft-spoken man.

"How," I asked, "did you become such a great runner?"

"By running in these hills as a boy," he smiled. "For fun, we used to race bicyclists on the road!"

Dan Buettner

"See Betty! I knew if we pedaled
fast enough we'd catch the sunset!"

Reprinted by permission of Bill Canty.

Maps

While hiking high in the Colorado Rockies one day, my son and I became lost.

I immediately went to work with my map and compass to determine where we had gone off course. My son, an electronics engineer, searched through his pack and took out a hand-held Global Positioning System device.

"I know exactly where we are," he proudly announced, after carefully locking the instrument on four satellites high above the Earth and checking his map.

"We're on that mountain over there!"

Norman Augustine

Wild Turkeys and Cat Calls

If you love it enough, anything will talk with you.

George Washington Carver

After studying wildlife in the hot, harsh African bush for twenty-three years, my husband Mark and I were sun-weary and snow-starved. We decided that it finally came time to trade our tattered desert tent for something more substantial and less sandy. So we relocated to a small, wild valley in northern Idaho.

Surrounded by mountains and forests, dotted with glacial lakes and lined with rocky streams, this land was the opposite of our African home, but we welcomed the change. Rather than observe lions, elephants and giraffes, we watched moose, white-tailed deer and black bears crisscross our meadows. But of all these animals, we became especially attached to the wild turkeys.

Several years before we arrived, the Idaho Fish and Game Department introduced wild turkeys to the area. These charismatic birds are not indigenous this far north and cannot survive without handouts during the long, frigid winters. We inherited a flock of about forty birds on our land,

and we gladly participated in the Department's program of providing food for them in the winter. I took this job very seriously, and clad in my new wardrobe of fleece, wool and down, I waded into the deep snow every morning and evening to feed the turkeys.

About the same time that I adopted the turkeys, Mark surprised me with two kittens for our anniversary. He knew that after watching lions and leopards for so many years in the bush, I longed for a cat of my own that I could cuddle. However, due to the high density of coyotes and the occasional cougar, the cats weren't safe outside at night. Every evening when I fed the turkeys, I would call, "kitty, kitty, kitty," and they would scramble into the warm security of our cabin.

The turkeys soon learned that shortly after I called the cats, I spread the corn onto the snow. All the toms and hens would come running from the woods whenever they heard me. And they were not the only ones. The white-tailed deer and the crows also thought that "Kitty, kitty, kitty" meant, "Soup's on!" So whenever I called the cats, we would have forty turkeys, fifteen deer and numerous crows munching in the yard.

Perhaps I was a *bit* overenthusiastic in my feedings. In a few years we had more than eighty turkeys glaring at us through our windows if I was late with their food. These "wild" birds would prance around the picnic table and perch on the porch, flapping their wings until I emerged with the bucket of corn.

During mating season, the toms, wanting to impress the females, became very vocal. "GOBBLE GOBBLE GOBBLE" echoed through the forests and meadows for most of the day. The slightest noise would set them off, and to our amazement, whenever I called, "kitty, kitty, kitty," they would respond, "GOBBLE GOBBLE GOBBLE."

One day a local sportsman drove down our road and stopped his rifle-racked pickup at our cabin. He had noticed our large flock of turkeys and wanted a closer look.

"You can call 'em, you know. I'm pretty good at it," he said. "Old trick I learned from years in the woods. Ya wanna see?"

Before we could answer, he pumped up his chest, twisted his fingers into some kind of complicated knot, puckered his lips and produced a loud "GOBBLE GOBBLE GOBBLE." Sure enough, the turkeys answered rather weakly from the woods: "Gobble Gobble Gobble."

"Oh, yeah?" I replied. "Watch this."

In my sweetest voice, I called, "Kitty, kitty, kitty."

And from the woods came a resounding thunder: "GOBBLE GOBBLE GOBBLE." Then, more than eighty birds came running toward us as fast as their scrawny legs could carry them.

Later I told Mark that I hoped I hadn't offended the old guy.

"I wouldn't worry about it. Just wait until his friends catch him in the woods during turkey season, calling, 'Kitty, kitty, kitty!'"

Delia Owens

Snow Days

Nature is always hinting at us.
It hints over and over again.
Until suddenly we take the hint.

Robert Frost

Most adults hate it. Granted, it causes problems driving and shoveling—it all seems like such a bother. But to some of us, the magic of "snow days past" lives on forever.

As kids, the winter held endless possibilities for unanticipated holidays—snow days. My memories of these blessed events range from the tingling of numb earlobes frozen from the biting wind to the distinct aroma of packaged soup mix simmering on the stove and corn muffins in the oven.

It began as a flurry several days before. All us kids talked about it. "It's supposed to snow on Thursday. Maybe school will be closed." Then the night before arrived, and I plotted what I was going to do and where I was going to go, while looking out the window every fifteen minutes at the unmistakable gray sky that promised a day's reprieve from school. The morning of an expected snow day is second only to Christmas in creating pure joy for a child.

After piling on old clothes, I'd dig through the bottom of

the coat closet for the winter boots and hope they still fit once I'd de-crunched them from last year's hasty discard. The first step outside must be what it's like to walk on the moon: an eerie silence, foreign terrain, no sign of life.

The neighborhood came out around nine. My brothers would set off with the two snow shovels we own to "make a killing" shoveling driveways. My mom had to pay the boys from the next block to shovel our driveway. My brothers would return around lunch, having shoveled a few driveways, vowing to get right back out there after they ate. Inevitably, they would fall asleep on the sofa, exhausted from their efforts.

As a young girl, I was not expected to shovel the driveway, but the front walk was certainly within my abilities. Of course, as the snow shovels were around the corner earning income, I had to use the old coal shovel we had carted to our suburban home many years earlier from a house with a coal furnace.

Little by little, I'd start to hear shovels scratching up and down the block, young boys parading through the streets looking for a gig.

Later, I would make my way to my friend Cathie. There were no longer any sidewalks, walkways or even streets— just one great field of sparkling white. Tiny birds flew about confused, skating on the new snow bed and leaving no proof behind. As I neared her house I could see her in the front door waving frantically and rolling on the floor in her landing trying to get her snowsuit on over a mound of clothes. I approached the door, and she'd be like a horse at the gate, waiting to spring free while her mom pulled a wool cap over her head.

She bolted out the door. I trounced around hitting branches on trees and jumping in snowdrifts, but when I looked back, I saw Cathie crying big, silent tears.

"What's wrong?" I asked. "Why are you crying?"

Through deep gasps she explained that I had "messed up her yard." To a kid this was a terrible violation.

I took my friend by the hand, and we trudged through the snow back up the block to my house. The front yard was already "messed up" from my earlier exploration, but I knew the backyard was still pristine. I led her through the back gate and exposed a blanket of snow, perfectly intact.

Cathie ran in circles, dragging her feet in order to disturb as much snow as possible. She bent down, lifting snow in her bright purple mittens and throwing it up in the air. A bold, low wind cut through the naked trees and carried the snow to my face, the cold spray stinging my cheeks and settling on my eyelashes. Cathie and I fell on our backs, kicking our legs and arms out to their sides. Now, we were four angels, and all slights had been forgotten.

When there was not a single undisturbed inch left, with our ears pained from the cold and our feet numb, we made our way home.

As an adult, I welcome the occasional snow day. I stay home from work, simmer a pot of soup and shovel the front walk while watching the local kids make their own snow-day memories.

The world seems to stop when there's enough of that white stuff. It's the closest we come to time standing still. I can't help but wonder if it's someone's way of saying: *Take a break and enjoy the beauty of nature that I have created for you.*

Marie Sylvester

Trouble on the Rips

Fortune and love befriend the bold.

Ovid

I didn't have to ask my wife, Debra, if the river was high that April afternoon; I could hear it.

The two dogs barked as we unloaded our canoe. Pee Wee, our fifteen-year-old sheltie, showed signs of excitement, and even Bronnie, my German shepherd, momentarily forgot his dignity as a Seeing Eye dog and tugged eagerly at his lead.

We never had the canoe out so early in the season. The Sebec was still swollen with snowmelt, but when Roland and Mary suggested an eight-mile run from our town to Milo, the next town downstream, we jumped at the opportunity.

Our friends followed us to the put-in, but before we could even get there I was already in several inches of water. I had never known the river to be so full!

"At least this should make the Rips smoother going," I reasoned. The Rips are a three-hundred-yard stretch of boulder-strewn rapids halfway between Sebec and Milo, the only tricky bit of navigation along our route.

I held the canoe steady as Debra climbed into the bow, then took my usual steering position in back. I am often asked how a blind man can steer a canoe. The answer is easy—Debra directs me. "Left!" "Hard right!" Why I do it is a harder question.

When I was a sighted person, I was an alcoholic, a dropout as a husband and father, a guy who lived only for himself. The first clear-eyed thing I had ever done was as a blind man, when I was miraculously delivered from drinking.

I had never paid any attention to the beautiful outdoors before that, but when I got sober I couldn't get enough of it. In fact, I became the first and only blind person to "thru-hike" the Appalachian Trail from Georgia to Maine. It took me over the roughest terrain in the Eastern United States, covering almost 2,200 miles.

It was this new world that beckoned as the two canoes headed along the deserted waterway. Roland and Mary were up ahead as Debra and I approached the Rips. The thundering sound of the water drowned out all conversation.

Suddenly, I felt our canoe go into a spin, whirling us round and round in a dizzying eddy.

The motion must have startled Pee Wee, and he started jumping. But when Bronnie did the same, his ninety pounds shifted. Before we could do anything to stop him, our canoe tipped sideways, and then over.

In the next instant I was tumbling and thrashing in the middle of the freezing river. I broke through the surface, shouted Debra's name and went under again. Something kept pushing me down. At first, I wasn't sure what it was, but then I realized it was the canoe forcing me underwater as the current propelled it downstream.

Struggling free, I thrust my head up. "Debra!" I snatched at the canoe, but the current tore it away. I hurtled through the water, slamming into boulders, rolling and spinning. As I bumped against a rock, I managed to grab hold.

At that instant I heard over the roar of the water the sweetest sound in the world—Debra was calling me.

"Baby," I yelled. "I'm over here!"

She answered something, but the noise of the river drowned it out.

In the near-freezing water my hands were swiftly going

numb. I let the current take my feet backward till they touched another rock downstream. Legs braced against the battering rapids, I shouted questions in the direction of Debra's voice.

Although I missed much of what she said, I understood enough to know that she had managed to get onto a boulder.

"Have you seen Bronnie?" I asked.

"No!" she shouted back.

"Pee Wee?"

"He went under!"

Poor little fellow . . . or maybe, I thought as the icy torrent pummeled me, a swift death was better than hypothermia's slow, inexorable shutting down.

After half an hour in the water, my legs were completely numb. I was sure Roland and Mary had reached Milo by now. How long before they could get a rescue team organized? Maybe in time for Debra, but certainly too late for me!

Another half-hour passed when there was a cry from Debra. She could see Bronnie's body on the bank . . . no, she could see *him* on the bank! Bronnie had made it!

By then I had lost all feeling below my neck. Debra was shouting something else.

"I'm going to swim for it!"

"Don't!" I pleaded. Roland and Mary would be coming soon.

The sun felt lower on my face. How much longer till rescuers reached us? Debra shouted again that she could make it to shore.

"No! Help will be here!"

"But they're gone," she cried. "I've been trying to tell you! They tipped over right after we did!"

Mary? Roland? Gone?

The first warmth I had felt since the accident was the sensation of tears running down my face. There was no hope. It would be weeks before anyone opened one of the summer cottages.

The next time Debra yelled she was going to swim, I didn't argue. "Okay, Baby," I called. "I love you!"

"I love you, too! Here I go!"

Lord, keep your arms around my wife, I prayed.

For moments that seemed like hours, there was nothing but the deafening tumult of the river, then a joyful cry.

"Bill, I made it! Bronnie's here! We're going for help!"

Four miles on a muddy logging road?

"Good, Baby!" I shouted, although "Good-bye, Debra" was what I meant. Running would at least keep her warm, keep her from having to see me swept from my rocky handhold. The familiar stupor of hypothermia was creeping upon me, numbing my mind as well as my body.

Debra was gone maybe twenty minutes when I lost my grip. The current whirled me downstream. A branch brushed my head, and seconds later I stopped moving. There seemed to be tree limbs around me. Had I reached land?

With no sensation in my lower legs, I pushed myself up on my elbows, then onto my knees until I was standing. I splashed a couple of feet forward onto flooded ground, then stopped. Directly in front of me, behind, all around, I could hear rampaging water. I must have been on a tiny, half-drowned island.

My chance of survival depended on creating body heat. Bracing my elbows on a limb, I began running in place in six inches of mud. I had been at this hopeless marathon for maybe an hour when, above the water's roar, I heard a shout from the bank.

It was a man's voice. "Hang on, help's coming! Just keep running. Your wife's safe. The dogs, too."

Dogs? Pee Wee made it?

"What about our friends, Mary and Roland?" I called to him.

"At our cabin. They're okay."

For another forty-five minutes, I ran in place on my brushwood island, every step a prayer of thanksgiving.

Finally, the local game warden reached me in a canoe tethered to shore. I had been rescued.

That night, in the emergency room at the local hospital, we pieced together the extraordinary series of events that had saved us.

A couple had come to open their cabin. They were the only people on the river that day. They were just about to leave when Albert went down to their dock and heard Mary shouting for help.

Had Mary not swam for land when she did, had Albert and his wife left a minute sooner, had Albert not been at the river's edge . . .

These questions ran through our heads—hard questions with no answers. But the questions I am asked most often are just as hard: Why do you do it? Why would you go out on a swift moving, rock-strewn river? Why would you put yourself in that danger?

Maybe it's because I know what it's like to have two good eyes and still end up on the rocks.

Bill Irwin

Fishing with Robby

My son Robby opens his tackle box and shows me his fishing lures. Each is in its own little compartment like an expensive box of chocolates. He names them, carefully holding them up between his fingers and turning them, like he is seeing them for the first time himself. Rapala, Broken Back, Jitterbug, Rattle Trap . . .

Fishing has brought out a new side to my son. He hoards his equipment like it's gold, preferring his old rusted fishing rod and reel than any harm coming to his new set. And this child, the same one who loses important math papers and tennis shoes, hates losing a lure to a branch on the bottom of the lake, so much so that he won't even use them.

The other day, I was stressed out and not looking forward to my evening, wondering if I would ever get to bed. Robby asked me to go out in the paddleboat with him and watch him fish. Torn, I sighed and began to apologize for how much I had to do that night.

"It's okay," he said disappointedly.

One look at his eyes and, reluctantly, I went along, all the while thinking of how much this little excursion was going to put me behind.

We paddled out to the middle of the lake, and he cast. It was long and smooth and landed with a plop about three yards from where a fish had just jumped.

"See, I don't want it right on top where that fish jumped because he'll know it's a fake worm. He won't believe a worm just dropped out of the sky right in front of him. You want him to swim to it," he explained in a low voice.

We sat quietly for a while, my son scanning the lake for his target before he drew back his arm and, in one fluid motion, floated his bait far out into the lake. I looked out over the water, beyond where he had cast. A blue heron was standing on a log by the shore, one leg pulled up under his body, his long neck smooth and elegant. He was still, like a statue. I pointed him out to Robby, and, as if the bird could sense that he was detected, it took off, its wings barely flicking the water. We watched him fly, his long neck curved in like the letter S.

"He likes that log over there," my son whispered. "He'll be back." I nodded, wondering why I'd never noticed the heron before.

"Here go the crickets," he said.

I was suddenly aware of crickets surrounding us from all sides, their grinding melody as deep as the woods themselves. I realized how much I'd been insulated by air conditioning lately, how little I'd heard of the outdoors. I closed my eyes and listened.

I heard the deep croak of bullfrogs and the far-away call of a morning dove. I heard a fish splash now and then, sometimes near us and sometimes far across the lake. And over and over, there was the slow squeak of my son reeling in the line, then a gentle whir as he cast it out again.

"I like this time of day," I said, my to-do list long forgotten.

"Just wait," he said. "In a little while the trees and the sunset will reflect off the water. It is so beautiful."

"I will wait," I said, and I thought about what I would have missed if Robby hadn't asked me to join him. I leaned back in my seat and watched my little boy, the one who, in finding his own way, is helping me find mine.

Ferris Robinson

Bypass

Where the willingness is great, the difficulties cannot be great.

Niccolò Machiavelli

All morning, while I was cooking, eating oatmeal and packing up my stuff, a grouse had been thumping its wings like a dramatic drum roll for my ascent of New Hampshire's Mount Moosilauke. It was the fourth morning of a six-week hiking trip on the Appalachian Trail. A weak spring sun threw filtered beams of light across the snowy hemlocks north of Jeffers Brook, and when I set out on the trail, I felt full and strong, ready for the climb.

But soon, the gentle sun turned harsh and glaring above the tree line, and I was kicking myself for the sunglasses I'd forgotten. Holding my eyes in wincing slits against the glare, I painfully made my way to the summit. Suddenly, a scrap of red material poking up through the melting ice caught my eyes.

Long ago, probably the previous fall, someone had lost a red bandanna and, as my luck would have it, a pair of sunglasses. I cleaned off the glasses, slipped them on and tied the bandanna around my head like a pirate. I had planned to camp at the next site, but living the pirate-with-sunglasses persona, I decided to move on.

Rounding a bend, I noticed another hiker farther up the trail. He was walking rather slowly, and I quickly closed the gap. We started talking, and he introduced himself by the nickname Bypass. He'd had a quadruple bypass operation three years before. He was sixty-eight years old, retired and had just started out on a ten-day hiking trip.

We chatted for a while, and like me, he was heading to the next shelter, which was about seven miles away. But first we had to climb up and over Mt. Wolf. He told me that I would soon outdistance him and insisted that I go on ahead. We bid each other good-bye, and I set off.

Most of the hiking was what's called post-holing, when you break through snow to the top of your leg. Sometimes the snow was firm enough to support my weight for a few steps, just long enough to get moving, and then one leg would crash through.

But now, as I struggled and slogged, gasped and grunted, I was conscious of Bypass. I found myself worrying, wondering if I should've stayed with him. It was snowing hard, and the trees were blanketed in sticky snow. I couldn't spot any of the white lines painted on trees to mark the trail.

The last mile and a half to the shelter was the toughest physical challenge I'd ever gone through. Post-holing became wading, bumping my shins on hidden branches and boulders. How was Bypass doing?

When I got to the shelter, I changed into dry clothes and got a fire going. I cooked dinner and got more nervous about Bypass as time went by. Finally, at dusk he arrived, proudly delivering my red bandanna, which I hadn't even known I'd lost.

I hugged him and shared my concern about how he was doing. He assured me he was feeling fine. He really did look quite invigorated.

When he was changing into a dry shirt, I could see his chest scars, deep purple crisscrossing dents. He caught me glancing, then he shrugged and smiled. "At first all I saw was the scars," he said. "But now I think of them as healed places. That's really what a scar is, you know."

That night, as I sat in front of the fire, I thought about the courage and perseverance Bypass had shown that day and wondered if I could be that strong. I realized that the real heroes are not the ones we see in the media or playing sports, but rather the people who toil unseen against personal challenges and triumph.

I hang on to some strange things—a small stone from the summit of Mount Katahdin in Maine, the collar of a wonderful dog, a special letter from my mom. And a found, lost and found again red bandanna that a hero picked up for me in the New Hampshire woods.

Lisa Price

Visiting the Edge of Death

Only those who dare truly live.

Ruth P. Freedman

Within six months of my father's death, I took up climbing. I had cared for him throughout his illness: planning and cooking meals, monitoring the myriad medicines he was taking, accompanying him to treatments and staying with him overnight. My father was a strong, dignified man, a private man. And it was painful, for both of us I suspect, to watch him wither away.

To digest those heartbreaking events, I had planned a two-week solo journey for the summer across the Great Plains and Rockies that finished with a backpacking trip into the Cirque of the Towers in the Winds. The stunning granite peaks evidently triggered some primal ambition to climb because when I returned home, I was studying rock formations and cliffs like a hawk eyeing its prey.

Fortunately, a writing project brought me to Lander, Wyoming, in the fall, and I found myself learning to climb with Steve Bechtel, a well-regarded climber. I instantly felt safe with Steve. Perhaps it was his experience or confidence or my own naiveté, but I felt his presence would ward off danger, the way a citronella candle keeps the bugs away. It was a familiar feeling: I had always felt my father would keep me safe from the world.

Standing at the base of the boulder looking toward the heavens, the rock stretched up only sixty feet, but in my novice state it could have soared 600 feet. What was I doing? Armed with some unexplained desire to climb, I grabbed a hold of the hard dolomite with my hand and hoisted my body along its face. The rock was damp and sharp and smelled like the earth—sensual and pure. About halfway up, I froze.

My hands, cold from nervous excitement, wouldn't move. I frantically waved my eyes across the surface, looking for a suitable hold.

"I don't want to do this anymore," I finally admitted.

"Okay," Steve said, but sensing my reluctance to quit, he coached me over to the right. "You'll be safe climbing with me."

Steve's words the previous day raced through my head. I took a deep breath and planted my feet firmly against the rock once again.

As the fear dissipated, I began to relax, and some other energy took hold. Instinctively, I sensed it was best just to keep moving. The quicker I made it to the top, the quicker I could come down. I moved with the abandon and determination of an eight-year-old climbing the backyard maple tree, desperately reaching and pulling for the next branch, too afraid to look down. Realizing I had actually completed the climb, I let out some kind of victorious howl. The sound of my uncontrollable, silly laughter tumbled across the canyon and faded into the cool evening air. I was completely exhilarated, filled with a sense of accomplishment and relief like nothing I had ever experienced.

When I returned home again, I immediately signed up for an introductory ice-climbing course. I had seen photos of Goretex-clad bodies unimaginably splayed across the frozen canvas. Ice climbing intrigued me. Besides, I live in Vermont where winters envelope us in powder, sleet, freezing rain and subzero temperatures for up to six months. Scaling a frozen cliff seemed like a natural progression of my new-found fascination with climbing. But with its sharp implements and precarious surface, I knew that ice climbing was especially dangerous.

Seconding my first multi-pitch ice climb, I stopped to take out the third anchor. My fingers were numb from the prolonged cold and constriction. Just as the screw released from the grasp of the ice, it rolled out of my lifeless hand like water spilling from a cup and dropped five feet below me, resting on the lip of the ledge.

Slowly, I down-climbed to within striking distance of the piece of metal. As I carefully reached for the screw, I made the mistake of shifting my focus past it, fifty feet down the frozen wall into the abyss. Like a lightning bolt, a rush of terror surged through my veins. Quickly, I retrieved the lost anchor and made my way toward the top, where the sound of flowing water beneath the ice nearly drowned out the "clunk, clunk" of the tools meeting the solid surface.

Ascending vertical ice for the first time, I found a physical power I hadn't known existed, like the emotional strength I discovered deep within my soul while caring for my dying father. Day after day I watched him fade, toxic treatments no match for the awesome force of his disease. Night after sleepless night keeping him company, the darkness was unable to conceal the terror that his impending death had etched on his face.

Perched on the ice, my arms felt like wet rags. I prayed the teeth of the crampons would clench me to the cold surface just a bit longer as I shook out my hands, anxiously hoping the circulating blood would infuse my useless limbs. It seemed impossible to extend my arms upwards, let alone form a fist. My silent mantra—"You can do it, you can do it"—played out like a well-worn record. With all the effort I could muster, and mental focus as sharp as the tool in my palm, I coached my hand to grip the axe and slowly began to

pull myself up. The seconds stretched on like a country bal-
lad, each muscle quivering with fatigue, as I struggled to
maintain my strength and courage. Finally, I reached the
ledge. I did it.

I had bagged my first slab of vertical ice.

Over the winter, I climbed again and again, my technique
improving and my confidence solidifying with each completed route. My obsession received mixed responses. Close
friends and family understood this as an extreme example of
my adventurous nature, an evolution of my compulsion to
push myself physically over the past few years. But for others, the queries about my pursuit were wrapped in judg-
mental tones.

"Why?" they inquired incredulously as if I had spit out
parental responsibility and sanity in the same mouthful.
Why was I climbing now, in my mid-thirties with a child to
nurture and protect, the moment for reckless, youthful ven-
tures seemingly long since expired? Why climb now?

Because I can. My body is still sufficiently strong and agile
to propel itself up an icy waterfall or rock face and not yet
crippled by a savage illness or the passage of time.
Gratefully, I trudge up the sloping mountainside in thigh-
deep snow, the wind slapping my face. Its chill penetrates
my torso even through layers of technical clothing. My
breathing is quick. I try to slow its pace to conserve the air
inside my lungs for each successively steeper step. At these
moments, I know I am alive.

With death surrounding me, absolute consciousness
of my pulsing heart is essential now, no different than
needing water or sleep. Each time we enter the nursing
home to visit my grandfather, I extract a promise from my
only child not to send me to one of these dreadful, forgotten
places. Just two years ago, my grandfather was hobbling
along just fine, muttering his usual curse words, when the
cat darted past him too quickly. After the death of my
father—his eldest son—and a second broken hip, he's

resigned himself to a hospital bed that he vacates an hour each day, waiting for his time.

I climb because he can't.

The day before my father died, he was moving in shaky, staccato steps, determined to walk to the bathroom rather than use the wheelchair. He was using me as a pseudo-crutch, as he had done with greater frequency throughout his illness. How strange to be his strength now when all these years he was mine. I climb for him, too. I climb because his adventurous spirit still lives on in me.

"Aren't you afraid?" I am asked about my climbing forays.

"Yes. Yes, I'm afraid. Yes, I'm afraid of dying," I want to scream. But my greatest fear is not living. Perhaps it is on the edge of death that we feel most alive.

Wendy Knight

Bill Magie

Opportunities are often things you haven't noticed the first time around.

Catherine Deneuve

Nobody ever knew the Minnesota north woods better than Bill Magie. After he died, the other guides and outfitters put a plaque on a boulder in the middle of a lake in the Boundary Waters canoe country. It says on the plaque:

> *Think on this land of lakes and forests.*
> *It cannot survive man's greed*
> *Without man's selfless dedication.*
> *William H. Magie,*
> *Friend of the wilderness,*
> *Devoted most of his life to this cause.*
> *Now, it is yours.*

I spent a day doing a story about Bill. He was already seventy-six. Every summer, he said good-bye to Lucille, his understanding wife, left her behind in Superior, Wisconsin, and went up into the Minnesota woods to camp alone beside a lake with his old dog, Murphy. He hired himself out guiding canoeists.

Bill Magie remembered everything that had ever happened to him in a lifetime of guiding in the Minnesota–Ontario wilderness. He told about the hunting trip he took Knute Rockne on back in the twenties, about the night he crawled inside a moose he had shot to keep from freezing and all about his mapping expeditions in winters past.

"I'm the only man alive that's walked from Lake Superior to Lake of the Woods on the ice and carried a transit on his shoulder all the way," he said. Bill Magie was a wonderful man and such a good storyteller that we were able to finish up our story about him before the sun went down.

Over supper, he said to me earnestly, "You know, I want to take one more long canoe trip before I get too old to carry a canoe on the portages. I believe I like you well enough to invite you to come along with me."

I could tell he meant it. I felt honored and a little abashed.

"I don't know much about canoes," I said.

"I could teach you everything," he said. "You like fishing, hell, we'll catch our supper every night and listen to the loons and live off the land the way I used to. I'll promise you this: I can take you to some lakes that damn few people have ever seen. I'd like to see them one more time myself."

"How long a trip are you talking about?" I asked him.

"We could do the whole thing in six weeks, maybe eight," he said. "We'll leave the Fourth of July next summer and be back the end of August. How about it?"

I didn't know how to answer. I could never take that much time away from work, but his invitation was so eager and heartfelt that I hated to tell him so.

I said, "Six or eight weeks is kind of a long time for me, Bill."

"The hell it is," he said. "It's six or eight weeks is all it is. What are you going to do for six or eight weeks that would be better than this?"

I told him I'd think about it and let him know.

He wrote me letters over the winter to make sure I was thinking about it. In one of them, he said if it was money I was worrying about, why of course he wasn't planning to charge me for guide service, he thought I understood that. "Just your grub is all you'd have to pay for," he said. "Write me soon."

But I never did write him, and after a while he gave up on me. I found later that he never made the long canoe trip. He spent the next summer around Moose Lake, guiding a few tourists on overnight outings, telling them some of his stories around the campfire and paddling them back the next day. A year or two later, Lucille Magie wrote to me from Superior to tell me that Bill had died.

I wish with all my heart that I had made the long canoe trip with Bill Magie. I can't remember what I was doing from the Fourth of July to the end of August the summer he wanted to go fish every night and listen to the loons and see those distant lakes one more time. What could I have been doing that would have been better than that?

Charles Kuralt

"I'm tellin' ya, Frank, that may have been Al
who went into the woods for firewood,
but that's not who came out."

7

THE HEALING PATH

I go to nature to be soothed and healed, and to have my senses put in tune once more.

John Burroughs

Summer Son

Love is the river of life in the world.

Henry Ward Beecher

While some kids have bar mitzvahs and others have con-firmations to commemorate the beginning of their transition into adulthood, my son Peter—twelve years old, tall for his age with size ten feet, short curly hair and round, wire-rimmed glasses—had a sea kayak trip. It was the first time either of us had ever taken a major outdoor adventure together. His goal was to paddle by himself in a solo kayak; mine was to let him.

Peter is my only child. His father and I have been divorced since he was five—we did not part well. He lives a hundred miles away from us and sees Peter when he can. I wish I could have given my son the mother and father combination I always wanted for him, but it didn't work out that way. After my divorce, I felt that I had failed as a person and as a mom. When Peter's kindergarten teacher called me in and suggested I get my son some counseling, I felt that my fail-ure at life had been passed on to him.

As I worked at shoring up the walls that had fallen around us, he tested their strength by trying to push them down. It took time for Peter to regain a sense of security. It took time for him to rebuild trust in me—and for me to rebuild trust in myself. Slowly, I learned to believe that I had made good choices in life as a person and as a parent, and that not all partings are abandonments—indeed, some are necessary and should be celebrated.

Still, learning to let go is hard, especially when you're raising a boy who's about to become a young man. Just when I thought I was getting the hang of being Peter's mom, I realized there was one more step I had to make.

Three days into our adventure, we slowly awakened inside our bright yellow tent on the small island of Tannøy in a fjord of the Norwegian Sea. However, it wasn't the morning light that had triggered the end of my sleep; the sun is up all night during the summer in this land above the Arctic Circle in northern Norway, and I had grown accustomed to its insistent shine. Rather, it was the smell of boy—campfire smoke in his hair, spicy mosquito repellant on his skin, dried sweaty socks on top of the clothes he had shed the night before.

Our breath had condensed while we slept, forming droplets smaller than tears that clung to the inside of the tent. They released and dropped like rain as I struggled to pull on my shirt and pants.

Peter suddenly sat up. The sun was finally above the mountains that had shadowed us to the east. It was unbearably warm. We needed more air. Both of us reached for the tent zipper at the same time.

"I'll do it, Mom."

The zipper stuck, and my reflex was to offer a suggestion, reach out to help, take command of the whole zipper situation until it was fixed. I caught myself and pulled back. I opened my mouth, then shut it. A moment later, Peter successfully dislodged the zipper, and we both crawled out into the fresh morning air.

We were accompanied by the trip leaders, Tim and Lena, and seven other participants. Everyone got along and shared a mutual appreciation for the dramatic pristine land and seascape. As we paddled, we often paused to take in the towering mountains of the coastal range, their chartreuse-green grassy backs sloping down to the narrow rocky beaches along the shoreline. The unusually windless conditions had made for a smooth passage over the blue-green sea.

From the start, Tim had taken Peter in his double kayak, but on this, the third day of our trip, Tim announced, "Pete, today you solo. Get yourself ready. Take the yellow kayak."

Peter moved quickly, donning the rubbery blue kayak skirt and cinching up the life jacket. I came forward and watched silently. Before he stepped into the kayak, he looked over and asked, "Can you hold these for me?"

His sweaty hands dropped a collection of white shells, worn black rocks and a long brown feather from a sea eagle into mine. I cradled these treasures of his in my hands.

This first attempt at paddling by himself would be an hour trip around the island we had camped on. He was joined by Tim and two other men from the group. After they returned, we would all paddle over to the next night's stop at the Tranøy lighthouse.

Tim pushed Peter's kayak off its sandy perch. With careful even strokes, Peter backed, turned, pointed the kayak toward the sea, then waited for the others. He slyly peered out from under a wide-brimmed canvas hat.

Everything looked big on him—the sleeves on his jacket were bunched at the cuffs, the thick orange life jacket hugged him front and back. And the way he sat made him look short. I wanted to say, "Be careful. Keep up with the others," but after everything that we had been through over the last few years, I had to show that I could believe in and trust him.

I smiled.

He smiled back.

Soon a flurry of white-tipped paddles rose and fell like a flock of seagulls. The men and the boy moved together out of the protective bay. I waved and waved. Peter didn't look back. I was afraid he would disappear from me without a good-bye.

The kayaks reached the open water and turned to the right.

I kept waving. Nothing.

Then the hat on the duckling-colored boat turned toward shore. Suddenly, Peter lifted his paddle overhead and pumped it up and down victoriously. Two strokes later, he slipped out of sight.

At my feet the sea gently rolled in and out. I was alone on a beach near the top of the world, holding the sharp shells, smooth stones and a feather left behind by a bird that had taken flight—finally able to smile back on the pain and the courage of a little boy and his mother who had lived on a different shore, in another time . . . long ago.

Jennifer Olsson

Reprinted by permission of Vahan Shirvanian.

Heaven on Earth

Not knowing when the dawn will come, I open every door.

Emily Dickinson

I had rarely seen an early November day as mild as that one. It was as though God had decided to grace those of us living in Michigan's snow belt with a special gift of balmy temperatures and gentle breezes before winter's descent. My friend Rick and I were walking the country road near my home, taking in the harvested corn and the autumn leaves still clinging to the trees.

Suddenly, Rick stopped in his tracks.

"Hey! We could drive to Lake Michigan if you want," he said excitedly.

My face immediately lit up. My friend knows what magic the "big lake" has for me, as it has the same effect on him. There's something so wonderful about being by water. It didn't take us long to pack a picnic lunch of tuna-fish sandwiches and chips, grab our fall jackets, and set off for the half-hour drive west to the lakeshore.

After parking the car, we wrapped our jackets around us to ward off the chill of the lake breeze. Silently, we walked across the white sand to the water's edge. The South Haven lighthouse stood sentry on the end of the pier as it had for over a century, providing a beacon for sailors to find their way home from stormy waters and starless nights. There was no need for a beacon now, though. The sun was shining brilliantly. The sparkling waves rolled in and gracefully slid back into deeper waters.

I knew that I needed this break, but Rick needed it even more. After a year of visits to the doctors and a plethora of medical tests, he still didn't have a helpful answer to the health problems he faced. He was given a couple of official diagnoses: Fibromyalgia caused his chronic pain, and peripheral neuropathy was the reason he was losing all of the feeling in his lower legs and hands. Although we now had labels, the doctors could find no cause and could offer no treatment to stop the diseases' progression. As Rick grew more unsteady on his legs, he needed to use his arms to get up on his feet and occasionally while walking he'd stumble or fall.

Looking at him, no one would guess he had any physical challenges. They would only see a man in his early fifties who looked strong. A strapping six-footer with a trademark baseball cap on his head, no one would guess how difficult it was for Rick to disguise the pain he was in. Likewise, they wouldn't know that my friend had spent years raising his eight-year-old grandson and now took full-time care of his ailing mother. An afternoon at Lake Michigan was not just a weekend outing for him; it was a brief and precious escape from his daily responsibilities and challenges.

And so we walked the beach, my friend and I, and silently let the symphony of waves and the beauty of Lake Michigan fill us with its healing power. We stopped for important things like finding round, flat stones that Rick skipped across the water. We examined seashells and driftwood and dodged the rogue waves that ran up the shoreline and threatened to drench our feet.

A few steps ahead of me, Rick suddenly turned around

and blurted out, "There's something I want to do that I can only do here on the beach. Do you want to do it with me?"

I hesitated. At my age I don't commit myself without knowing details. "What do you want to do?" I asked.

"I want to run. I don't know if I'll ever be able to run again, and I want to run along the beach," he replied. "It won't matter here if I fall because the sand won't hurt me, and there aren't many people around to see me if I do."

Although I'm not a runner, there was no way I could refuse his request. Slowly, we picked up speed until we were moving at a brisk pace, jogging along the shore. I could see the smile on Rick's face; if there was any pain or doubt, he wasn't showing it.

Not to my surprise, I stopped before he did, breathless from the run, breathless from the sight that met my eyes. Up ahead of me he kept going, sprinting along the beach, legs pumping, strong and sure under a cloudless November sky. For an instant, the world slowed and stopped, and the image before me engraved itself in my mind.

I can still see Rick running down the shore, the waves sparkling like diamonds in the sunlight, and the copper and gold of the remaining autumn leaves swaying in the trees atop the dunes. In slow motion I saw my dear friend finally stop and turn, legs planted firmly, arms raised high with clenched fists, face turned toward the sky, exuberant.

"Yes!" he shouted. "I did it! And I didn't fall!"

"Yes!" I yelled back. "You did it!" I laughed, but I could just as easily have cried.

I had always imagined that one day when we were both in heaven, I would see my friend running the bases on a ball-field, unencumbered by any pain or dysfunction, strong and whole and flying like the wind. On a glorious autumn afternoon, for a brief moment in time, I think I saw this world softly touch the one beyond. God graced me with a glimpse of heaven on Earth.

Anne Goodrich

Hold Your Breath

Without wildlife
Where would we learn about ourselves?
Without nature
How could we survive?
Without wilderness
Where would we be?

Cindy Bradburn

Skiing is a simple sensation, sliding down a mountain while turning left and right, but it's been my addiction for forty years. My wife Chris is also a skier, and when our children finished college, we moved to a mountain town with tall peaks and abundant powder. In January 1997, Chris, a few friends and I climbed to a high ridge on a remote mountain in British Columbia. Winter sunlight refracted rainbows from the new snow, even though the temperature was so cold that my breath froze to my cheeks.

I pointed my skis downhill, felt the speed, then arced into the first turn. Suddenly, the snow settled almost imperceptibly. For an instant, I thought I had imagined the sensation, but no—it was real. The smooth white surface crinkled, and I looked frantically for an escape route, but there was none.

When the snow fractured and disintegrated into jumbled blocks, I knew with a horrible certainty that an avalanche was about to engulf me. I looked over my left shoulder, then my right to gauge the magnitude of the slide. One thought filled my brain: *This one is big enough to kill me.*

The churning snow swept me off my feet and into an airless darkness. I accelerated, somersaulting madly down the mountainside at fifty miles an hour. Darkness, speed, horror! I envisioned the consequences and ending, struggling for breath and then gradually losing hope. But despair is such a useless emotion in times of danger, and right then the line between life and death depended on my ability to stay alert, keep track of my body position and try to swim toward the surface. An intense pain raced through my lower abdomen, then the churning snow ripped my left shoulder out of its socket, but I kept fighting for my life. The avalanche washed me half a mile, then slowed and stopped in the valley floor. Due to my frantic efforts or, more likely, to blind luck, I lay miraculously on top of thousands of tons of snow, not buried beneath it.

I looked around at the silent peaks and said a grateful prayer. Then, instinctively, I wanted to stand up and walk away as if nothing had happened—but my legs wouldn't move. Perhaps it was just shock, so I tried again, but my legs absolutely wouldn't move. Could it be? Was I a paraplegic? No, impossible, it hadn't happened! I calmed myself and reasoned that if I could wiggle my toes, I wasn't paralyzed. Maybe I'd wait and live a few moments with the hope. But I couldn't wait and quickly transmitted a signal down my body, "Hey, you—toes—wiggle!" The toes bumped comfortingly into my ski boots. Whatever was wrong with me, I wouldn't spend my life in a wheelchair. I looked around and spoke directly to the silent peaks that surrounded me, "Okay, my friends, I'm injured, but I'll be back. Wait for me."

Then panicked voices started calling. "Jon, can you hear us? Jon!"

I called back, "I'm alive, but hurt."

Linda had a radio and called for rescue, while Chris and Mitch hiked up and cradled me in their arms. A snow machine from the ski area hauled me to the road, and an ambulance carried me to the local hospital, where the doctors ordered immediate helicopter evacuation to Calgary.

I had suffered a separated pelvis, internal bleeding, hypothermia and a dislocated shoulder. The next day, after the surgeons had bolted me back together, I lay on my hospital bed, dazed on morphine, staring at all those tubes transporting fluids into and out of my body. I pushed the call button and asked the nurse to bring me a pad and pencil. Even though I couldn't think clearly and my hand was shaky from the drugs, I started writing about my past adventures and dreaming about what I would do when I was whole again.

When I returned home, Chris rented a small hydraulic crane from a hospital supply company. Every morning she jacked me out of bed, lowered me into a recliner and spread all the necessities around my chair—lunch, a few cookies, a water bottle, a telephone, a book and a laptop computer. Then she put on her parka and left to ski powder. I wanted to leap out of the recliner, put on my ski clothes and join her, but I told myself quietly, *Stay strong, keep your mind active, and your time will come.*

After six weeks, we returned to the hospital. The X-rays looked good, so the doctors sent me downstairs to physical therapy. For a moment, I was afraid to rise from the security of the wheelchair, but when I stood, I could imagine hiking or skiing through remote landscapes again. I was shaky, I needed crutches, but I could walk.

Four months later, I still wasn't strong enough to climb mountains, but I could sit in my kayak. To paddle a kayak, you need to balance the boat with your hips. My hips were held together with bolts and scar tissue, but I managed a few small rapids without mishap. I paddled every day, slowly graduating to more difficult rivers.

In May, a group of my friends planned to kayak the

Selway River. I have paddled the Selway every year for two decades, and I knew that I would feel whole again if I kept my annual rendezvous with the river, so I asked if I could join them.

After the first two days, I started to feel my natural rhythm. On the third day, we beached our kayaks above the most difficult rapid. My friends asked if I preferred to portage. I scanned the ancient ponderosa pines and dark spruce trees. If I subdued my fear, I could rekindle my old confidence. I quietly shook my head no, slipped into my kayak and pulled my spray skirt tight.

The first wave hit me hard in the chest, but I managed to maneuver between obstacles with inches to spare. The four of us rejoined at the bottom of the rapid and congratulated each other on the run.

I felt exhilarated that I had completed the run, but I had to remind myself that we still faced four more treacherous rapids downstream. I continued down the river, navigating the first rapid and then the second. As I approached the third cataract, I glanced at a phantom motion in the cliffs. I paddled to shore and found myself staring into the eyes of a young deer.

She stood in a small cave where spring moisture dripped off the green moss. The doe had an ugly wound on her right shoulder. Her ribs protruded through taut skin, and mucus oozed from her nostrils. I guessed that she had fallen in the river, been swept through the rapids, then clambered to shore, trapping herself in the cave. She was starving, sick and too frightened to jump back in and swim the tumultuous rapid below.

I whispered quietly to her, "I've been where you are. I know the helplessness you feel."

The doe backed against the rock until cold water trickled down her emaciated body. Her ears stretched straight out. I climbed out of my boat and stepped into the cave. She tried to inch backwards again, then looked nervously side to side, but she had nowhere to go. As I looked into her terrified eyes, my mind raced back five months to the fear and pain I felt at the bottom of that avalanche gully.

"You'll die if you stay here. I had snow machines, ambulances, helicopters and doctors. All you've got is me." I paused for a short moment. "I'll throw you in the water. You'll have to swim the rapids. Hold your breath when a big wave hits you, then head for shore."

Her ears twitched. I lunged. My left hand pressed against the sticky wound on her shoulder. My right tried to grasp her hind leg, but she was alarmed and she jumped. A rear hoof bashed painfully against my cheek, but then she was in the water, swimming strongly. As she floated toward the rapid, I reminded her one more time, "Remember, hold your breath."

Easing myself back into my boat, I saw her disappear into the last bit of rushing water, her head held high, and I knew that everything was going to be all right—for her and for me.

Jon Turk

Hemlock Trail

Doctors will tell you that a walk outside is good for your health. Outdoorsmen will tell you that a walk outside is good for your soul.

Shannon Sankar

I remember it well, that morning back in '75. After a restless night of fruitlessly pursuing sleep, I rose early with thoughts of the quiet trails of Big Creek Park in my mind. Maybe I could walk off the tension even though it was January. I needed the inspiration of being alone with God, the invigoration of a winter walk. Pulling on a pair of boots, I headed for one of my favorite trails, Hemlock.

The large snowflakes were falling gently, drawing me into a pensive mood. As I walked along in the three or four inches of new fallen snow, I pondered my restless night.

Emily, my two-year-old daughter, was recovering from her most recent of many surgeries. It was so good to have her home, even with her head shaved. Her smile was the light of my life. Born five weeks early, the doctors had doubted that she would live through even her first operation.

The prognosis given by the team of neurosurgeons at Rainbow Babies & Children's Hospital in Cleveland, Ohio, was devastating. A cyst had formed on the back of Emily's brain sometime during her fetal development. The cyst had grown, crowding her brain, which did not fully develop before birth. "There are only two other recorded cases like your daughter's," the doctor explained solemnly. "Both of those babies died. Your child will probably not survive the multiple surgeries she will need. If by some chance she does live, she will be retarded and have a variety of handicaps."

Four long and stressful months later, Emily had proven the doctors wrong, at least in part. My little six-pound daughter was still alive. She had survived more operations than I'd been able to count, so I took her home for the first time. But the all-consuming demands of her medical condition left little time for a relaxing hike in the woods, or even a moment to stand still and enjoy a bird's song.

By the time Emily was two, she'd been home for several months, but her cyst required another trip to the hospital, another date in the operating room. Spending long weeks in the hospital by her side, I needed a break and longed for trees, trails and fresh air.

I ambled on, down Hemlock Trail.

The starkness of the tall trees stripped of their leaves reminded me of life's fragility, as Emily and I had experienced over her first couple of years. I had walked this trail while Emily was growing inside me, yet during her life-and-death struggles, I had given up my dream of her ever walking alongside me.

As I viewed the tangled vines, so evident now that the trees were bare, my mind flashed back to the hospital room and the tangled tubes and monitor wires attached to my little daughter as she lay on her bed, weak and confused. Her eyes darted about in fear, like the rabbit I had just startled.

After weeks of prayer, her health had finally returned. The pink flowed back into her cheeks, the sparkle to her eyes. With great joy and thanksgiving, I brought her home once again.

By the time I reached the hemlocks on the hillside, nature

had released the tension in my spirit. My walk down Hemlock Trail had renewed my appreciation of the many forms life takes. As I began my walk back, I pictured in my mind a gift twice given—Emily. My tenacious little child had overcome once again. She was home, safe and warm, snuggled with sweet dreams in her bed.

By fifth grade, thoughts of Emily being mentally challenged gave way to the realization that she was in fact a gifted child. And after many precious years of hiking together along the Hemlock Trail, my little girl is now working for the Parks District.

Sharon R. Haynes

Lake Therapy

Imagine for a moment the feel of water rushing across your feet. Imagine the flow of cold that would travel to your knees, across your back and into your growing smile. Stop. Listen and feel it.

Carla Green

My vision of heaven never included streets paved with gold. I picture it with the cypress-lined lakes of Louisiana—the murky water that hides all creatures below and the slightly fishy smell that is strongest in the late afternoon when the sunset glows through the green leaves draped in moss.

My love for the water started at a very young age. A fearless tomboy, I was springing off the high dive at age four. Whether I was following or leading my older brother Bruce didn't matter, as long as we got wet. Living in the South, the only way to endure the heat of summer is in the water. If a puddle of water was around, we would find it.

Eager to be on the lake, my best friend Gail and I spent most weekends and holidays camping and fishing with my dad. If he minded that only us girls wanted to go, he never said anything.

I guess the need to be on the water stayed with me, because after I finished my studies in nursing my first purchase was a used boat. It was questionable whether my ratty, old car would even last to pull it. But my dream was realized. I could go to the lake whenever I wanted! Waterskiing became a passion as my girlfriends and I took every opportunity to go for "lake therapy."

My tomboy traits never subsided as I continued to enjoy all the outdoor sports I loved so much. If it was outside in the sun, I loved it. Tennis, biking, softball, Rollerblading, swimming and skiing—I loved them all.

At thirty-one, I started sharing my love of outdoor sports with my boyfriend Ronnie. Three months after our wedding, I was diagnosed with a brain tumor. Surgery and radiation removed most of it, and I thanked God that I could continue to work and enjoy life with my new husband. We had eight glorious years and a beautiful son, Aaron, before the tumor came back.

The surgery was more aggressive this time, and I suffered a stroke during the operation. Even with intensive rehabilitation, I was left with no use of my left arm and limited use of my left leg. This level of disability would be difficult for anyone, but I felt especially wounded because of my love for the outdoors. I was never a spectator; I wanted to play!

Gradually, I learned to walk again, but I was still essentially one-handed; my left arm and hand never recovered. The words "accept" and "adapt" were thrown at me like snowballs. I found some peace in going to the lake with family and friends, but riding in the boat just couldn't measure up to flying across the water on skis. Then, in a fit of determination, I decided there had to be a way for me to ski again.

After many phone calls, I found the disabled division of USA Water Ski. Denise and Bill, two very kind and compassionate members, agreed to meet us in Mississippi and teach me how to use a harness designed for one-armed skiers.

I arrived very excited and nervous. With my bad "wing" tucked in my ski jacket and the sling attached to the rope, I jumped in ready to conquer the lake. I jokingly laughed about skiing under the water and drinking half the lake before I got it right. The boat driver gave me a pair of nose clips, and Ronnie and Bill cheered me on.

With Denise behind me holding the skis and giving encouragement, I would tuck my head, take a deep breath and prepare for another nose full of water as I heard the engine accelerate to pull me up. My good arm clinging fiercely to the handle, my legs would tense and attempt to direct the skis. With each failed attempt, I became more and more determined to ski again. Stubborn by nature, I was not going to give up.

And then, after what seemed like a hundred tries, I came out of the water standing up. Though wobbling and falling quickly, my heart soared because at that moment I knew it was possible. I was going to ski again! The cheers from the boat echoed my elation. I was on top of the water! It may have been only a few seconds, but it felt magnificent. It was a moment of success that could only be compared with the rush of a first solo bike ride or dive into the deep end.

We left armed with information and hope. Returning home, Ronnie made the adaptations and the equipment I needed for one-armed skiing, and we were off to the lake. Having no difficulty learning to ski as a strong, agile child, I finally understood how hard it sometimes was for others. My Louisiana lake wasn't quite as beautiful when I was swallowing most of it.

It wasn't easy, but with each lake trip my wonderful husband, beautiful child and loving friends cheered me on. They patiently and lovingly pulled me around the lake until I could ski on top of the water rather than under it. The sensation was glorious. Each trip across the water brought on the same thrill I felt the very first time I ever skied as a child. It is a feeling of fear mixed with delight as the water seems to rush by with great speed. The pure fun of it helped to make the physical challenges of weakness and partial paralysis much easier. Once again, I could share the activity with friends and family as a participant, not just an observer. The beauty and peace of the lake spoke like a message from God, reminding me of all I have to be grateful for. Once again, the water was working its healing magic.

Over the coming months, "lake therapy" took on a whole new meaning as skiing strengthened my leg in ways regular physical therapy never could. But I think that what healed the most was my spirit. Skiing brought back a sense of motion and connection to the outdoors, recharging not only my body, but also my soul. It gave me hope.

Janice Duvall

Back to Nature

I have walked myself into a less safe life. I walk on unsafe streets and in unsafe jungles. Mostly I walk to get where I want to be. I hope I can keep walking until I die. I'd like to be climbing a mountain when that happens.

                                                    Judith McDaniel

At one time, my friend Paul was sitting on top of the world. He was a graduate student working toward a doctorate in computer science at a prestigious university, an accomplished musician and a successful triathlete. He had achieved extraordinary heights in his intellectual, creative and physical powers, and he was climbing higher still.

Then one morning, he noticed a strange weakness in his muscles. An unusual difficulty climbing stairs became, by nightfall, an inability to walk. Twenty-four hours later he was completely paralyzed, unable even to breathe without the aid of a respirator. Paul had contracted a grave case of Guillain-Barré Syndrome, a medical condition in which the body's own immune defenses attack and partially destroy the patient's nervous system. For most GBS patients, recovery is slow and terribly difficult. Nerves regenerate, but not quickly. Some patients suffer relapse, and many take years to recover full use of their hands and feet.

Nearly a year after the disease's onset, Paul began to take his first tentative steps with the aid of a walker. His progress was agonizingly slow to those of us who knew him before GBS, but it was reassuringly steady. A month later, he was able to replace the walker with two ski poles, although curbs and similar obstacles remained a challenge. He didn't talk about it, but it was easy to see that merely walking in his own neighborhood was exhausting, disheartening and dangerous.

Nevertheless, Paul insisted that he was ready for backcountry hiking. And his friends agreed.

Before his illness, Paul had been an avid wilderness camper. Preparing for an overnight hiking expedition became the primary motivator for his recovery efforts. He was convinced that nothing could be more therapeutic than hard, directed, physical effort in a peaceful and unpeopled natural setting. He made it clear to his friends that a hiking trip would help him prove to himself that he was still in charge of his own destiny. Above all else, the trip would just get him out in the wilds again.

We didn't worry about whether Paul could handle the challenge. He is a fighter like no one else we have ever known.

Three of us made the trip: Paul, me and another friend named Lukman. We chose a wilderness region near Idyllwild, California. None of us had visited this area before, and we were impressed by its harsh beauty. The wilderness in and around the San Jacinto range looks very much as if you took a huge chunk of the High Sierra, transplanted it to the desert and left it there for a century or two. The dramatic alpine topography is the same, the panoramic views are similarly spectacular, and many of the trees are as large—but the region is as dry as old bone.

Let me be more precise: Lukman and I were impressed; Paul was intimidated.

The trail climbed steeply upward from its head, the ground uneven and loose. Deep ruts, thick gnarled roots and great slabs of upthrust rock made the trail all the more difficult to negotiate. As Paul set out, Lukman and I sighed with deep satisfaction and shouldered our packs, heavy with three men's gear, food and water.

The first thirty yards were the roughest. It was really hard for Paul to raise his feet high enough as we headed uphill. His poles provided woefully insufficient balance and support. To make matters worse, the ground continuously crumbled and slid away under his feet. Burdened as we were with heavy packs, it was difficult for Lukman and me to maintain our own footing as we tried to help our friend. We concealed our concern with a constant stream of gibes and encouragements. Finally, we reached a saddle-point where Paul could rest.

After that strenuous beginning, we covered only half a mile the first day. We found a lovely, sandy clearing where we relaxed for the rest of the afternoon and prepared a leisurely dinner. As the sun sank over the horizon, we shared a bottle of wine and sang our favorite songs to help shepherd in the night with grateful revelry.

The second day dawned bright and beautiful. We took our time breaking camp and getting on the trail, but once we started we were relentless. The trail took us mostly uphill, but occasionally down, with scarcely any stretches of level terrain. Paul found the going difficult. About half a mile into the walk, he indicated that he was wary of pressing further and preferred to turn back.

We marched onward. Lukman and I each supported one of Paul's elbows as we walked, Paul complaining all the while that we were trying to kill him. We traveled about another quarter-mile in this fashion before Paul told us again that he was nearing the end of his strength and had to stop to rest.

We paused for lunch at a glorious spot overlooking the wide valley below. There we regained much-needed energy and restored our flagging morale. Looking back on the hill he had just crested, Paul simply could not believe he had come so far.

"Paul," I said, "what you are doing now may seem incredibly difficult, but after this, the curbs and sidewalks back in the city will seem like nothing."

But he hardly heard me. He was too overwhelmed with fatigue and preoccupied with the challenges being imposed on him.

After lunch we pressed further, insisting now that Paul walk unsupported, with merely a hand on one of our shoulders for balance. By the time we had covered another quarter-mile, he was shaking with weariness, his face drawn, his skin shining with sweat.

Having traveled far beyond what was reasonable to expect from a patient in Paul's condition, we finally turned around. He had another mile and a half to go to return to our starting point. By day's end, that hike would cover more than twice the longest distance he had walked in over a year.

Except in the very toughest stretches, we insisted that Paul walk the rest of the way down alone. Lukman and I remained nearby to catch him if he fell, but we left it up to him to maintain stability and recover from stumbles. Halfway down, we were astounded when Paul broke into song, an improvised ditty honoring our glorious surroundings.

When we reached the car, and Paul's long, weary ordeal was over at last, he recognized that he had surpassed the perceived limits of his strength and endurance. Part of him knew that his soul had been vitally restored by the wilderness, part of him raged against his friends for pushing him so far, and most of him was too tired to think at all.

We drove back to San Diego nearly in silence, and the very next day I returned to my home in Michigan. Over the course of the next few days, I wondered whether we had pushed Paul too hard. Had we trusted too much in the healing properties of exertion, fresh air and beauty? Had we been foolish, even cruel, to trust our own judgment of Paul's capabilities?

Then I got Paul's call.

"Steve!" he exclaimed. "You won't believe it! Since I got back, walking around town is nothing! I can't believe that just last week it was hard for me to walk down to the store!"

He had no recollection that I had used almost those very words to encourage him during our hike. I didn't remind him. It was enough that we both knew the words were true.

Stephen Leggatt

Plodging in the Pacific

I only know there came to me a sense of glad awakenings.

Edna St. Vincent Millay

I kidnapped my mother-in-law one California morning and fled Los Angeles down Pacific Coast Highway 1. I didn't know where we were going exactly, but I knew I was taking her to the beach. I had decided that what Mama needed was to dip her toes in the healing waters of the mighty Pacific.

Mama proved a willing participant in this abduction. Her spirits had been desperately low at the prospect of having a toxic soup of chemicals pumped into her on yet another sunny day. While we couldn't speak each other's native tongue, we had conspired to outwit her daughter, with some help from my eleven-year-old nephew Jamie, who speaks both Farsi and English.

I selected a solitary place. Mama needed nature's peace and quiet, the plaintive cries of gulls, and the pounding of blue and white surf in her ears, not blaring traffic, yammering humans and sterile, metallic hospital noises. Jamie consulted the map. If we stuck to Pacific Coast Highway 1, he assured me, we were bound to find somewhere. And as we curved out of Newport Beach, we did. Suddenly, before us, the vast ocean glinted like a metal sculpture carving the land into a perfect crescent.

"Bah, bah," murmured Mama. "Oh my, oh my."

The sparkling, deserted bay stretched below us. I pulled into the first parking lot I came to. "Crystal Cove State Park" the sign said. As if to bless our playing hooky, a swallowtail fluttered onto the white hood of the car and took a breather, yellow and blue wings flapping in the intense, hot light. Mama's face glowed like a little girl's on Christmas morning. I grinned at Jamie, who giggled. We hadn't seen Mama's face so animated for months. We waited for the butterfly to resume her journey, then Jamie and I yanked the wheelchair out of the trunk and helped Mama into it. Drowning in dancing pink and lavender wildflowers, we headed off into a piercing sun, along a path winding steeply down the bluffs.

Once we arrived at the beach, the wheelchair presented problems, but Mama laughed out loud as we bounced her over gray pebbles to the tide-line of dried seaweed and on to flat, moist sand recently bathed by the tide. We parked near an outcrop of boulders, Jamie flinging himself flat on his back onto them.

"These rocks are so warm," he sighed, as comfortable as a cat.

Mama gazed out to sea, and my heart warmed to see golden light reflect off silver waves onto her deeply smiling face. *"Bah, bah,"* she mumbled and reached for my hand. We sat holding hands a long time, just watching the ocean. Although I'd been raised in England on the shores of the bleakly beautiful North Sea, the untamable Pacific has truly captured my heart.

As the tide ebbed, I spied tide pools. "Hey, Jamie."

All Jamie could manage was a grunt in reply.

"You ever seen tide pools?" I asked.

He bolted upright. Sea creatures fascinated my city-bound nephew. I pointed to islands of brown-green seaweed.

"Wha-a-a-a!" he yelled, leaping off the boulder.

"Tell Mama we're just going to wander over there."

Jamie crouched beside his grandmother and explained to her. She stroked his curly black hair in reply.

I pounded down the beach to crash through foam to the rocks.

"Wait," Jamie shrieked, hopping about on one foot as he yanked off enormous sneakers.

I turned to wave to Mama, who waved back. It pained me to see how much effort that simple motion ate up.

"Do you think Mama would like to plodge?" I asked Jamie.

"To what?" He bent like a hairpin over a puddle of tiny crabs who scuttled away from his shadow to hide under curtains of pungent seaweed.

"It's a word the English use for dipping your toes at the edge of the sea," I explained.

He glanced over his bronzed shoulder back to Mama, a little old lady swathed in a black shawl; she looked so frail. Eyes sparkling, he beamed at me.

We splashed through the waves, then cut up the beach. Before Jamie had even finished explaining it to her, Mama had impatiently unwound her shawl and was lifting her feet off the wheelchair footrest.

I kneeled to remove her velveteen slippers, and she nodded with glee.

Jamie and I pulled her up, waiting for her to feel secure. She took a deep breath, focused on the distant horizon, and out shot one small foot.

The slope wasn't of any consequence to Jamie and me, but Mama's toes groped before she dared venture each step. She almost toppled a couple of times, and I regretted my idea as I saw her breathing labor, but she gritted her jaw. She couldn't vanquish the cancer, but she could and would do this.

As soon as icy spume flooded between her toes, her body melted. Jamie and I were able to move slightly away as she stood on her own. Eyes closed, Mama tilted her face to the sun and breathed deeply. As her lungs released the cleansing air, she moaned a soft sigh of such contentment, and my eyes welled with tears.

We arrived back in L.A. after dark, sneaking into the apartment like three naughty mice. My sister-in-law was frosty: What on Earth had we been thinking?

Mama, Jamie and I exchanged conspiratorial glances.

We knew.

Christine Watt

Breaking Up the Ice

The care of rivers is not a question of rivers, but of the human heart.

Tanaka Shozo

I'd been up since dawn composing repair lists for the broken-down cottage I'd moved into. When my dog Teco dropped her leash at my feet, I initially ignored her. I was busy feeling sorry for myself because I had lost my house and everything else I had, including my marriage.

I yanked open the door to a warm, cloudless March day. Arriving at the neighborhood ball field, I stopped scowling long enough to let Teco off her leash.

We played catch. I threw balls of soft, end-of-winter snow, and she caught and swallowed them. We walked for a long time along the frozen Souhegan River, and when we returned, we sat on the cottage's rickety deck and looked at the ice on the river. It was as white and opaque as milk glass.

I made a cup of apricot tea and sipped it; Teco chewed a Milk Bone. The sun was high, and the air had that tender, soft feel that says winter is truly over.

I was slouched in a porch chair, my feet propped against the deck rail, when I heard a loud popping noise like a gunshot. At first I assumed it was a car backfiring, but I heard another pop and still another. Then the rumbling began. It was as loud as thunder at first, and it became almost deafening. I stood up, wondering where all the noise was coming from, while Teco stood quivering, nose in the air. Then I saw water gushing out of the ice.

I watched as the frozen river broke apart. It was as if an invisible giant was dancing across it: Parts of the river suddenly sank down under what seemed to be a great weight, and then an entire sunken section crackled into an ice mosaic. As suddenly as the mosaic formed, it broke into pieces, and the broken ice collage rushed away. I watched lumps and chunks and slabs of ice crash into each other and form floating ice rafts. Then the rafts raced downstream, forming new islands of ice.

The ice islands kept careening down the river, and I could hear the roar of the falls increase as more and more water, frozen and liquid, spilled over the rocks.

While I watched the ice breaking, I felt the part of me that was so worried about making my home perfect again start to break up and float free.

Teco and I watched until the river ran clear. It was still moving rapidly, but it was singing, not roaring. I could see through the water to the river's fine, sandy bottom.

It looked as if there would be good swimming, whenever I was ready to get wet.

June Lemen

Bells in the Night

Let us add this one more night to our lives.

Suetonius

On March 13, 1989, seven months after my husband, George, died, I woke from a dream. As usual, I took a few minutes to realize he wasn't lying beside me and will never lie beside me again. Often when I can't sleep, I read awhile or walk on the deck looking at the stars over our cattle ranch and talk to George. Under the star-filled South Dakota sky, I can believe he is listening.

I got up to open the curtains and noticed that the sky was light in the east. I checked the time: 1 A.M., too early for dawn, and the moon had set in the west some time before. I couldn't explain the light, but its soft glow made the garage and the van beside it, the woodpile, the whole hillside, completely clear.

Barefoot, in my long flannel nightgown, I went to the frost-covered deck and realized I was seeing the Northern Lights more brilliantly than ever before. Waves of blue and white swept up from the northern horizon to a spot almost directly overhead to meet in a whirlpool of mingled lights. I got a blanket and put on the sheepskin-lined moccasins

George had made for me. My activity woke the dog, and together we walked to the waist-high cairn of rocks on the hillside near the house. The light began to flow faster, in long streaks of blue and white; each streamer of light seemed to flare more brightly as it moved toward the south, then diminish as it slid back north. All at once the pulses paused, and I began to gather the blanket around me, thinking the show was over.

Then the northern horizon glowed red, and a single shaft of crimson light shot up, ending at the whirlpool above me. Then came another, and another, until the whole sky pulsated like a heart with red veins. I felt like crouching and gibbering, as a primitive woman might have done. Behind the fires in the sky, I could see stars shining calmly in the deep blue.

Once before I had seen red Northern Lights, when George and I were newly married. This time, the lights seemed to streak up the sky faster and faster, changing from red to blue to white to green without pause. Once or twice I craned my neck to look behind me as a single spear of green shot from the vortex of light to the southern horizon. I heard a coyote howl once to the east, a gentle creaking as the wind pushed softly at the snow fence, and the rustle of grass nearby. No cars passed on the highway. No other person was within a mile of me. The wind was gentler than breath.

Then the light wind died completely; all sound ceased. I leaned back against the pile of rocks, expecting thunder, expecting the sky to open, expecting a majestic voice. Nothing happened, only the cadences of light continued. I felt not only safe, but as if I were in a great cathedral, watching a performance so holy that no harm could even be thought about me.

Suddenly, I heard a distant tinkling, like bells. I sat straight and thought carefully. I might fantasize about a miracle, but this was serious. Rationally, I considered the possibilities. No wind blew. The sound did not resemble any other I had heard that night: the snow fence, the coyote, the breeze. It came again, louder, just as a curtain of green light swept the entire width of the sky from north to south. Again and again, the horizon flowed green. Each time green flushed the sky, the bells rang, the sound softening to a gentle tinkle as the light died. I shut my eyes—I could still see a green glow—and waited for an image of what might make that sound. All I could visualize were dozens of tiny glass bells, rung softly by delicate hands somewhere in the darkness.

I pictured the pasture that lay around me: each post, each strand of wire, each tree, the electric pole. I have sat and paced for hours on this hillside, in all weather. Nothing exists here that could make that sound. No one else was near; no cars passed. The sound could not exist, and yet it did.

Finally, I remembered reading that arctic explorers insisted they could hear the Northern Lights; they had given no description of the sound, which they declared to be audible only in the far north.

I watched the lights and listened to the bells until three, drifting into waking dreams. Do good souls get to orchestrate the light show? Do several spirits play together, like an orchestra? George could be happy in such company.

Later the same year, reading a scientific magazine, I learned that sunspots large enough to contain seventy Earth-size planets had come into view on the sun in mid-March. Giant solar flares erupted; the sun threw radiation and billions of tons of matter tens of thousands of miles into space. The Earth's upper atmosphere was struck by solar particles carrying electrical currents that created magnetic fields; among the results were interruptions of power and communications, garage doors spontaneously rising up and coming down—and the phenomenon we know as the Northern Lights.

Not a single scientist mentioned the bells.

Linda M. Hasselstrom

"No Aurora Borealis 'til your homework's done."

Reprinted by permission of Dave Carpenter.

8

MAKING A DIFFERENCE

Do not go where the path leads; go instead where there is no path and leave a trail.

Ralph Waldo Emerson

The Pelican

This is our purpose: to make as meaningful as possible this life that has been bestowed upon us; to live in such a way, that we may be proud of ourselves; to act in such a way that some part of us lives on.

Oswald Spengler

Malibu Beach, before dawn. My friend Louise and I tightened our goggles and slid our feet into the surfline. For the past six months I was her coach. Today we would swim fifteen miles, from Malibu pier to the Santa Monica pier—the longest distance Louise had ever swum and the ultimate test to determine whether she would be able to reach her goal of swimming across the channel from Catalina to the mainland.

Swimming was a hobby for Louise. By profession, she was a deputy district attorney in Los Angeles. She was dedicated, driven and relentless in the courtroom—all attributes that easily carried over to the sport of long-distance swimming. But Louise was wound up tight, way too tight. If I didn't calm her down and reassure her, she would quickly burn herself out through nervous energy.

"Louise, let's put this workout into perspective. The

longest you've ever swum is ten miles. We're adding five, and that's a big stretch. If you can complete even eleven or twelve miles today, you've done a great job. Just remember, whatever distance you do today will bring you closer to your goal."

She took a deep breath. "I understand, but I want to swim the distance."

We decided to unwind a little by watching the sunrise. Rosy light spread across the cool blue Pacific, washing over the old wooden pier and highlighting a flock of pelicans that silently glided toward us in single file and perfect formation, riding on the air current created by the breaking waves.

We dove beneath the waves, swam around Malibu pier and paralleled the coast. As we swam south just outside the surfline, we watched the Earth awaken.

Sunlight poured slowly over Malibu Canyon's undulating walls, saturating the soft green grasses, silver shrubs and wild mustard in warm morning light. A breeze stirred the hillsides and carried the fragrances of sage and rosemary mingled with rose. We drew in deep wonderful breaths, and the breeze-beveled water sparkled like diamonds.

Light streamed below the surface, illuminating silvery bubbles rolling rhythmically off Louise's fingertips and out of her mouth. She was feeling great. She even smiled. She was precisely on pace.

Then out of the corner of my eye, I noticed something in the water. It was a young pelican, a fledgling, paddling directly toward me.

"I think something's wrong with that pelican," I said to Louise. "They don't usually swim with people."

The pelican moved closer. It seemed as if it were asking for my help. I swam around the bird. Surprisingly, it didn't move away. I moved closer to take a better look and spotted a fishing line tangled around its beak, breast and wings.

If I could guide the bird to a rock, I thought, it could climb out and I could unsnarl it. With Louise swimming just ahead of me, I spotted a rock rising from the water. The pelican paddled right along beside me until we reached it. But when the bird tried to leap onto the narrow shelf, it flailed; its legs and feet were also caught in fishing line. I tried to get out of the water, but the rock was covered in barnacles.

I continued swimming down the coast, searching for another rock on which to land, and the pelican followed. Louise looked back.

"What are you doing?" she shouted. She sounded annoyed.

"I'm trying to find a place to free the pelican from the fishing line," I replied.

I thought of going ashore with the bird, but I wasn't sure whether I should leave Louise swimming alone, and I knew she didn't want to stop. I was torn between ensuring Louise's safety and saving the poor pelican's life.

About a mile ahead was Las Tunas beach. I knew Louise could swim safely there. I gave her a choice to continue swimming to Las Tunas or to come ashore right then with me.

"I want to keep going," she said. "I'll be fine."

But I could tell she wasn't happy about going alone. I felt like I was letting her down, but I couldn't just let the pelican die.

I turned to shore at Big Rock beach and guided the bird in with me. The swells began lifting us four and five feet up, then dropping us down again. Sensing the danger of the waves, the pelican suddenly veered away from the surfline. If I were going to help this bird, I was going to have to pull it to shore.

I looked at its pouch and neck covered in lice and large, black ticks. The pelican had been unable to preen itself because of the fishing line. An enormous wave rose above us, and the bird started to panic. I grabbed its giant, soft beak and started swimming with one arm and kicking as fast as I could. The wave caught us and tossed us over the falls, whitewater crashing around us. I tried to hold on and keep the bird's head above water, but the wave tore it from my grip.

Desperately, I scanned the water. Finally, the young pelican emerged in the surf. I grabbed its beak and rode with it on the whitewater into the beach.

Onshore, I saw it had a deep gash in its leg from the fishing line. Its whole body began to tremble, and its eyes began closing, as if it were going into shock. Stroking its feathers, I gently tried to open its beak.

The fishing line was tangled so tightly that I could open the beak only a few inches, but it was enough for me to see a three-pronged hook imbedded inside, the fishing line attached. I tried to pull out the hook, but couldn't grip it. Clearly, I couldn't save the pelican alone. Louise was swimming just offshore.

I called out her name. She didn't hear me, so I shouted it again. "Louise, I need your help!"

Immediately, she swam to shore and ran over to us.

"I need you to get some scissors from one of those houses up the beach so we can cut the line."

Louise took off across the beach and climbed a steep embankment. After trying a couple of houses unsuccessfully, she called on a third, and an elderly man answered. He grabbed a pair of pliers, and the two of them hurried down to the beach.

The pelican was going into deeper shock. They held the bird while I used the pliers to cut the lines. Carefully, we freed its wings, breast, beak and, finally, its feet.

When I opened its beak to remove the hook, we saw there were two more inside. Using the pliers, we pulled out all three. The pelican blinked and squirmed a little, but didn't try to get away.

We examined the bird's body. All the lines were gone, and the hooks were out. We were worried about the gash in its leg, but decided that the saltwater would heal it. Then all three of us carried the pelican to the water's edge.

The bird stood on one leg and then the other. Cautiously, it lifted its wings, testing them one at a time. Then all at once, it pushed off the beach, flew above the waves and out to sea.

With a great sense of satisfaction, the three of us smiled at one another. Soon after, Louise and I climbed back into the water and continued our swim down the coastline.

It was hard to get back into the rhythm, but our time with the pelican seemed to spur Louise on with even more determination.

Then, as we neared Santa Monica pier, a pelican splashed into the water nearby and paddled over to us. We looked closely and saw a gash in its leg. It was our little patient.

The bird followed us right to the pier, then left to join a flock of fellow pelicans flying north. As he flew off, he looked back and seemed to nod his head as if to say "thanks."

Two months later, Louise swam across the Catalina Channel in just over fifteen hours. I'm sure our feathered friend was somewhere overhead.

Lynne Cox

A Coyote Named Promise

Love the world as your own self, then you can truly care for all things.

Lao Tsu

I awoke to a violent, unearthly cry—like the sobs of a tortured demon.

On our remote cattle ranch in Arizona, night sounds are common: the hoot of a great-horned owl, the yowl of a bobcat, the electrifying squeal of bats racing the dawn. But for sheer shock value, nothing equaled the terrifying but unmistakable din of voices beneath my window. Coyotes!

The coyote makes about a dozen different sounds that range from a high-pitched yelp to a low, haunting howl. One coyote can sound like a pack, and when two or more echo against the mountains and cliffs, it's like a symphony gone wild.

Coyotes can be a threat to farm animals, so we were fortunate to see one rarely. Still, I missed the presence of this wary, elusive creature slinking among the mesquite.

As I sat in bed, the fiendish din reached an earsplitting crescendo, then stopped. I looked out the window, expecting to see a battleground strewn with dead animals. Instead, I saw only tufts of rabbit fur scattered like dandelion down.

My gaze shifted to Bill on his tractor over a mile away. His headlights were still on as the early-morning mist crawled over the sweet-smelling alfalfa fields. The day before he'd oiled and sharpened the gleaming, scissor-like blades on the swather, a huge mower pulled by the tractor to cut the hay.

The coyote was far from my thoughts as I prepared breakfast for Becky and Jaymee, ages twelve and nine. They were outside feeding their 4-H calves and rabbits before school. Suddenly, Jaymee burst into the kitchen, horror in her eyes.

"Mama!" she yelled. "Daddy killed a coyote! Just now—out in the field. I saw it thrown in the air!"

Bill had no patience with animals that got in his way when he was mowing. Each tractor pass left arrow-straight windrows or evenly spaced bales. But ever since Becky and Jaymee had found a dead duck inside one of the bales, Bill hadn't heard the end of it. Each time he prepared to make hay, the children began their warnings. "Watch out for quails' nests, Daddy," Becky said, "and the cats and kittens."

"And there are baby bunnies out there," Jaymee added.

"But they're eating half our crop!" Bill said. "I'm trying to raise decent feed for our cattle—not baby-sit birds and rabbits!" He continued cutting unforgiving rows.

Fortunately, the duck had been the only tragedy—until now.

When Bill came in for breakfast, he hung his sweat-stained hat on the rack and sank into his chair by the wood stove. "I think I clobbered a coyote," he said.

"I know. Jaymee told me." I could see how much it bothered him.

"For the past few days, I've seen a coyote watching me from the edge of the field—a pitiful-looking creature, scrawny and sick. I saw her once in the rearview mirror catching mice behind the baler. She didn't seem the least bit afraid. Now this had to happen." He was silent for a moment. "She must have dragged herself off and died in some other part of the field."

"How do you know it was a she?"

"Big belly," he said, sighing. "Pregnant."

I shuddered. "Maybe you just thought you killed her."

He shot me a hard glance. "She's dead," he said. "All we can do now is watch for the buzzards."

The buzzards, however, never appeared. Maybe the coyote was still out there somewhere, suffering. I couldn't stop thinking about it.

Summer slipped into autumn, and thoughts of the coyote dimmed. Winter closed in. Now hunger stalked the wild animals on the surrounding desert. In search of food, they moved closer to our buildings. Often at night, I caught sight of a hooded skunk or a raccoon-like coatimundi, or a porcupine emerging for a starlit shuffle, searching for loose kernels of corn.

January brought icy winds, heat lamps in the hen house, blankets on the horses—and the return of the coyote. It was midnight when I heard the first diabolical shrieks and howls near my chicken coop. I dressed quickly and dashed outside. There in the beam of my light was an old coyote—with three legs. The left hind leg was missing below the knee.

So Bill's tractor took only her leg, I thought. *But how did she survive? Can she still catch a rabbit?* She was a pathetic, skeletal creature, with ratty-looking fur. She showed neither fear nor surprise, only a woebegone expression that tore at my heart. It had to be the same coyote that had wandered into Bill's path.

What about her pups? I thought. Under the circumstances, probably only one or two had lived and, if so, would be weaned by now. I glanced around but didn't see any.

Enormous ears cupped the coyote's dainty, intelligent face. Her amber eyes, veiled in cataracts, glowed like tiny blue gas jets in the darkness. *Poor thing,* I thought. *That's why she got hurt. She's probably blind!*

As if in answer to my thoughts, her lips parted, revealing a flash of fangs. Now I knew she could see a little bit and was reacting like any mother, protecting her young. Perhaps a pup was nearby.

We stared at each other, neither of us moving, until gradually I felt she sensed I was not a threat. I clicked off the light so she could shrink unobserved into the moonlit shadows.

Suddenly, I grasped the full extent of the tragedy that had befallen her. I didn't care that she was a predator; she was starving to death. Her natural diet was birds, rodents, rabbits and insects. But I had also heard that coyotes like fruit. Maybe she'd eat dog food with apple slices on top.

I couldn't help wonder what Duke would think of that. Duke was our timid, 206-pound English mastiff, and he ate and slept on the front porch only a few feet from where this same coyote had killed a rabbit all those months before. Duke sometimes let the barn cats finish his food, but how would he feel about this wild animal eating from his bowl? I had to try, so I prepared the first bowl.

A short time later back in bed, I heard strange sounds on the porch. Peeking out, I saw the wild and the tame, hair raised and tails clamped, cowering on opposite sides of the bowl. The coyote, ears pinned back, crouched low on her belly, yapping and scolding, while Duke trembled and whined. Finally, Duke sank heavily to the ground, dropped his huge head between his paws and moaned while the coyote crept toward his bowl and dug in.

When I told Bill, he shook his head. "We shouldn't interfere," he said. "This is a wild animal that can't take care of herself. We should put her out of her misery—or at least let nature take its course. We shouldn't be interfering."

"She has survived this long," I countered. "If it's survival of the fittest, maybe she is the fittest! We're just giving her a little help."

The coyote appeared several times during the following three months. And as she fed at Duke's bowl, I was always aware of a mournful howl from the barren plains to the north. Could it be a pup crying for her? Or possibly even the father of her pup? Coyotes usually mate for life, and the yearning wail was almost heartrendng in its plea.

Eight weeks after her first feeding at Duke's bowl, I

noticed a glint of brownish red and black tinting her silver-gray fur. And her body was filling out a little more. One morning I told the girls, "Our coyote looks much healthier. I think she's going to make it!"

"You promise?" Becky asked.

"Promise," I said, crossing my fingers. Jaymee, who liked giving every living creature on the ranch a name, smiled at me. "That's perfect," she said. "Let's call her Promise."

A warm and unusually wet spring brought swarms of beetles, moths and flies that clung to the screen door like barnacles. When they started slipping into the house, Bill installed a zapper light. As the bugs hit its electrically charged mesh, they sparked and fizzed, then rained onto the concrete in smoldering piles. Barn cats arrived in droves to eat them.

Then one evening the familiar yelping began again. We all peered through the living-room window to see Promise snapping eagerly at the smoking bugs in midair and gobbling them down.

"I'll bet she likes them cooked better than raw," Jaymee murmured.

Bill peered over the top of his newspaper. The laughter in his eyes said he was becoming more and more intrigued by this survivor. A few days later, he bought a book that told how, in times of drought and famine, the cunning coyote will outlast all creatures because it can smell water just below the earth's surface and dig to it. After satisfying its thirst, the coyote pounces on smaller animals and birds that come to drink from the same hole.

Promise appeared only one more night after that. I saw she was pregnant again. Her fur was healthy now, her tail magnificently bushy.

From Bill's book, I knew that Promise—being pregnant—was the number-one female of her pack, the only one reproducing. Late in her pregnancy, the coyote holes up in a den. There, she is fed by her mate and other members of the family—but only until her pups are weaned. After that, Promise would be on her own again.

Soon I noticed a change in Bill. It began one day when he left a patch of alfalfa uncut. "Another dumb duck built her nest out there," he grumbled. Then a week later a jackrabbit sat in the alfalfa and defied him. So once more, Bill's straight-arrow cutting veered off at an angle.

Finally, one scorching day in August, Bill had an even bigger surprise when he was baling. A three-legged coyote appeared on the edge of the field with a young pup. Promise hobbled toward the tractor, totally unafraid.

As Bill watched, the pup began chasing mice that had lost their hiding places to the baler scooping up windrows. After he had eaten several mice, Promise waited until he caught one more—then she grabbed him by the neck and threw him to the ground. He let go of the mouse in his mouth, and she ate it herself. As mother and son lay down near the edge of the field, Bill marveled at what he'd seen.

"Did they go to sleep, Daddy?" Becky asked that evening when Bill told us the story.

"Not right away," he said, "at least, not the pup." Now his voice took on a warmer tone when he talked about the coyotes. "The pup chewed on her nose for a while and nipped at her ears. But he finally curled up right next to her and settled down. Even though she was old and frail, she looked so darned content, just like your Mama did when you kids were little and finally fell asleep." Bill glanced at me and grinned.

As winter approached, we wondered what would happen when our crippled coyote weaned her pup, and the pack no longer helped her. Would she turn to us again?

Each night, I put extra food in Duke's bowl and slices of apple on top. It was still there the next morning, but distant howling and yelping were more prevalent than in the past. Was it Promise? Her pups? Her family?

The months hurried by, and alfalfa season came again. More and more, Bill's windrows zigged and zagged. When I commented on the scattered patches of uncut green dotted with lavender blossoms, he grumbled, "I had to steer around a quail's nest and a couple of dumb rabbits." But the sudden twinkle in his eyes said a few detours were okay.

Near the end of April, he saw a coyote bounding along beside him, inches from the razor-sharp blades. It was a female—young, healthy and pregnant.

"She followed me for over an hour," Bill told us. "She wasn't the least bit scared of me. And she caught mice like an old pro."

An old pro? Could this have been another of Promise's pups—the one I had never seen? Had she witnessed, from her hiding place in the shadows near a chicken coop, my first meeting with Promise? Had she watched the next summer as her mother and younger brother caught mice in our fields?

That night I heard a coyote howl, and recalled Promise's amber eyes veiled in blue, the small sad face and quick flash of teeth. I realized then what a stalwart our crippled coyote really was. Against tremendous physical odds, and the threat of nature and man, Promise had raised her pups.

"I guess you were right," Bill said, grinning at me. "They are survivors, aren't they?"

"Yes," I said, smiling. Promise had taught us all something about hardship, perseverance and the value of a helping hand. No wonder coyotes have so much to sing about. And so do we.

Penny Porter

Mr. Bucky

I live not in myself, but I become a portion of all around me.

Lord Byron

"One of your fawns has been hit by a car." The man's voice on the other end of the phone jarred me awake. Bleary-eyed, I focused on the clock radio: 2:07 A.M.

"Where is it?" I asked, nudging my husband John to wake him.

"Just up the road from your place," he said. "On the black top, about halfway up before the highway, on the right." The line disconnected. I still hadn't recognized the voice.

"John, wake up," I nudged harder.

"Uh huh," he mumbled. "Whaaa?"

"Someone just called to tell us one of our fawns has been hit by a car." I was halfway out of bed, my stomach clenched with dread.

"Who? Where?"

"I don't know who. He hung up too fast." I pulled on socks.

By now John was wide awake and moving. "Is it still alive?"

"I don't know that, either," I said. I wished I had more information.

We finished dressing quickly. John grabbed essential items: blankets, my basic medical kit, flashlights and his .22 rifle, just in case. I woke our oldest son to tell him where we were going.

"I hope it's not Yoda," Johnny worried, mumbling sleepily.

"Me, too."

We had released five rehabilitated fawns that year. Yoda, the only buck, had remained the most tame. He had become our favorite and assumed leadership of the orphaned herd. I didn't want any of our fawns to be a car casualty, but especially not Yoda.

John and I were out the door within minutes of receiving the phone call. On the short car ride, I couldn't help but think of another fawn hit by a car, years ago.

The little buck, unimaginatively christened Mr. Bucky, was the first orphaned fawn we ever took in for rehabilitation. The situation had been thrust on us unexpectedly, and we hastily made a fawn pen and hut. All of us fell in love with the baby in his spotted plush coat. Mr. Bucky was a learning process for John and me, and a wondrous experience for the boys, then six and four years old. He basked in our love and attention.

"My own fawn," Johnny bragged.

"He's mine, too." Jesse was determined not to be outdone.

Even as novices, we knew it was better to raise deer in a group. We attempted to locate other orphaned fawns for Bucky to grow up and be released with. We called other rehabilitators, who promised to call us back when and if they took in fawns. No one called. Even if they had, I don't know if we could have been unselfish enough to let Mr. Bucky go to them. We thought of him as our deer.

A half-grown yearling buck shared Mr. Bucky's pen once, for about an hour. Spike had been confiscated by the authorities from someone who'd tried to domesticate him by confining him to their barn. Independent and willful, Spike wanted nothing to do with Mr. Bucky. Spike was old enough to be on his own, and Mr. Bucky seemed relieved when his cantankerous companion leapt the six-foot fence for freedom.

By September, Mr. Bucky was also free, but chose to remain on our property. He'd follow Johnny down the driveway to the bus stop.

"Hey, look at that!" The schoolchildren would rush to one side of the bus to watch Mr. Bucky trailing Johnny, a ritual repeated every school day.

"Wow, awesome!"

"Neat-o!"

Johnny proudly accepted the status his "pet" gave him, while his schoolmates were amazed.

As winter closed in, Mr. Bucky would wander off for hours on end, exploring. He never assimilated into the wild herd, but always came back each evening to spend the night bedded down along the chain-link fence of our dog kennel. Max, our big Labrador, would forsake his cozy doghouse to lie next to Mr. Bucky, fence between them, sharing their warmth. The fact that they were dog and deer never bothered either of them.

One brisk evening, I informed John that Mr. Bucky hadn't come home yet.

"He's a big boy now, Lin," John responded. "One day he's not going to come back, but stay out there and be wild."

"Maybe so, but I'm worried," I replied. Something didn't feel right to me.

"Come morning, he'll be here looking for his apples," John assured me.

But Mr. Bucky didn't show up that morning, or the next. I searched all his favorite spots. Throughout each day I'd go out and call to him, hoping he'd come back. We told the boys we hoped he'd gone off with the other deer, a closure they could accept. Meanwhile, John and I both watched the road for a body.

"He's not coming back," I told John flatly, resigning myself to the realities of rehabilitation and release. Setting deer free, compared to some of the other animals we care for, is emotionally harder for us. We are supposed to raise wildlife to become independent, I kept reminding myself. But a piece of my heart had left with Mr. Bucky. And what was left of my heart broke as I had to keep explaining that situation to the boys.

As hunting season approached, John and I began our annual chore of posting the bright orange "No Hunting" signs. Our neighbor had given us permission to post on their property, too, which would effectively provide a safe, adequate buffer zone for Mr. Bucky if he was still in the area.

In the far corner of the adjoining land, we came across the body of a spring buck. He was lying in high underbrush, facing our house. He had been hit by a car yet made it off the busy roadway.

It was Mr. Bucky.

"No!" I denied it, convulsive sobs wrenched from me as I knelt by the body. "Why? How are we going to tell the boys?" They were unanswerable, futile questions.

I cried against the truth, the unfairness, the carelessness of cars.

"I'll never, ever raise another fawn," I choked out to John. "I can't. Not if this is going to happen. Oh, God, it hurts so much!" I doubled over with the agony of it.

Silent tears slid down John's face as he gently covered Mr. Bucky with dirt and leaves. We held each other by the graveside, almost wishing we'd never learned this fate.

Jerked back to reality by the cold wind hitting us as we got out of the truck, I ran to where tonight's fawn lay. Playing the flashlight beam over her, we knew there was nothing we could do to save her.

"Thank God," I told John. "It's not Yoda."

Morning light confirmed my identification. We took the dead, nameless doe far up into the woods, where she would provide nourishment for the other animals in the circle of life.

As we pulled into our driveway, we saw our son, Jesse, extend an apple-filled hand to his favorite fawn, Yoda. With trust-filled eyes, the deer gently plucked the fruit from his fingers and nussled his face against Jesse's warm, mittened hand. John and I looked at each other and smiled as we remembered a special deer who inspired us to extend our hearts to nature's creatures.

While we still mourn Mr. Bucky, we also honor him by nurturing more fawns each spring—in his memory.

Linda Mihatov

Reprinted by permission of George Crenshaw, Masters Agency.

Ladybug and Cricket

What feeling is so nice as a child's hand in yours?

Marjorie Holmes

She wanted to do what all the other kids did; she wanted to go to summer camp. But Erin was born with cystic fibrosis, and much of her energy was spent in the simple exercise of breathing. Within her frail body lived a keen mind, a strong will and a lively spirit invigorated by her love for God's wonderful world.

She would never accept what she was told she could not do. She set her own limits in a continuing battle between weakened capacity and robust determination. I remember the night she wanted to sleep outdoors in the backyard tent with her sister. The night air turned cool and damp, so I carried her indoors. As I entered the house, she awoke, turned to me and said, "Mama, you worry too much," and back to the tent she went.

She had just turned eight years old the fall we moved from the suburbs to wooded rolling acreage in the countryside. There, on the farm, was a creek to play in, animals to care for, a garden to grow and the pleasure of wide-open skies. But after only two months in the third grade, it became impossible for her to attend school. With the long hours and her shortness of breath, it was just too much for Erin. She became my constant companion, and I teased her about being a third-grade dropout.

Our conversations were often more friend to friend than mother and daughter. One time when I made the comment, "I wish this week were over," she quickly replied, "Oh, Mama, don't say that. Time goes too fast."

Our best times were shared outdoors. Together we milked Nelly the goat, fed the chickens and took walks to find wildflowers. Delicate springtime blooms of trillium, Dutchman's britches and bloodroot faded in summer heat, making way for the hardier orange day lilies and purple Joe Pye weed. Bright red jewelweed attracted the hummingbirds. In the lane we gasped breathless at the beauty of the shy bluebirds, bright blue with robin's red breast.

Erin joined a 4-H club and grew sunflowers as her project. She dropped the seeds in the row I had dug, and, as best she could, she watered and cared for her crop. I'll never forget her 4-H leader driving to the county fair with the long sunflower, roots and all, tied to the top of her car. Of the 4-Hs—head, heart, hands and health—Erin had all but health.

All these things she did with zeal, but the greatest desire of her ninth summer was to go to camp. It seemed an impossible dream. Her twice-daily treatments were time-consuming and required specialized equipment. In addition, she slept in a "mist tent" at night. It seemed there were no camps that could accommodate her special needs.

Then we heard about Campfire Girls' day camp. Erin was a member of Bluebirds, the younger set of Campfire Girls, so she was eligible. The local chapter responded to our plea and accepted Erin as a day camper.

Each morning an excited little girl smiled and waved good-bye as she climbed into the camp bus. She greeted every day with eager anticipation. At day's end, a weary child related stories about her wonderful time. She loved

Ladybug, the camp director, and glowed when she spoke of Cricket, her counselor.

"Cricket carries me when I get tired," Erin smiled. "Cricket showed me a bird's nest with speckled eggs. We found a praying mantis, but we left him alone 'cause he eats bad bugs. Do you know how to tell a boy turtle from a girl turtle? A boy turtle has red eyes. I brought you a leaf picture I made today."

When an activity was too strenuous, the counselors found a way for her to be a part of the event. "Guess what?" Erin reported one evening. "We had races today, and I got to hold the stopwatch."

One scheduled event was an overnight campout. I was reluctant. Then I remembered my own camping experience and how much it meant to sleep under a cover of stars, the glowing embers of a campfire warm upon my face. I could not deny her this one night of childhood.

When she got home, her enthusiasm overflowed and fizzed like a shook-up pop bottle. She gushed, effervesced and then went flat in exhausted slumber. I watched her labored breathing as she slept and knew then that one night, one tenuous link to generations of campers, was all she would ever have.

She asked if she could go again next summer. She hoped all the friends she had made would come back. Most of all, she wanted Cricket to be there. "I hope I don't get too big," she said, "or Cricket won't be able to carry me."

In late November Erin came down with pneumonia. After a month in the hospital, she returned home, two days before Christmas. Her body had not responded to treatment. A hospital bed with an oxygen tent was set up in the family room. She was too ill to get up, but still wanted to put on a new dress I had bought her for Christmas. I pulled the dress over her head, but it would not fit. Her brave heart had worked so hard that it had enlarged and pushed out the walls of her chest.

Two weeks after Christmas, she lapsed into a coma. One

week later, on Sunday, the sixteenth of January 1977, the ground frozen white with snow, she took her last breath cradled in my arms.

She's resting still in a plot on the farm, on a hillside along the road across from the river. In the spring the wild phlox bloom, the creek rushes into the river and Erin remains forever nine years old.

Lois Donahue

The Solo Club

*Paddle a hundred (miles) in a canoe and you
are already a child of nature.*

Pierre Elliott Trudeau

I was a rather chunky ten-year-old, spending my summer
at a camp in the Laurentian Mountains north of Montreal. I
wasn't athletic or particularly well-coordinated, but I was
tall, and therefore, everyone assumed that I'd be good at bas-
ketball or some such sport. I wasn't. In June 1971, I was an
awkward preteen, and with no desire to play baseball or
shoot hoops in the hot sun, I made my way to the camp
docks and a head counselor by the name of Jim.

Jim was a stout, bearded guy with the beginnings of a
belly. He was also in charge of the waterfront. That morning,
he was milling about, arranging water-ski equipment and
portaging canoes from the beach to the storage sheds.

He called me over and asked for a hand with one of the
larger canoes. It was heavy but I managed, and as we lay it
carefully on its designated rack, he asked if I'd ever canoed
before.

"Nope," I replied.

He motioned for me to follow him. Pulling the one canoe

that was still in the sand out into the water, he said, "Get in."

I did as he instructed, stepping cautiously out of the water and onto the wooden seat in the bow. The canoe felt tippy, and I wasn't sure how or where to sit. He assured me that where I had plunked myself was fine.

As we drifted off into the open water, he slid a paddle my way. "Come on," he said, "you've got to do some work here as well."

I grabbed the paddle and broke the surface of the water. Proudly, I took that first swath of the lake.

"Not like that," he said calmly. "That's lily-dipping. Turn your thumb away from you and make it count. Like this," he demonstrated. "You need to make a small whirlpool."

With that admonition, I shifted my weight to the left, leaned over the paddle and dug into the water, my thumb forward and down. I felt the power of the paddle and then, in its trail, I saw my first whirlpool.

"Keep going," exclaimed Jim, "that's it."

Thumb down and forward. Whirlpool. Thumb down and forward. Whirlpool. Thumb down and forward. Whirlpool.

I did it again and again. No more lily-dipping for me. With each proud stroke, we slid across the lake.

The next day, I was down at the water bright and early, eager to do what I could to help Jim. I cleaned out the canoes, swept the dock, put away life preservers and dragged all kinds of water-related matter up and down the beach. And then, late in the day, after all the other campers had left for dinner, Jim and I headed out on the lake where he taught me essential strokes like the sweep, the draw and the j-stroke.

Days passed, but Jim wouldn't let me take a canoe out on my own until I had passed my Solo Test. Only a handful of campers reached that level, and I was determined to be one of them.

Every day I practiced the essential strokes, and Jim took the time to teach me some advanced tricks. Before I knew it, with Jim's encouragement, I could even right a tipped canoe in the middle of the lake.

By the end of July, I felt, and more importantly *Jim* felt, that I was ready to take my Solo. I took to the water, paddle in hand, and later that same day, with the scent of fresh pine in the air and a cool lake breeze at my back, my name was one of only five called that summer to accept the Solo Club designation.

As I rushed on to the dock in front of my fellow campers, I was greeted by Jim, a proud smile on his face, his hand out-stretched toward mine. He presented me with a small wooden paddle, lightly varnished. Inscribed in red lettering were the words "Solo Club" and on the other side, my name and the year '71.

More than thirty summers have passed since I won that award, and I still have the paddle. It's been with me in spirit through dozens of canoe trips and countless other nature adventures as a precious reminder of the man who steered me in the right direction.

Steve Zikman

Terrified on Timpanogos Mountain

To experience the fullness of our humanness, we need to turn again to nature and open ourselves to what it has to say to us.

Margaret P. Stark

During the summer of 1993, my thirteen-year-old son Andrew and I headed out on a four-week, 6,000-mile return trip across America from Wisconsin to California. In the Timpanogos mountains outside Salt Lake City, Utah, we decided to take in a cave tour. A wooden sign warned:

To reach Timpanogos Cave, visitors must hike the 1.5-mile Cave Trail. The hard-surfaced path rises 1,065 feet and is considered a strenuous hike. Anyone with heart trouble or walking or breathing problems should not attempt the hike. Allow three hours for the round trip, including an hour in the cave. Individuals under 16 must be directly supervised by an adult at all times.

It was a warm, sunny July afternoon, and since it was only 3 P.M. we had plenty of time before dark to walk up the trail, catch the last cave tour of the day and hike down. We bought our tickets and started to climb.

Even though we were in good shape, loose gravel and the steep switchback path that zigzagged up the mountain took its toll. Every quarter-mile or so we'd sit down on a bench to catch our breath. Enormous pines hundreds of feet below, sheer slate gray cliffs, cream-colored rocks that stretched to the heavens and a clear blue sky that went on forever greeted us at every rest. After an hour of exhaustive climbing, we reached the entrance to the cave.

I plopped down on a bench just outside the cave entrance next to an older man wearing a beige one-piece worksuit and a miner's hat with a light attached. He spoke in a very thick Spanish accent, telling me that it had taken him over two and a half hours to climb up the mountain. He was exhausted and upset that he'd missed the scheduled time for his tour. His name was Emilio, and he was originally from Madrid, Spain. He was seventy years old and said he had no idea how steep the climb would be.

Then our tour guide appeared. She welcomed Emilio into our group and opened the entrance to the cave. An hour and a half later, after exploring the cave and its winding paths punctuated with stalactites and stalagmites, we stepped back into daylight. Only it wasn't bright and sunny like before—it was cloudy, windy and starting to sprinkle.

Andrew didn't like the looks of it. "Mom, hurry up. It's raining. We gotta get down. It could be a big storm."

I glanced behind me toward the cave exit, looking for Emilio.

"Mom! Come on! Look how windy it's getting! We gotta get down!" Andrew was starting to panic.

"Andrew, wait a minute. Emilio's right behind us."

"Who cares? Mom, it's really starting to rain! Let's go!"

I had no idea why I couldn't leave without the old man, but I wanted to wait until Emilio was safely out of the cave and walking with us.

I tried to reason with Andrew. "It's going to take us at least an hour to get down, maybe longer. We're going to get wet no matter what. Let's just wait for him."

"Mom, do you see those black clouds over Salt Lake City in the distance? That's rain pouring out of them! And they're moving this way! It's getting darker!"

I could see that my son was really scared. I certainly didn't like what I saw ahead of us either. A steep, narrow mountain path with no guard rail and littered with rocks was not where I wanted to be during a thunderstorm.

Just then Emilio stepped out of the cave. Andrew skittered down the first leg of the switchback path. I walked slowly, just ahead of Emilio. Within a few minutes, Andrew had disappeared around the first sharp turn.

"Mom! Hurry up!" Andrew yelled. "I can see lightning in the distance!"

Suddenly, a giant sharp cracking noise slammed into the mountain. It wasn't the rolling thunder I was used to in Wisconsin. This sounded like ten thousand bull whips had snapped right in front of us into the side of the rock, a nasty heart-stopping sound. Then a giant rod of white light zigzagged just ahead of us.

"Mom!" Andrew screamed. "Hurry up!" I knew my son wanted to run and not stop until he reached the bottom where the car was.

The wind roared, and I crouched behind a rock outcrop. As the sky turned black, the clouds let loose, pelting us with pouring rain and wind. Stones and small rocks flew off the mountain and smashed at our feet. I could feel my heart slamming against my chest. I closed my eyes tight and prayed as more lightning flashed in front of us.

"Ouch!" Andrew let out a yelp. "Mom, I just got hit in the head by a rock the size of a baseball! Can't you go any faster?"

I couldn't move. I started praying again. *God don't let us die out here. Protect us and keep Emilio's legs strong.* I shouted over the wind, "Stay calm, Andrew! We'll be okay."

Another giant crack. This one sounded like the mountain

itself had split in half. Then more lightning, closer this time.

Andrew was fifty feet ahead of Emilio and me. In some places on the path, a blue line was painted down the middle. A sign said that those were the areas where rockslides were likely to occur. Andrew was on one side of a rockslide area; Emilio and I were on the other.

I was shivering as cold rain ran down my neck. Finally, I looked up to make sure no large rocks were falling, raced across the blue-line section and caught up to my son.

"We have to wait for Emilio," I said matter-of-factly.

"Why, Mom? He can make it by himself. He got up here, didn't he? I don't like this. Let me go by myself. You know how long it took Emilio to get up this mountain! I can't stand this!"

I yelled over the howling wind, "Andrew, think of all the things that could happen to Emilio. He could lose his balance and slip on a rock. He could have a heart attack from exhaustion. He . . ."

Andrew pulled away from me and interrupted. "Okay, okay! Geez, Mom, this is going to take forever!" He wasn't happy, but I think he was starting to understand.

"Andrew, you're strong. You're five feet, nine inches, a little shorter than Emilio. How would you feel about letting him put his hands on your shoulders from behind for support?"

I looked back up the path at Emilio. I could see clumps of wet white hair under the child-size miner's cap. He was bent over, hands on his knees, panting for breath. I looked at the dark clouds. It was still raining, and the path was wet and slippery. Andrew was looking at him, too . . . then at the black clouds, at the bent trees blowing wildly in the wind, and then back at Emilio.

Then his voice softened. "Okay, Mom, I'll do it."

Emilio liked the idea of using Andrew's shoulders for support as the two of them baby-stepped down the path while the rain soaked their backs. Shuffle, rest. Shuffle, rest. Emilio could only take twenty or so steps before he had to lean against the mountain and rest his knees.

As we shuffled along with me in the front pushing rocks off the wet path and Emilio's hands on Andrew's shoulders, we looked like the blind leading the blind, leading the blind. Andrew thought we looked so funny that he started whistling the song from *Bridge on the River Kwai* where the prisoners did their single-file death march. In a few seconds Emilio and I were whistling along with him.

Then Emilio started teaching Andrew to speak Spanish. *"Esta es una montaña grande! Vamonos amigos!"* He'd say phrases in Spanish, and Andrew would repeat them.

Next he told Andrew tales about his life in Madrid, about his Cuban wife, how he'd lived in New York for many years and the three years he worked as an auditor on a Norwegian ship.

As I walked ahead kicking stones and rocks out of the path, I could tell from Andrew's comments and questions that he was genuinely starting to like this old guy. Even when they had to stop every few minutes to give Emilio's knees a rest, they joked back and forth until we'd hear Emilio's loud voice echo through the mountains, *"Vamonos muchachos!"*

After an hour, the black clouds moved further south. Our slow procession continued as the pounding rain gradually slowed to a drizzle. For three and a half hours, as we inched our way down that steep, slippery mountain path, Emilio and Andrew were glued to each other, Emilio's hands on Andrew's shoulders.

Ten feet before we reached the bottom, Emilio pulled away from my son and stood tall by himself. In his loud, clear voice with the thick Spanish accent, he proclaimed, "I do the last steps myself! So, Andrew, when we reach the bottom, shall we purchase the tickets to do this again tomorrow?"

We all laughed. When Emilio reached level ground, we cheered. I gave him a hug, and we walked him to his car in the dark of night. By now it was after 9:30 P.M., and our two cars were the only ones left in the parking lot.

Before he opened his car door, Emilio shook my son's hand and said, "Andrew, you are a fine young man. I could not have made it down without your help. Thank you."

Later, as we drove back to Salt Lake City, Andrew said he felt sad when Emilio drove away. He wanted to talk to him some more, to hear his big belly laugh again. Then he thought for a moment and continued, "You know, Mom, as soon as Emilio put his hands on my shoulders, I wasn't afraid of the storm anymore."

A bridge had formed between two strangers, and my boy was becoming a man.

Patricia Lorenz

Nice Bird

It is our business to go as we are impelled.

D. H. Lawrence

Having always loved the outdoors, it was inevitable that I would leave my longtime job as a secretary and find myself the founder of a wildlife rehabilitation center. Somehow the paycheck earned from my dreary nine-to-five job did not come close to the "paycheck" earned by watching a wild thing fly away—healed, wild and free.

One sunny Saturday late afternoon, our center received a call from the local police department reporting that a goose had been hit by a car near Otter Pond.

We arrived to see one of the officers holding a very large brown and white domestic goose. Blood was oozing from the wound on its leg. Luckily, the bird suffered only a broken toe, minor abrasions and a bruised wing.

Bringing him to the center, we taped his toe, cleaned his wounds and made him comfortable. He looked grateful and even nudged my arm, seeming to say "thank you."

To comfort him while tending to his wounds, I told him what a nice bird he was and soon started calling him Nice Bird. Hearing this, he'd cock his head, looking at me out of one eye and then the other, as if he were sizing up the name.

During his rehabilitation, I grew attached to this big brown and white goose. If I didn't set his food dish down fast enough, he would gently nip my legs. When the dish was empty, he'd honk loudly! Whenever anyone passed his pen, he would honk, demanding some attention.

Soon it was time to release Nice Bird. Usually a happy occasion with wildlife, it isn't as joyful with domestic waterfowl since the wild is not their natural habitat. But it was this bird's home, and I'm sure that all his waterfowl friends were there, wondering what had become of him. So, sadly, I brought him back to Otter Pond, left a big pile of food and quickly drove off.

Nice Bird looked puzzled, honking loudly, even running a few steps after the truck. But twisting my neck around to view him for the last time, I could see he had settled down to eat.

The days passed, and several times during our travels, my coworker Jim and I would pass Otter Pond and see Nice Bird happily grazing with his friends. We would even stop to give him and his pals some nourishing cracked corn. The weather was growing colder, making it hard to find food. Nice Bird always recognized us and would run from wherever he was to greet us.

One day Jim and I passed by and didn't see Nice Bird. Concerned, I asked Jim to stop. We got out.

His friends ran up to us, but there was no sign of Nice Bird. Growing alarmed, I walked further to the water, even calling to him. Nothing.

Suddenly, in the distance, I heard his familiar honking. As my eyes scanned the pond, I saw his head far down in the shoreline vegetation. Moving closer, I could see him running back and forth, honking frantically. Something was wrong.

I worked my way through briars and brambles, finally reaching a little clearing where he stood. To my amazement, among the thorns lay a young herring gull, starving, weakened and very frightened, with the big brown and white goose standing protectively over him. Stooping to pick the gull up, I felt how dangerously thin he was. With Nice Bird following curiously after me, I ran back to the truck with the sick gull. We rushed back to the center to give him emergency treatment.

On the way, I wrapped the sick bird in a warm towel and reflected for a minute. *Could it be?* No, it was just a coincidence. It simply wasn't possible that Nice Bird tried to get our attention to rescue the sick gull. *Or was it?* Could it really be that he stayed by the gull's side, comforting him and then calling us to come and help his feathered friend?

Back at the center, we began emergency treatment. A heat lamp was placed near the bird's cold body, and fluid therapy was started. Later that day, we went past Otter Pond again. Nice Bird was grazing happily with the others, his mission accomplished, his good deed done.

Sadly, despite our efforts, the gull passed away. But as life left him, peaceful and warm, his last breath was drawn with the knowledge that someone cared about him—those of us who tried to help and a big, gentle brown and white "nice bird."

Virginia Frati

Marigolds and Memories

Forgiveness is the most tender part of love.

John Sheffield

I've seen sweet little bunnies in the early evening hours and smelled the perfume of skunk through the open window of my bedroom at night. I've watched, helpless, as flocks of birds descended upon my almost-ready-to-eat vegetables.

I've tried my hand at a vegetable garden a number of times. It seems that just as the crop begins to ripen, and I begin to imagine the many ways I'll soon be able to enjoy the fruits of my labors, the same thing happens.

It serves me right, I suppose. I did my share of garden-ravaging as a child.

I remember the summer I was six. That was the last summer of freedom before I started school. My friends and I spent lazy days at the pool or building forts—and we generally ended up in the backyard of one of our neighbors.

Now that was a garden! During the day, the elderly Portuguese lady worked long and hard to coax the carrots, beans, rhubarb and every other vegetable imaginable to grow. Some days, I'd see her come out the side door of her house as I passed by on my way to play with my friends. She always wore a big straw hat and carried a woven basket when she was gardening. Once, I crept up the driveway to watch her work.

The sun was blistering hot, but she didn't seem to mind at all. She knelt down between the rows of baby plants and began to work the earth with her hands, pulling weeds and placing them in the basket beside her.

For an old person, she sure could work hard. She could work longer than I could stand and watch. I left, cutting across the grass in the front yard, wondering absently what she did to the grass that made it so soft and greener than anybody else's.

By the time August came around, my friends and I could resist no longer.

The first time we raided the garden, we went for the rhubarb—picked a few stalks each and ran to our fort to eat them. It was sour, and I didn't much like it, but I ate it anyway. Next time, I decided to try the carrots, and they were good. I picked a few, only to look up to see my friends making a mad dash for the fence.

"Wait for me," I called out to their retreating backs. Too late, they were gone—and no one would be able to help me over the fence. I'd have to take the more dangerous route down the side of the house.

As I turned, I saw the reason my friends had abandoned me. The old woman was coming. Waving a straw broom in her hand, she lumbered toward me. I swung my head around, terrified, and looked at the fence. No way could I make it. I raced past her and ran down the driveway.

"You! You want to steal from old woman, huh?" She could run pretty fast for an old person. "You no take my carrots again!"

"I'm sorry!" I screamed, feeling the rough straw of the broom scrape against the backs of my legs. I ran all the way home. She had stopped at the end of her driveway and did not follow me. It was then I realized I still had the carrots in my hand. I dusted one off and munched at it, not enjoying it nearly as much as I had anticipated. I ate all three, though—after all, I had risked my life for them.

The following Monday brought the first day of kinder-garten. I put on my nice new clothes, picked up my pencil case and scribbler, and started bawling. I hated school. It was dumb, and I didn't have to go if my stomach hurt—and boy, did it hurt. My poor pool was leaning up against the shed in the backyard, looking as dejected as I felt. The days of sum-mer and carefree childhood had come to a bitter end. Mom called my stomachache "butterflies," but it felt more like ele-phants running around in circles.

As my friends and I made our way to the school, I lagged behind, fighting the tears that threatened. Before long, they had rounded the corner and forgotten all about me. Now I started to cry in earnest.

"Why you crying?"

I looked up through my tears and saw the garden-lady. She didn't have a broom, and she was smiling.

"I don't wanna go to school," I replied, sniffing loudly.

"School is good. You learn reading." Taking me by the hand, she led me up her driveway. "Come, I give something to you—your teacher like you, and you like school."

I sat on the step while she went inside, coming back with a sheet of aluminum foil and a wet napkin. As I watched, she fashioned a cup from the foil and put the soaking napkin inside. "You pick some flowers for teacher," she said, pointing to her flower garden.

"I can't. I stole your carrots," and, as an afterthought, "and your rhubarb, too."

I could see she was trying not to laugh. "You say sorry, right?"

"Yup."

"So pick flowers. I say it's okay."

I looked at the vast array of colors spread before me. The biggest flowers were in the back—bright reds, pinks and yel-lows. Then there were the snapdragons, flowers you could play with, watching their little mouths open and close. I twisted a piece of hair around and around my finger, trying to decide, and pointed to the smallest ones, the marigolds—bright, yellow ones.

She put them in the foil and handed them to me. "Now go to school—you get smart—grow up and maybe be lawyer or something."

I hugged her and ran to school, carrying the flowers proud and high.

Even now, thirty-five years later, I smell marigolds and remember the lessons on forgiveness and kindness she taught me. Not many people like the scent of the "stink flower," but I love the memories they hold. I bring one to my nose, and I'm six years old again.

Hope Saxton

"Now isn't this better than bringing
the Christmas tree to us?"

To Plant a Tree

You and I are suddenly what the trees try to tell us we are: That their merely being there means something.

John Ashbery

Years before I traveled to Hispaniola, I came across a famous aerial photo of the island in *National Geographic* magazine. In the photograph, one half of the island is green with trees, the other side a collage of browns and gray. The stark meeting of the two sides marks the boundary between the Dominican Republic and Haiti. One half of the island is lush with verdant forests; the other half is barren.

Most Haitians must walk miles to find even an occasional dead limb to heat their family meals. They cannot afford the charcoal that brings more money when exported to the country on the other side of their island. During my stay in Haiti, we would sit on the sands and watch one tired, weathered boat after another, laden with burlap bags full of charcoal. They told me that it takes several medium-sized trees to process even one bag of charcoal, and we saw hundreds of bags pass the tourist-deserted beach clubs destined for other shores.

In its own small battle against the inevitable, the hospital where I had lived and worked in Haiti for two years had a tree-planting project. Tiny seedlings of acacia, mango and almond trees were tended and nurtured by hospital employees until they were ready for planting. One afternoon, I accompanied a group of students from the community as they spread out across the hillside around their village planting these small trees.

I followed the line of children in brightly colored school uniforms and bare feet singing in Creole as they walked along dusty paths balancing boxes of seedlings on their heads. When we arrived at the dry plot, we struggled to dig up the rock-hard soil to make a pocket for the roots of each young tree.

A year later, I hiked back up the mountain with the young women who ran the reforestation program. Out of the two hundred trees planted, we could find only ten that had survived. Some of the trees were brown and brittle, no bigger than when we planted them, the result of too little rain.

Ironically, others had been washed away as water flooded down the mountainside during a capricious rainy season. Still others had been eaten by the livestock, primarily goats that are allowed to roam freely.

I wondered what it would take to plant even one tree, let alone enough trees to reverse the sure path of ruin that was too far underway.

Whenever I went for a hike in Haiti, I would tell my colleagues I was going to "the place with two trees." Everyone knew what I meant because on all the mountain slopes surrounding our village, there was only one place where as many as two trees stood together. It was the place where those going up and down laden with supplies or a sick relative could stop for shade and a few minutes relief from the tropical sun. I am told that today, even though one of the trees has died and been cut down, that place is still known as "the place with two trees."

One day, when trekking with a friend, we walked for several hours in intense heat under the clear blue sky and had long since passed "the place with two trees." Haitian peasant women in ragged dresses passed us on the trail. They carried buckets of water from the nearest supply, miles away, and trudged upwards, expressionless. Their bare feet were callused as thick as the souls of my hiking boots, with crevices as deep as those in the earth they trod.

Nearly to the top of the mountain, we rounded a bend in the path, and a cluster of several mud huts came into view. In front of the huts stood five round white stone structures I had never seen before. My curiosity piqued, we continued toward them, thinking perhaps they were some sort of grave markers or ovens for bread. They were deceptively far, and they disappeared and came back into view as we trudged over ridges and around more bends. The closer we got, the more curious we became.

The structures were larger than I had initially thought. Each one was about four or five feet high, and we thought they might have been used for grain storage or were some kind of rainwater collection system. Or maybe they were shelters for a small animal or pet, or some aspect of a child's sport. But they were constructed of large rocks and had involved heavy work. Perhaps they were created for a religious purpose.

Finally, we reached the plateau where the forms stood, and by then we could tell that the round enclosures were open to the sky. Like a child now, forgetting my thirst, I could barely contain my curiosity and hurried ahead of my partner the last few feet to the nearest ring of stones.

I peered over the top of the first sun-bathed white wall. Amazed by what I had discovered, I quickly checked the other four tiny shelters. Sure enough, they all contained the same thing.

Inside of each grew a single, healthy young tree—five trees planted at the top of a dusty, dry mountain in an act of diligence and hope. At last, I knew what it took to plant a tree.

Karen Lynn Williams

$\overline{9}$
TO THE LIMIT

*W*here else can the limitless landscape match
the greatest reach of the human spirit?

T. A. Barron

Expedition Inspiration

The mountains reserve their choice gifts to those who stand upon their summits.

Sir Francis Younghusband

In 1989, I started planning a trip to Africa to climb Kilimanjaro, the highest mountain on the continent. I was as intrigued with climbing this exotic peak as I was with the culture—both the two-legged and the four-legged kind. This would be my foray into another world—a world of high altitude, wild animals and Masai tribesmen. I hoped that Kilimanjaro would be the first of many high mountain climbs.

The seeds for my African expedition were planted during my recent journey to Nepal where I had spent six weeks trekking over rarely traveled footpaths en route to the base camp of Kangchenjunga, the third highest mountain in the world.

I fell in love with the extraordinary and rugged beauty of the mountains, the rustic villages through which our small team traveled and the sing-song voices of the local children with their big smiles and tattered clothes. I reveled in a culture that was so very different from my own. Even before I left Nepal, I knew that I wanted to travel to more villages, more voices, more smiles. I also knew that I wanted the challenge of climbing to be part of my experience.

Ambitiously, I set my sights on six of the seven continental summits. The challenge would afford me the opportunity to see Africa, Alaska, Russia, New Zealand, Argentina and Antarctica.

Kilimanjaro, more of a trek than a climb, was a logical place to start. As I set the wheels in motion, I thought about my grandmother, a major influence in my life. Grandma also liked to travel, but rarely made time for the trips she envisioned. She died with a very long wish list in small type.

I was determined not to have the same thing happen to me.

What did happen, however, I could never have expected. Two weeks before that Christmas of 1989, I was diagnosed with a rapidly growing breast cancer that had metastasized to my lymph system. I was told I had a 15 percent chance of surviving three to five years. In a matter of hours, I went from feeling as healthy as I ever have in my life to fearing I might not make it through the New Year.

After much research, I decided to take part in a clinical trial that would give me the best chance for long-term survival. The treatment would include three months of outpatient chemotherapy, seven weeks of radiation and two months in the hospital undergoing intensive chemotherapy, followed by a bone-marrow transplant. I would be one of the first people in the country to go through this particular protocol.

In March 1990, I entered Pacific Presbyterian Hospital, where I spent seven weeks in a sterile room the size of a closet. My only human contact came in the form of hugs delivered through plastic sleeves that protruded into my room. Food was administered through tubes running into my chest, and exercise consisted of frequent trips to the basin to throw up. I grew weaker and weaker. From my bed, I would stare at the park outside my window and dream of walking through it.

As I slipped into a drug-induced slumber, I would visualize myself on the summit of Kilimanjaro and McKinley and peaks I didn't yet know the names of. But as I dreamed, my muscles atrophied, my immuneless body became wracked with fever, and I almost died.

But I never stopped hoping and praying that one day I would walk out of that hospital and through the park I viewed from a distance every morning, noon and night.

Finally, miraculously, the fever broke, and I was released. The first thing I did was to walk through that park. It took every ounce of energy I had to walk the four short blocks, but I was elated. Each day I walked a little more. Over the months that followed, I began to slowly and painfully put the pieces of my life back together. As I grew stronger, so did thoughts of my unfinished goal of traveling to Africa and climbing Kilimanjaro.

A year after treatment, I hiked up Baldy, the local ski mountain. My legs and lungs fought against the exertion, but after four long hours, I stood on top. It was then I knew I would go to Africa.

So once again, I started making plans. After several more trips up Baldy and every inoculation in the book, I boarded a plane for Nairobi, excited and nervous about what lay ahead. I could hardly believe that my long-awaited adventure was about to become a reality.

The trip began in the Serengeti Plains where lions, hippo, cheetah and elephants share the rugged landscape with the African natives. It is a sight that stirs the blood, and it took me back to an earlier, less complicated place in time. For three days, our group of nine was on safari, happily lost in another world.

On the night before we were to leave for Tanzania to begin our climb up Kilimanjaro, the Masai danced. Circling us in the darkness, each of the warriors began a chant deep from within their stomachs. As they circled faster and faster, they became a mesmerizing blur of sound and movement. With each step, they increased their concentration until I could feel nothing but the energy being forced outward from their bodies.

I reflected on their concentration, their ability to focus their power. I had needed that kind of focus to get well, and I knew I would need it again to reach the summit of Kilimanjaro. Like the Masai, I would have to draw from an inner resource. My chemo-battered lungs were untested at high altitudes, and I suspected that if I was going to stand on the roof of Africa, it was going to take a great deal of mental and spiritual fortitude.

The next day, we started our trek up the "Shining Mountain." For four days, we meandered through jungles of hanging moss, towering groundsels and cactus. The foreign food wreaked havoc with my newly enhanced immune system, and I fought diarrhea the entire way, but with each step I got closer to the top.

When I weakened, I would chant, *"Hakuna Matata, Hakuna Matata,"* which is Swahili for "No problems, no worries." On day five, we set out for the summit. Two years earlier, it seemed I was on my deathbed, throwing up the insides of my lungs, but now I was strong again, recapturing a dream I thought was lost.

As I approached the 19,000-foot rim of the crater, I could no longer contain myself. With a sudden burst of energy, I ran to the top, thrusting my fists skyward, Rocky-style, exulting in my victory.

Standing there in that fresh mountain air, I knew for the first time that our bodies can rebuild if our minds allow them to. On that mountain, in that moment, I was the luckiest person in the world. I wanted to share that feeling with others— that there is life after a cancer diagnosis, that we can go on and achieve whatever had seemed impossible at one point.

After two and a half years of hard work, I co-led seventeen breast-cancer survivors up 23,000-foot Aconcagua in Argentina. We called our project Expedition Inspiration. Our shared goal was to raise $100 a foot per team member to fund breast-cancer research, so every step counted. I was one of three to make it to the top, but, as my team member Nancy Knoble said, "We all reached important summits for ourselves."

Since then, I have traveled around the world, and I have now stood proudly atop five continental summits. As long as I am able, I will be out there, focusing my energy on one more adventure, one more mountain, one more dream. I'm going down my wish list, checking things off and making sure that little, if anything, is left in small type.

Laura Evans

Going Like Sixty

*Life is like a ten-speed bicycle. Most of us have
gears we never use.*

Charles M. Schulz

A month and a half after my sixtieth birthday, I, a devout
nonathlete for most of my life, found myself at the starting
line of the 26.2-mile New York City Marathon. How did this
happen?

It's a long story.

Fourteen years earlier, lured by the promise that a daily
jog would counter the mounting consequences of chocolate-
chip cookies, I found myself running two, then three, miles a
day. I soon realized how precious these runs had become to
me.

Aside from the triumph of knowing that determination
could win out over minimal athletic ability, I reveled in the
bouquet of sensory experiences my morning runs gave me.
Before I began to run, I had never seen the sun blaze up
through the trees at daybreak over the little pond below the
house where I live and work. I had not viewed the different
moods of the early morning sky over the bay across the road,
now pale pink with promise, now a jubilant azure. I had not

heard the joyful singing of the birds as we greeted the day together. I had not drunk in the lush scent of the honey-suckle that grows in such profusion around the corner from my home.

Before I ran, I had viewed the rain and the cold from inside as often as possible. I went out in bad weather only when I had to. Now I found myself running all year round, in every kind of weather, down to zero degrees. No day was a bad day for running. I dressed for it and made each day mine. I embraced the caress of snowflakes drifting onto my face on chilly winter days, the sweat drenching me on steamy summer mornings, the sting of rain on my cheeks, the gentle breezes fanning my hair, the wind against my chest. All these sensations were mine in the ever-changing world that now belonged to me every day.

Over the years people would ask me, "Have you run a marathon?" I would laugh and say, "No—and I never plan to. People aren't meant to run twenty-six miles—especially middle-aged people who have more sense." Mostly, I didn't expect ever to run a marathon because I was sure I couldn't do it.

One day a friend talked me into running a ten-kilometer race. Emboldened by my survival, I ran a half-marathon. Then, the spring before my sixtieth birthday, I was trekking in the Himalayas. I had been climbing up and down steep rocky paths for six hours. I was more exhausted than I had ever been in my life. My back ached from my pack, and my shoulders were sunburned. My heart was beating double-time, and my head was on fire from the relentless sun. *If I can keep going for another two hours,* I thought, *I can run the New York City Marathon in November.* I kept going. I came home and signed up.

What a way to turn sixty—to herald this new stage of my life not as a slippery slope of deterioration, but as a new beginning! I would confront myself in a way I'd never been challenged before. What would I do when the going got tough? Could I keep up the training? What about the day itself? Now that I was of an age when my character should be well formed, who was I?

I enrolled in a training class. I did one long run every week—ten miles, then thirteen, fifteen, sixteen, eighteen miles. Each time I ended up feeling, in the words of an Arkansas friend, as if I'd been "rode wet and then hung out to dry." How would I ever do 26.2 miles? In October I joined a twenty-mile group run in Central Park. I started out with the slowest runners, slogging eleven-minute miles, got separated from them and ran alone for four hours.

Running the serpentine loops in this great city park, I was totally directionless. For much of the time I was in a dream, in an altered state in which my body moved on its own. I felt a delicious solitude, a pleasure in moving over these paths on this glorious fall day, in seeing the scarlets and golds of the trees in this urban sanctuary, in breathing in the winey aroma of the autumn leaves underfoot.

Then I came home and slipped getting off the train, a moment of carelessness that left a shoulder and a knee sore and aching. In fairy tales I had read, when something bad happens, it means something new has to be tried, a new energy has to be found. I needed to find a healer. And I needed to look within myself for my own magic force. I found it all. Two weeks, two doctors' visits and three physical-therapy sessions later, I felt fine.

What is the gift in my wounding? I asked. I was forced to think about how I'll adjust to the inevitable physical reversals of aging, what I'll do when I can't run anymore or can't even walk. Will I find new outlets for my energy, creativity, life force? Will I keep going? Will I find a new purpose in life? I knew these questions would remain long after the marathon was only a memory.

And now here I was on November 14, running the first mile, over the Verrazano Bridge, the highest elevation of the race. I wasn't worried about the unseasonably high temperatures that would soar to well over seventy degrees. I had trained all summer in the heat.

I didn't feel the uphill surge at all. I moved effortlessly, with the gentle wind at my back and the balmy blue skies above me, looking down at the tugboats spouting red, white and blue fountains in the shimmering water of the East River, at the runners coursing all around me, at the soaring supports on the largest single-suspension bridge in the world, at the photographers perched precariously on the steel railings of the bridge, at the Manhattan skyline ahead.

I was astounded to see runners wearing headphones. I didn't want to move on automatic. I wanted to be totally here, in the full richness of every moment. I felt my body tingling as all my neurons and dendrites, for every sense, reached out to be open to all the sights and sounds and smells that were part of this full day, this crowning event.

I ran through Staten Island, Brooklyn and Queens—and then onto the 59th Street Bridge into Manhattan. This—what many marathoners consider the true halfway point—is the hurdle to overcome. This rise, the second highest elevation of the route—although less than half the height of that first mile—now felt like Everest. Even over the plush carpeting laid down the length of the bridge for the sake of the runners, my legs protested, and I did my first walking except for water stops. Walk fifty steps, run 100; walk 100, run fifty. Then with a burst of newfound energy, I ran, ran, ran as I faced a roaring wall of spectators.

At mile nineteen, the sun blazed in this record-breaking heat. I had to be careful not to slip in the slush of discarded paper cups and puddles of water. My quads ached, and the soles of my feet burned. I remembered my coach's words: "When your body hurts, welcome the pain and the tiredness, because you'll know you're pushing yourself to do more than you've ever done before. Smile, knowing you're getting a really good workout." I smiled.

Just before mile twenty-one, I was on the final stretch toward Central Park. I knew now that I would finish. Boom boxes blared, and I almost broke into dance as the music put a new, needed spring into my step. Then it was into the park at 102nd Street, where I had walked so often before, to the encouraging cheers of people lining the roads. When did that hill become such a mountain?

Finally, I heard the public-address system: "If you can hear my voice, you can finish in under six hours." In the dusk I saw the glittering lights on the trees creating a fairyland outside Tavern on the Green, and then at last the rainbow of balloons arching over the finish line. I came in just under six hours—no prize except the medal given to all finishers—but for me the doing was the prize.

The race has been over for eight years now, but I still lace up my running shoes almost every day, year round, whether the morning temperature hovers at zero or zooms up to eighty. I still relish the different sights and sounds and smells of each season, no matter where I find myself—on the streets of my own suburban neighborhood, on the rural roads near my daughter's house where I'm likely to be outdistanced by deer bounding through the woods, or in some foreign city where the outdoor aromas come from breakfast sizzling on sidewalk stalls.

I'm not the same woman I was before the marathon. I have a new respect for my body, as a good place to live, a good instrument for insuring my health and fitness. I have a new respect for my mind, too, for what it did to transform a dedicated couch potato into what my medal proclaims is now an athlete. And I have a new sense of my capacity to change—no matter how old I get.

The day after the race, a young friend in his thirties said to me, "I couldn't run twenty-six miles."

"I couldn't either—at your age," I told him.

Sally Wendkos Olds

In My Father's Footsteps

We reached the summit almost together.

Sir Edmund Hillary and Tenzing Norgay Sherpa

My father, Tenzing Norgay Sherpa, discouraged his children from becoming mountaineers because it was dangerous. He knew, since he and Edmund Hillary were the first men to reach the top of Mount Everest in 1953.

Despite my father's caution about mountaineering, and for reasons I myself do not fully understand, I had dreamed about climbing Everest ever since I was six years old.

In 1996, it looked as if my dream might come true. David Breashears, the leader of the Everest IMAX Expedition, was making a documentary about the Everest region, and he offered me a central role in it. Finally, after years of dreaming, training and planning, I hoped to achieve my goal.

However, once we were in the mountains, things quickly began to go wrong. On the day we were preparing to ascend from Camp III (24,000 feet) to Camp IV (26,500 feet), we noticed that there were about thirty-five climbers ahead of us, also on their way to Camp IV. David said that we couldn't join them because our plan was to film when only two or three climbers were on the ridge as they made their way to the top. He didn't want to shoot with that crowd crawling up.

The next morning, there was more bad news. At ten o'clock, a Taiwanese climber at Camp III slipped and fell sixty feet into a crevasse. Some of our Sherpas who happened to be coming down the mountain at the time helped rescue the injured climber, but he died later that evening.

The following day, about one o'clock, using binoculars, we observed the climbers making their way toward the summit. They were very slow, and we became uneasy.

Around three in the afternoon, we heard on the radio that everyone had finally reached the top. But this was not good news. The rule of thumb on Everest is that you do not attempt to summit past one-thirty. After that, you must descend.

Like an avalanche, bad news began to roll in. Sherpas at Camp IV radioed to say that only one or two climbers had returned from the summit, and that many were missing. To make matters worse, a fierce blizzard had developed higher on the mountain where the climbers were floundering. Winds howling at sixty to eighty miles an hour would quickly reduce visibility to a few yards.

At our camp, things were chaotic and frustrating. While I was translating messages radioed from Sherpas about missing mountaineers, it was already dark, and we were helpless. There was nothing we could do except wait and pray that somehow the climbers would either find their way back to their tents or somehow survive the night outside.

Naturally, sleep was out of the question. At three or four in the morning, we started getting more calls. Many climbers were still missing or dead. The blizzard had died down, so four of our members headed up to Camp III to establish emergency relief.

I don't recall the next two days because we were so busy doing rescue work. We were no longer climbers but emergency medical personnel. Near Camp I, at 19,500 feet, members of our expedition flattened out a helipad, pouring

Kool-Aid into the shape of a cross to mark the landing spot. At Base Camp, ten different expeditions merged into one huge rescue effort. In those forty-eight hours, we helped many survive, but not all.

After the helicopter left with the casualties, we assembled at Base Camp to recuperate and prepare for our own attempt to summit. Even though much of our supplies had been used up, we gathered what we required from other expeditions, two-thirds of which decided not to continue. We remained optimistic, and five days later, we headed once again for the summit.

At Camp IV, our final rest before the climb to the top, I woke up at 11:00 P.M. after only five hours of sleep. I had some *tsampa* and dried meat, and washed it down with a bowl of soup. Next, I packed my equipment. My fifteen-pound pack was the only thing I would carry. I adjusted my oxygen mask and harness, clipped on my crampons, put on my hat, and switched on the headlamp. Then I grabbed my ice ax and stepped out into the clear, cold night.

As if to make up for its part in the recent tragedy, the weather was now ideal. The wind, which can be the curse of climbing, was gentle, like a refreshing breeze. All around, it was calm and quiet. I felt the mild weather was a good omen.

Ed, David and a few Sherpas had left an hour before and broken the trail.

The first half hour was a gradual climb on rocky, icy, crevasse-splintered terrain, but this gentle sloping ended abruptly at a steep, straight ascent. The easy part was over. For the next ten hours, I was going to have to use every resource I had, every trick I had learned as a climber. This was the final test of all my years of learning. It was going to be climb, clutch, trudge a few steps, pant for breath and rest for a few seconds, and then start all over again using hands, feet, ropes, ax—everything at my disposal to go up and not crawl back down.

As I climbed, I took every step with care, especially when it was still dark. I did everything deliberately. In these massive mountains, I was nothing. A splinter that could be blown away by a whiff of breeze. I said my prayers.

David and Ed were waiting on the South-East Ridge for the Sherpas who were carrying the camera equipment. Resting on the ridge, we witnessed a gorgeous sunrise and spent the next two hours filming and fortifying ourselves with water, tea and chocolate bars.

Throughout the climb, I felt strong and confident. It was the strongest I had ever felt in my life. Of course, along the way, I thought often of my father. He had been on this mountain forty-three years ago. I felt his spirit and his support. That is why I knew in my heart, *This is it! I will be on top, too!*

I knew I was doing well, yet at the same time, I felt anxious. I just wanted to get to the top, to *be* on top. But I told myself to be careful. You look to one side, you see Tibet, and on the other side, Nepal. Each is a scary, sheer drop of eight thousand feet. I got a little unsettled looking down and around. So I just looked up, waiting to see the summit, but it wasn't there.

Three hundred feet from the top, and I still couldn't see the summit. I negotiated the treacherous traverse to get to the Hillary Step, a very precarious spot totally exposed to the elements. I was climbing landmarks I'd heard so much about.

And then, just when I thought I would never get to the top, I saw Ed coming down, pointing into the whiteness ahead.

"Hey, it's right there."

We hugged each other and, with renewed spirit and strength, I continued.

I realized I was on the summit when I spotted the prayer flags left by Sherpas before me. I saw David and gave him a hug. I thanked him because he had made it possible for me to fulfill my childhood dream. Then I cried.

I thought about my mother and father and prayed. I scattered some rice grains in the air and did *puja*. I left a prayer flag, a *khata*, and pictures of my parents and His Holiness the Dalai Lama. Then I raised the flags of the United Nations, India, Nepal, the United States—and Tibet. It was the first time since 1959 that the national flag of Tibet had been unfurled on its own soil without fear of persecution, and I felt very proud. Finally, I left a small toy of my daughter's, just as my father had done.

I looked around. The summit sloped gently. The view was spectacular. I felt I could see everything everywhere stretched out far away and far, far below—little puffs of clouds and gleaming Himalayan peaks, all beneath my gaze.

I called Base Camp and asked to be connected to my wife in Katmandu. When I heard her sweet voice, I was so happy, but she was even happier. I had promised her a long time ago that after I climbed Mount Everest, I would never climb another mountain again.

And now that I have walked in my father's footsteps, I will not break my word.

Jamling Tenzing Norgay

Faith of a Child

The woods would be silent if no birds sang there except those who sang best.

Henry Van Dyke

Maura was only thirteen years old. Could she really do this? Did she even realize at her tender young age exactly what she was getting into? Would she be one of the youngest American females to ever accomplish this seemingly "impossible" challenge in the great outdoors?

Everyone was worried except Maura. This was not going to be an ordinary soccer game or middle-school cross-country meet. She was engaging in the most challenging endeavor of her young life, something that most people would never attempt or even contemplate at any age. With only one full week to prepare after finishing seventh grade, Maura Ratcliff from Bloomington, Indiana, started pedaling her bicycle from sea to shining sea across the entire continental United States.

What? Coast to coast by bicycle? A thirteen-year-old? A girl? It does seem impossible, but Maura and her family have always used that word with the greatest of caution. It certainly wasn't going to be easy, especially riding with the deCycles, a group known for rugged long-distance bicycle adventures.

This was not going to be a leisurely vacation on a bicycle. In one short month, the deCycles were scheduled to cover 3,300 miles from Huntington Beach, California, to Atlantic City, New Jersey, averaging 125 miles a day. She would face the heat and dryness of California and Arizona deserts. Climbing several mountain passes in the Rockies and Appalachians would make her teeth grit and muscles ache. The headwinds in the Great Plains would be unforgiving. The heat and humidity of the Midwest would be oppressive. And the motorized traffic in the eastern states would be a challenge to her safety. In addition to these outdoor difficulties, Maura was going to share the road with a bunch of cycling powerhouses, including veterans of the Indiana University Little 500 and the world champion Bloomington South High School solar bike team. This group was the "dream team" of local and area cyclists.

Tiny Maura was just a youngster with the physical attributes of an average middle-school student. Fortunately, she did have some background. As a twelve-year-old, she was the youngest person to ever ride on a deCycles trip, pedaling 1,200 miles in twelve days from Florida to Indiana. The organizers of deCycles were initially hesitant to have her on that trip because of her youth and inexperience. But Maura quickly established her credibility as a rider and covered the entire distance without a whimper. As stronger and more experienced riders engaged in their daily complaining rituals, little Maura quietly pedaled her bike with incredible attitude and character.

And so, after dipping her back wheel in the Pacific Ocean, Maura began her transcontinental adventure of a lifetime. Riding through Los Angeles and Southern California was a battle against traffic, pollution, increasing temperatures and hill climbing. She ended the first day in Palm Springs, riding 125 miles with temperatures reaching 110 degrees. She was totally wasted, dehydrated and unable to keep food in her stomach.

Miraculously, she bounced back to tackle the second day of 120 miles to Blythe, California, the hottest town in the United States. At midday, the temperatures soared to 117 degrees with the group riding on Interstate 10 through the Mojave Desert.

By the third day, after pedaling 122 miles in 113-degree temperatures, everyone wanted to go home. *Is this crazy or what?* they thought. But when the group would start complaining, they'd look over at Maura on her bike, and that's all it took to keep everyone quiet. Despite her exhaustion, she never registered a complaint. Incredible! When she called home that evening, she told her parents, "This is the hardest thing I have ever done, but I'm having fun!"

The deCycles escaped the scorching desert by climbing Yarnell Pass and Mingus Mountain in Central Arizona. It took forever, but finally they were free of the oppressive heat and enjoyed the wonderful ponderosa pine forests near Prescott. Maura had survived her ordeal in the desert and conquered some pretty big mountains up to this point. But the steep and winding downhill descent from the top of 8,000-foot Mingus Mountain to Cottonwood and Sedona was something she never encountered before.

My fervent warnings to all the riders to keep their bikes on the road and under fifty miles per hour seemed to go unheeded except by Maura. The racers flew down that descent like it was a thirty-minute-long roller-coaster ride. But Maura clamped down and burned her brakes, actually going slower down the mountain than she did climbing up on the other side! She was white-knuckling all the way to the bottom, and it took her forever. From that point on, however, Maura had no problems with any other downhill coasts. She just needed to test this out and be cautious. Another lesson learned, another challenge met.

Day after day, Maura and her fellow cyclists hammered out the miles across northern Arizona and southern Colorado, climbing Wolf Creek Continental Divide and La Veta Pass. The riders were getting stronger every day.

Favorable tailwinds helped the group crank out a 160-mile day from Alamosa to La Junta. Bikers and spirits were flying high. With the major challenges behind us, the prairies were calling, and our intrepid group delighted in answering the call.

Little did we know that on day thirteen, this call would be abruptly halted by a screech of tires, a sickening thud, a shower of flying debris and a wildly weaving pickup truck. A survey of the scene moments later showed a demolished bicycle and the dreadful image of a rider slumped over on the grassy shoulder of the road. There she was, our little spark-plug rider, our never-quitting Supergirl, lying motionless in a fetal position.

On the ambulance ride to the hospital in Lakin, Kansas, thoughts started creeping in my mind. *Why Maura?* Her challenging cross-country adventure now seemed trivial compared to the crisis at hand. The other riders were visibly shaken and emotionally drained by this accident. But the purpose of deCycles is to venture outside our comfort zone with courage and determination and to appreciate all things.

There was much to be grateful for. Fortunately, the elderly, vision-impaired driver whose vehicle struck Maura had been driving rather slowly. Although Maura had been tossed some thirty feet after impact, nothing was broken. However, a deep puncture wound all the way to the pelvic bone in the left buttock would require two surgeries before Maura would be able to leave the hospital, and the road rash would need care and attention. The wounds would heal with time.

But I wondered about the healing of the spirit, the mending of broken dreams. How long would that take? What words could I say to ease the disappointment? My heart ached as I thought of the sacrifices Maura had made in order to prepare for this trip.

She would squeeze pre-trip training rides in between her soccer and track practices. She would get up at 6:00 A.M. on weekends for practice rides, when all of her thirteen-year-old friends were sleeping in for five more hours. She even gave up her first-ever pop concert to do a 100-mile ride to prepare herself. And even as she lay in the hospital bed connected to tubes and monitors, sedated by pain pills, she was asking if she might be able to ride in the support vehicle for a day or two, and then get back out on the road to resume her transcontinental task.

She had an injury to her hind end, no less, to the very body part that touring cyclists sit on for ten to twelve hours per day! The surgeon advised her to forget biking for the summer. "Plan a trip to Disneyland," he said. "Yes, you'll probably ride again, but not this coming fall. Rest! Let your body heal."

Maura's dreams of a coast-to-coast bicycle ride were dashed. But the spirit that initially led her to believe she could do this trip was not curtailed. Instead of sulking, Maura focused on healing herself . . . a concept foreign to some of us. Back in the fourth grade, she and her classmates had apparently dug a hole in the schoolyard and buried a sign inscribed: "I CAN'T." She certainly took this lesson to heart and has applied it ever since.

Upon returning home from Kansas, Maura found a doctor and sports therapist willing to work with her in rehabilitation. Maura refused to let her dream dwindle; she merely reshaped and renamed it. Incredibly, one short month after her accident, she surprised everyone and showed up for the second leg of the transcontinental bike trip, from Bloomington, Indiana, to Atlantic City, New Jersey. No one could believe it.

Looking ahead to a thousand miles of rugged hills and mountains, she proceeded to ride the entire distance. And yes, as you might suspect . . . without complaint.

It has been said that "there is more distinction in scars than in medals." Maura has her share of each. And yet, it is not distinction that Maura seeks; hers is a deep-seated desire to challenge herself, accompanied by an equally passionate belief that so much in life depends on one's mind-set.

Along her "almost" transcontinental bike trip, she spent a lot of time with health-care workers. Now she aspires to be a physical therapist, helping patients conquer their own health challenges. Maura will do well and will be a wonderful example for others. And no one will be surprised if, during her pursuit of that career, she were to travel back to western Kansas and start where she left off, completing her goal of pedaling every inch of the way from coast to coast.

Dr. Norman Houze

Mount Vaughan

Beautiful in its stark snow loneliness, the mountain waits.

Elizabeth Knowlton

"I have named a mountain for each of you Three Musketeers," declared Admiral Richard Byrd to Norman and his two friends. It was 1931, and Byrd had just designated three Antarctic peaks in honor of this trio—Eddie Goodale, Freddie Crockett, and my husband, Norman Vaughan.

"That's great," Norman replied, feeling honored. "One day, I've got to go down there and climb it."

"I suppose you will, Norman," laughed the Admiral, "I suppose you will."

The five-word headline of the *Boston Transcript* forever altered the course of Norman's life. In September 1927, while a student at Harvard, he opened the paper and read the words: "Byrd to the South Pole." Although Norman didn't know how, he knew he had to go.

Richard E. Byrd was already one of his heroes. The previous year, Byrd had made a historic first flight over the North Pole. Now he was leading a team to Antarctica, intending to stay on the virtually unexplored continent for fourteen months. The next morning Norman headed for Byrd's home in Boston.

Norman made Byrd an offer: He would leave college and work for the explorer for a full year without compensation, training his dogs to go to Antarctica. After a year, Byrd could decide if he wanted to take him. There was no obligation.

Days later, Commander Byrd accepted Norman's proposition.

Norman traveled over 1,500 miles with dog teams across the Antarctic. It was the adventure of a lifetime, and he didn't think he'd ever have another experience that would come close to his time with the Byrd Expedition.

Years went by, and Norman didn't have the opportunity or the money to live out his dream of climbing 10,302-foot Mount Vaughan. Until the 1980s, except for scientists, no one could even reach the interior of Antarctica.

Nevertheless, through the decades, Norman continued to challenge himself. At seventy-two, he entered his first 1,151-mile Iditarod trans-Alaska dogsled race. He competed in twelve more annual runnings, despite injuries that left him with a plastic knee, a fused right ankle and a permanent limp. In 1990, at age eighty-four, he finished his last Iditarod, making his mark as the "oldest and slowest" musher in Alaska, and probably the world.

Yet Norman's dream remained. He still longed for the opportunity to return with a dog team and climb his mountain.

In 1993, he got his chance. But after much preparation and financial wrangling, the DC-6 carrying six crew and all of their supplies crashed six miles short of the runway. While nobody was killed, Norman mourned the loss of four of the dogs who ran away from the wreckage, never to be found. It was a sad and traumatic time, but despite his frustration and disappointment, Norman never spoke of giving up.

The next year, we set off again, traveling 500 miles across the frozen continent toward Mount Vaughan, hoping to reach the mountaintop on December 19, Norman's eighty-ninth birthday.

On December 7, we took our first steps on Norman's mountain. As I watched my husband walking along, my heart began to beat with pride. Although he never complained about physical limitations or asked for extra consideration, we took it easy and constantly checked his pulse monitor. We had to keep slowing him down. He was so excited that he wanted to run up the mountain.

That night, Norman gathered us together and read thoughts from his diary, explaining why the trip meant so much to him and his strong desire to reach the summit on his birthday. Norman is a big dreamer, and the word *can't* is simply not part of his vocabulary. As he finished, he broke down and cried. The rest of us were in tears, too.

We waited three days at Camp Crockett. The day before we left, our teammates Gordon and Vern climbed ahead, marking the trail by chopping and kicking in footsteps.

"It's much steeper than we had expected," Gordon said when they returned.

The final push to the summit was going to be fourteen hundred feet. That was too much to do in a day, so we had to set another camp eight hundred feet below the summit.

We realized that Norman had not taken sufficient breaks the first day. He hadn't eaten enough, and the ordeal had sapped his energy. His body hadn't had time to recuperate for the climb.

We faced another unexpected difficulty. We had relied on Norman's pulse monitor to let us know when he should rest. Now, when we needed it most, the monitor failed.

So on our way up to the camp, we went slower and took more water, food and rest breaks. We reached camp in about five hours.

For the first time, we felt the severity of the cold. It was about twenty degrees below zero, and we were now in the shadows, with no rays from the sun to warm us. Lower on the mountain, our green tents had absorbed the rays that beamed down twenty-four hours a day, keeping the interior relatively warm.

We received reports of bad weather from the National Science Foundation pilot who had flown over our camp. A total whiteout was predicted, and we could see clouds forming in the distance. Gordon urged us to continue.

"If bad weather rolls in and we haven't gone on," he said, "we'll have to abort the expedition and return to base camp."

We were running out of time—and food. The pilot and crew at base camp had been eating more food than anticipated. We couldn't afford to get stuck on the mountain and face the shortage of food rations.

As the weather continued to worsen, we considered our choices. We could try for the summit, or we could stay where we were and risk aborting the climb because of the weather. I knew what Norman's response would be—this was his climb, his moment of glory.

Norman decided to go. We began to push for the summit late in the afternoon. As we trekked on, we stopped often for water and food. We climbed a forty-degree slope most of the way. The weather looked ominous on the horizon. Clouds rolled toward us. Six and a half hours later, we were close to the summit.

Vern pointed and yelled, "Fifty feet."

Seeing the summit, Norman took the lead, and we followed directly behind him.

As Norman took the last step, we were all screaming as loudly as we could, and then Gordon shouted, "You did it, Norman, you did it!"

Standing together at the summit, we could see for hundreds of miles all around us. Mount Goodale lay to the north and Mount Crockett to the south—the other two "musketeers." I could picture the six dog teams crossing below, with six young men—Norman among them—skiing alongside as they passed before this magnificent mountain range for the first time. In my mind's eye, it was 1929 again.

"By climbing this mountain, for my eighty-ninth birthday, I dared to fail and met success," Norman declared proudly. "I fulfilled a sixty-five-year-old dream."

It was the first time this peak had ever been summited.

From my backpack, I pulled out eighty-nine colored sparklers with streamers. I placed all eighty-nine in the snow and tried to light them, but the wind blew too hard and our hands were too cold. Instead, we enjoyed the streamers waving in the wind and sang "Happy Birthday."

"Norman," I cried, "today the whole mountain is your birthday cake!"

We had reached the top on December 16, 1994, three days before Norman's birthday. On December 19, we flew back to Patriot Hills. The people there had prepared a birthday cake made out of a circle of cream puffs, with candles on each one.

"We did it," Norman said. "We finally did it!"

His words summed it up well. Norman Vaughan had fulfilled a dream born sixty-five years earlier.

"What's next?" someone asked.

Norman, his eyes twinkling, only smiled.

Carolyn Vaughan

Mud Trials

We're backpacking on the West Coast Trail of Vancouver Island in British Columbia, which is blessed (or cursed) with an annual rainfall of 106 inches. The Trail is considered one of the most challenging in North America thanks to slippery log crossings, gnarled root systems, steep ladders, hair-raising suspension bridges, hand-powered trolley crossings and mud—lots and lots of mud.

I had been enlisted to participate in this forty-seven-mile, father-daughter hike by my fourteen-year-old niece when her father couldn't make it. I suppose I was the natural choice. I had introduced Chelsey to camping and the out-doors when she was just seven years old, and we had been adventuring together ever since. To boot, I was her youngest aunt, and I didn't have kids of my own. This meant our rela-tionship could crisscross between roles, from that of aunt and niece to acting like sisters, friends, or even mother and daughter—or, in this case, father and daughter.

Joining us on the trail were Chelsey's three good friends—Lindsay, Rebecca and Amanda—and their fathers: Ken, a commercial mortgage broker, John, a psychiatrist, and Mike, a retired chief financial officer. Having never met most of my fellow hikers, I was quite nervous about intruding on a father–daughter bonding adventure. Thankfully, the dads welcomed me as I donned my Groucho Marx glasses with fake nose and mustache, transforming myself from "Auntie" into "Uncle Nan."

Prior to setting out, a ranger made it clear that there was no way for us to get off the trail unless someone was seriously injured. On this trail, bad weather and blisters don't warrant an evacuation. We all nodded our heads.

And so, the next morning, with the sun shining overhead and backpacks loaded, we embraced our walking sticks, took the prerequisite "before" pictures and off we went. Day one would be an easy hike, a warm-up of sorts, just over eight miles on a relatively flat section of the trail. Hiking from Bamfield to Port Renfrew meant hiking the easier sections first.

That night, we camped on the beach at Orange Creek, where everyone felt great, and enthusiasm for a new adventure still hung fresh in the air. Our excitement grew the next day as we worked our way through a dense forest of Douglas fir, western hemlock, Sitka spruce and western red cedar. Where the trees gave way to meadows, there was thick underbrush filled with salal and salmonberries. Ferns hung lushly in moist, dark areas. We zigzagged between forest and beach, spotting deer skirting the forest edges, sea lions, whales and bald eagles along the way.

The next afternoon a drizzle began. Before long it was a downpour. We stopped to put on raingear and backpack covers, and for the first time, I noticed Ken's face went from a smile to a grimace. I tried to cheer him up, but a few hours later, my own smile also turned downward.

Hiking in the rain in a rainforest is like walking through a Midwestern blizzard. Roots, boardwalks and ladders become as slippery as ice; the mud like untracked deep snow. Water drips down the back of your neck, your shoes and socks get soggy, making them more prone to blisters, and wet shorts chafe against your legs. Trying to stay dry is a losing battle. Our goal was Cribs Creek, our next camp, where we'd be able to sit in our tents in dry clothes and sip hot tea. I could hardly wait. This trip was turning out to be a lot more challenging than I had expected.

I wasn't the only one feeling the rainy-day blues. We all were thrown off by the reality that it really *does* rain on the West Coast Trail. "I'd rather stay in the tent," Chelsey whispered under a steady beat of raindrops. Those were the first words I heard on the morning of day four. Unfortunately, that wasn't an option.

As Chelsey and I took turns getting ready (our "two-person" tent was too small for both of us to be moving around at once), I pulled on my soaking wet clothes from the day before. Dry clothes were at a premium and to be saved for nighttime. The tent oozed condensation, and everything felt damp and cold as the outside temperature lingered around fifty degrees Fahrenheit. By 9:00 A.M., we had resumed our silent single-file parade, the prospect of breakfast at Monique's propelling us onward.

Monique is a Ditidaht Indian, whose reserve we were hiking through, and her diner is truly unique. Made of tarps, solar panels and a dirt floor, it provided shelter from the rain, and therefore a heavenly place for us to regroup. We ate a warm breakfast of eggs and bacon, savoring every bite, and stocked up on extra treats.

Dry and full on home cooking, we left Monique's in good spirits, optimistic about the day ahead. Mud bogs that covered the tops of our gaiters quickly sucked away our joy. Our pace varied, with everyone taking turns leading and then falling to the back of the line. Ken's face wore a permanent frown—almost everyone's did. I made an effort to stay upbeat to help keep us moving as stops became more frequent for boot adjustments, water, snacks and encouragement. Although our daily distances were decreasing, the trail was getting consistently harder.

By the evening of day four, panic set in. We set up our tents under tarps at Walbran Creek and started talking. We weighed the pros and cons of a mad two-day dash to the finish versus waiting the rain out. We had less than fifteen miles to go, but Ken had blisters the size of silver dollars on his heels, and Mike and Amanda's tent leaked, and their sleeping bags had been wet for two nights. We were miserable.

"I want to go home," Chelsey said, creating a domino effect. Ken agreed. We had made a valiant effort, but if we could make it to Logan Point and get a water taxi, we should get the heck out of there. Lindsay felt that since she didn't think we could continue, she would come back another time to finish the hike. It seemed unanimous.

"We're going to finish," said John and Rebecca defiantly. The rain didn't bother John; he was happy just to be out of the office. Rebecca was equally determined.

The pendulum was swinging back and forth in my head. I didn't know what to think. Although the dads considered me a peer—I hiked as fast as they did and held my own in the campground—I was still a younger woman who was in some ways also under their wings. Ken seemed to assume that Chelsey and I would be exiting with the rest of them. But Chelsey and I still had dry clothes to wear at day's end, even though most of our gear was damp. We weren't cold yet. And though our tent was a pain-in-the-you-know-what, it didn't leak. I considered my responsibility as an aunt (er, uncle) and the lessons these girls were supposed to bring home from the trip. We had known the risk of rain when we started. Likewise, we'd been warned that once you're on the trail, you're on it.

I decided that we'd continue on with John and Rebecca even if the others left. When I discussed this with Chelsey, quiet preceded an explosion of tears. I stood behind my decision. This was one of the lessons of the trail. We walked in silence.

Much to my relief, we soon learned that there was no water taxi available at Logan's Point—we would all have to continue. And for some reason, now that we knew there was no way out, our spirits lifted. We still fought frustration and fatigue as the trail became even more arduous, but we also laughed more and embraced our muddy, dirty, smelly selves. As I crossed a particularly slimy log, I slipped and found myself beached like a turtle with my backpack underneath. Suddenly, the absurdity of the whole trip caught up with me in fits of uncontrollable laughter. This was not a good place to have a laugh attack, but it couldn't be helped. "Auntie Nan" being stuck on the log helped to lighten the load.

On our final morning, with a little more than four miles to go and the rain still drenching, we hiked with such fervor that we almost floated over the roots and mud that had for the last few days been tripping us up. Several times we thought we were at the end only to have the trail continue. At last, we began our descent toward the water.

Waiting until we were all together, we hiked our last steps and raised the buoy to alert a waiting water taxi to ferry us across the crossing. With just fifty meters of water between us and our waving families, we stood there, like drowned rats, looking pathetic, but with smirks on our faces.

"So kiddo," I asked Chelsey, "are you glad we stayed on the trail?"

She just smiled.

So did I, my favored-aunt status still intact.

Nancy Coulter-Parker

Two at Sea

For whatever we lose (like a you or a me),
it's always ourselves we find in the sea.

e. e. cummings

On Christmas Day, thirty-five-year-old Englishman Pete
Goss was one of sixteen competitors in the Vendée Globe, a
nonstop round-the-world solo yacht race. Sailing in the icy
Southern Ocean 1,300 miles south of Australia, close to
Antarctica, he was overtaken by a severe storm with hurricane-force winds and seas that quickly grew as high as sixty-
five feet.

In this last great wilderness on Earth—the realm of ice and
the wandering albatross—storms and waves roll around the
world unimpeded by land.

The race receded into the background as Goss tried to stay
alive, his boat, *Aqua Quorum*, screaming and surfing down
six-story waves at up to twenty-eight knots under bare
poles—no sail up.

In the middle of this mayhem, Goss's computer beeped.
Someone had set off a Mayday. Then a fax came through
from the race director asking Goss if he could try to rescue
one of the other racers, the Frenchman Raphaël Dinelli.

Goss and Dinelli had had no chance to meet before the start, but they had something in common: They had both had difficulties raising money for the race. Goss had only a slower fifty-foot boat in a fleet of sixty-footers; that was all he could afford. Dinelli had such a hard time funding his campaign that he missed making the necessary qualifying sail and was an unofficial entrant—the French press called him the "pirate" of the Vendée Globe.

Now Dinelli was positioned 160 miles upwind from Goss. Dinelli's boat, *Algimouss,* had capsized and flooded. The sailor was tethered on deck, his boat sinking. He didn't have much time left.

He had stayed that way for thirty-six hours without eating or drinking. His eyes were burnt by the sun, the wind and the salt. His feet were freezing. He was too remote for pick-up from land, and Goss was the only competitor within striking distance.

After the race director's fax, Goss thought about things for a moment. He knew that returning to Dinelli would be extremely risky. He might not survive. He might never again see his wife Tracey and their three young children—Alexander, Olivia and Eliot.

But Goss also knew it was an unwritten law of the sea that aid be rendered to anyone who asked for it, even if it meant risking the rescuer's own life. It was an extreme demand but the only one that made sense, or that had any honor, on the dangerous ocean.

He faxed the director: "I have no choice; I'll do it."

Goss hoisted a small storm jib and turned his boat into the full weight of the hurricane-force winds. As *Aqua Quorum* made its slow progress, climbing one mountainous wave after another, Goss kept wondering if it would hold together. No Vendée Globe boat could be counted on to withstand the shocking loads this violent motion inflicted on it.

To his relief—and surprise—however, *Aqua Quorum* remained intact during the two exhausting days it took him to get back to Dinelli's position. By then, the hypothermic

Dinelli was in a life raft dropped by an Australian search-and-rescue aircraft just ten minutes before his boat sank. It had been that close.

But even though he was in the life raft, Dinelli was desperately cold and wouldn't last much longer.

With growing desperation, Goss hunted through the valleys and crests of the big seas for the tiny, eight-foot-diameter raft. Dinelli's Mayday fix kept jumping a quarter-mile here and there, which may as well have been a hundred miles in the gale-force wind and bad visibility. In the Southern Ocean, untamed nature made a mockery of modern electronic equipment.

Finally, the Australian plane had to guide Goss to Dinelli. It radioed Goss the good news that Dinelli had waved to them. He was still alive.

Goss maneuvered alongside the raft. Stricken though he was, Dinelli welcomed him with panache. To Goss's astonishment, Dinelli handed him a bottle of champagne. Through everything, he'd managed to hang onto it in a pocket of his survival suit. Goss hauled him aboard.

And the two men hugged each other.

Goss had trouble bending Dinelli's stiff arms and legs to angle him in through the small hatch into the cabin. He stripped off Dinelli's sodden survival suit and got him into his own thermal suit and then into his sleeping bag.

In an exchange of national stereotypes, Goss replied to Dinelli's gift of champagne with an English cup of tea. It was a cyclist's bottle to be precise, filled with warm sugary tea to help restore Dinelli's body temperature.

And then Goss was absolutely exhausted. He hadn't slept for more than two days. He was battered and bruised and drained of nervous energy by the ordeal of getting back through the storm. He thought he'd take an hour's sleep before getting back to it.

But Dinelli was high on the adrenaline rush of his own unexpected survival. He wouldn't shut up.

"He was bloody rabbiting away," said Goss.

"Poor Pete," Dinelli said. "He had to look after me during the day, and then I kept him up all night talking."

Then, just as things seemed to be improving, they were overtaken by the heavy weather of another frontal system. Dinelli, still in shock and severely hypothermic, was fearful and at times almost panicky in the too-familiar din and clamor of a sixty-footer in a storm. He wondered if he had escaped only to delay his inevitable death at sea.

Goss soothed him. "We'll survive," he said reassuringly.

And they did.

But for the next five days, Dinelli couldn't feel his hands or feet. He was a helpless invalid. Goss had to feed Dinelli every four hours and give him muscle relaxants and pain medication.

Goss couldn't speak French, but Dinelli had some pidgin English. The two men drew pictures and mimed what they could. By the end of their ten-day sail together, they were having deep conversations about their lives, families and the sailing they still wanted to do. The beautiful, though perilous, wilderness of the Southern Ocean still fascinated them.

"It was ironic," Goss said. "You start off sailing around the world by yourself, and you come back with a good friend."

In June, President Jacques Chirac bestowed on Goss France's most distinguished award, the *Légion d'Honneur*. In August of that year, Goss was best man at Dinelli's wedding. And two months later, Goss and Dinelli sailed *Aqua Quorum*—this time together—in a transatlantic race for two-person crews.

"We're like brothers now," said Goss, "friends for life."

Derek Lundy

Making Peace

Peace is the fairest form of happiness.

William Ellery Channing

I have river sand in my pockets and pink canyon light beneath my eyelids. I can recall at will the milky consistency of the waves rocking the huge pontoons of our raft—feel the power of the water pushing in constant birth to move the river along.

My first night in the canyon, meteor showers rain down, keeping me awake all night. I can't close my eyes. It's too dull inside my head when the sky is raining stars. My tent is up, but I sleep outside anyway. In all my years I can't remember sleeping out much. Even though my family spent countless days fishing northwest lakes, we'd pass the night in old wooden cabins or in our car.

At 2:00 A.M., the wind kicks up, blowing its hot dragon's breath and sand through the canyon. Rock walls contract and expand, wheezing the sound of a million crickets' ceaseless buzzing. My former life seems nearly unimaginable, but I can't quite shake the feeling that I'm not supposed to be here. Sheer cliffs, canyon walls, whitewater rafting—my mother would not be happy about this. This is especially true given that nine years ago she and my father lost their lives when their small boat capsized during a routine outing.

I've been terrified for months since agreeing to do this trip. It's not just my parents' accident or the trip itself that has me going. Rather, it's that and all the stuff I've gone through to get here. Like the airplanes—I don't like them, especially the real small ones. I am claustrophobic, due in part, I think, to a cousin who once stuffed me into a duffel bag, locked the top and left me for a while. The idea of crawling into a handbag-sized plane gives me the willies. Then there is the hiking featured prominently in the brochure. I don't hike. I like to walk, but not straight up. I lack affinity for high places, which is another reason that I don't like to fly. And the bathroom—where will it be? God knows, if there is a category in the world for "girls least likely to go down the river on a raft," I am in it.

I've never been in a boat on a river. I'm from a family of black Southerners who I would describe as still-water people. Where I come from you sit still and fish. Going fast in a boat for any reason is just not done. My mother would think this a daredevil scheme, as would most of my relatives, so I avoid telling them. It sounds so ridiculous that I hesitate to say it out loud, but I don't think this is something a black person is supposed to be doing.

Even the old bus driver, the only other black person I've seen anywhere near here, drops his jaw when he sees that I am part of the group. As soon as I see him, I know he is going to say something to me, so I wait until the last minute to throw my knapsack into the back of the canyon airport bus, hoping I can slip past him.

I have no such luck.

Without missing a beat, he stops arranging the bags and looks straight at me. With his head cocked to one side, he says with eyebrows arched in disbelief, "You goin' down the river?"

Here I am caught in the act. I put my head right down on his shoulder and, in desperate confession, I say, "I know I'm not supposed to be doing this."

Puzzled, shaking his head, he shuts the doors. "Goin' down the river? Umph. Well that's somethin' that ain't never crossed my mind."

Is this an omen—a last chance to bolt and save myself? I think of my mother and father. Life is cruel, but if I am tempting fate, it's not death I fear so much as life's irony. I could not bear the thought of my family having a shoe drop in the same pond twice. If my mother were alive she'd say, "Have you lost your mind? Did you know life is short and hard enough without adding crazy stuff to it? And besides, it's only fools and people with too much money who'd pay somebody to scare them into death if they don't drown them first."

I am left on my own to make peace with my fear and to sort out for myself the difference between taking a chance and using good sense.

My eyes open at sunrise to a flurry of black butterflies. Moving silently in undecipherable patterns just above my head, they circle, float and then disappear into the canyon light. Simultaneously, I catch the sounds and smells of our camp waking. Counting our river guides, we number more than thirty—a group of young and old, randomly thrown together to form an impromptu family. The canyon defines our universe. We are the only people in it.

Light is the subject of the canyon's morning drama, and it recasts each moment. A sun flash startles, momentarily backlighting the canyon walls, flattening them into one massive silhouetted cutout. I want to kneel, pray and scream all at the same time. My sense of life is too small, my human circuits too weak, to contain the scale of this beauty. It rushes in and breaks me down. Suddenly, I'm inside of Bernini's *Ecstasy of Saint Teresa* when the golden rods of divine light pierce her marble body, rendering her limp. A person could die from too much of this.

Scrambling to keep up, I quickly sort out what I need for a day on the river. Shaking shoes and opening bags away from my body, I want to avoid seeing what might be sleeping inside. At breakfast I tell everyone, "I saw meteor showers last night, and this morning there were black butterflies you wouldn't believe!"

Tom, our river guide, says, "No, actually what you saw were tiny bats, not butterflies, come to eat insects that would otherwise be eating all of us."

When I protest, he says, "Plenty more to worry about here besides bats. Anyway, they're gentle creatures—fly by radar, haven't ever heard of 'em crashin' into anybody unless they were ill."

My brain can't translate butterflies into bats, so I decide to pray for their perpetual health instead.

Out on the river, anticipating the rapids, the energy is high. Tom narrates canyon geology and throws in a few tall tales just to see if we're listening. Under the day's mounting heat, I listen with my entire body, but my ears pick up only the familiar words. Grateful that I will not be quizzed, my mind merges history and lore. I roll the words around on my tongue and come up with my own version of what I'm seeing—Bright Angel Shale, Vishnu Schist and Angel Rock become the hymns I sing as we float down the river in our motorized gondola, flanked by majestic cathedral walls.

The closer we come to the churning water, the more the youngsters bounce, scream and vie for the best position. The rest of us grow giddy. I search Tom's face for a sign to help me gauge the seriousness of our predicament.

It's not lost on me that our guides have not once let slip a promise that we would survive it all. Kim didn't say it when, on my first hike, I found myself precariously perched on a narrow path surrounded by sheer cliff drops. She didn't even say it when I collapsed to my knees petrified and crying. What she did say was, "Hold my hand and keep your eyes on your feet. You can do it." I wanted to say, "Do you promise?" But I knew that wasn't part of the deal. There is nothing in the canyon or this life, it seems, that can be reached or fully expected without hanging your body over something a little terrifying.

By the third day I've taken up the lead position on the raft. I want to look inside the thing that scares me. I strap a small tape player to my body to record our voices as we go through the rapids. I will listen to it later, to decipher a mystery, and it will sound like passion captured on tape.

We hit the rapids. The water drops, and the boat plunges. Navigating huge rocks, we bounce inexplicably from crest to crest. The waves arc; we go under. Icy water walls hit, break and pound us. My internal organs are rearranged. Hysterical laughter seizes me with such intensity that it makes everyone laugh. Whether a gift or a curse, I am keenly aware of the role chance plays, which makes me doubly thankful when we pop out on the other side.

By the sixth day I've hiked over hill and cliff. I've taken on the waves and gone under the water. I've accepted help and forgiven myself for human weakness. I've survived beauty and peril to see the world in canyon light, only to learn how many small but important things in my life I've left undone out of fear. I am mindful of my mother's voice in the canyon wind, whispering safekeeping.

To make peace with fear, I turn it inside out. It's the best I can do. It's more than I believed possible.

Barbara Earl Thomas

10

NATURE'S WISDOM

Come forth into the light of things. Let nature be your wisdom.

William Wordsworth

A Fresh Start

We don't receive wisdom. We must discover it for ourselves.

Marcel Proust

We had dealt with the worst of it—the lawyers, the creditors and the endless explanations to Margaret, our teenage daughter. Our fourteen-year-old family restaurant business was no more. With no prospects on the horizon, we headed north to the Texas Panhandle, hoping to distance ourselves from the sting and stigma of bankruptcy.

Two days later, we entered Palo Duro Canyon State Park, thirty miles south of Amarillo. While checking in, I noticed a flyer recruiting park hosts. The position offered a permanent campsite in the park, and in return, the hosts served as a link between the park's guests and the rangers stationed on the rim a thousand feet above. It was the perfect solution for us: a rent-free place to reorganize our lives. I made an appointment for the following day.

That evening we camped surrounded by mesquite brush and tall grass on a small rise overlooking the vast canyon floor, the most remote site available. The camper popped up with ease, and we were soon in fine spirits. I fired up the

Coleman lantern, my wife Leigh opened the beer, and we clinked bottles, toasting our "fresh start."

Soon we were alone in the lantern's greenish hue, surrounded by a wall of darkness. As we finished our spaghetti dinner, Leigh heard a rustle in the nearby grass. "What's that?" she asked.

Out of the shadows, two large skunks in full winter coat waddled toward our picnic table. "Oh, how cute!" Margaret exclaimed.

I shushed her and froze, knowing exactly what brand of misery a startled skunk can bring to the table. We watched the pair investigate the campsite and shuffle toward us. One of the little stinkers approached me and began sniffing and clawing at my boot.

Leigh silently mouthed, "What are we going to do?"

I slowly shrugged my shoulders, expecting a noxious discharge any moment at point-blank range. After a forty-five-second eternity, the skunk, snorting in disgust, left my foot in search of something more edible. We hastily climbed onto the table and, for the next four hours, waited for the nocturnal scavengers to vacate our camp.

Having survived the "night of the living skunks," we were confident that everything else would be all right. We met with the people who ran the park. They explained our responsibilities and assigned us a beautiful campsite. Then we spent the rest of the day hiking the canyon's trails, marveling at its stratified beauty and our good fortune in securing such a wonderful place to reinvent our lives.

That evening we learned about the canyon winds. I had barely fallen asleep when the first gust shook the camper. Tsunamis of air roared through the canyon walls.

"This isn't good," Leigh whispered.

Blast after blast rocked the little trailer, as the frame groaned against the pressure. We lay shaking in the dark, visualizing our camper cascading through the canyon like a tumbleweed. Several hours later, the cold front passed, coyotes howled, and we slept soundly.

During the weeks that followed, we learned to survive in our camper. We stretched our budget with meals of beans and rice one night, and for variety, rice and beans the next. I learned how to secure the camper against the violent winds, and Leigh earned a little money by substitute teaching. The trauma of the bankruptcy had so strained our marriage that I thought I might lose my family as well. Building a successful business and then losing it had left very little time for building a successful family.

In the tiny camper, living elbow to elbow with no television to distract us, we spent our nights huddled together against the cold, reading and talking. It was there that we ate, played, laughed and cried. And one evening, standing under a jeweled sky listening to coyotes, I found myself thankful for the bankruptcy, the miserable little camper and all the hardship. We had hiked the trails, climbed the canyon walls and become good friends. We had become a family.

Robert Hedderman

The Secret to Fishing

At a certain point you say to the woods, to the sea, to the mountains, the world, "Now I am ready. Now I will stop and be wholly attentive." You empty yourself and wait, listening.

Annie Dillard

"Good morning, are you . . . ?"

"Yeah, I'm awake," I shot back through the early-morning fog of half-sleep. I glanced over at the clock—4:30 A.M.

"Oh, it's soooo early," I grimaced.

Sitting up in the bed, I reached toward the steaming mug of coffee held in my son's outstretched hand. I sipped it slowly, allowing its warm aroma to drift up into my face. Setting the mug down, I asked him, "Why are you up at this hour?"

"Let's go," he replied with his wide-toothed grin.

By three years of age, James could cast a crank bait using a spinning rod with a closed-face reel by himself. And he never missed an opportunity to accompany me on a fishing trip. He would throw a fit in front of his mom, stamping his foot on the kitchen floor if I ventured down to the lake without including him.

Usually going fishing meant we were headed to Lake

Edenwold—the four-acre lake behind our home in the tiny borough of Butler, New Jersey. The lake still teemed with fish. We had a beautiful canoe that we kept tied to a floating dock at the foot of our backyard from April through October. It was a perfect place to raise two boys.

By this time, John, my older son, was stirring under the covers. He reached over and gave his younger brother a shove, getting his attention in a hurry.

"James," he complained, "you woke me up. Why do you have to make so much noise?" The question hung suspended in the air momentarily until finally dissipating unanswered. It hadn't been ignored—I don't think it ever could be really ignored.

Thirty minutes later, the three of us stepped outside the trailer on to the wooden deck in front of our camper and quietly donned our waders and fishing vests. James had left his rod strung from the previous evening's fishing, so he was the first to be ready.

"See you later," he said over his shoulder as he disappeared into a stand of maple saplings.

John's eyes followed his younger brother as he quietly walked off into the woods toward the river. "There he goes. He's got a one-track mind when it comes to trout."

"Trout, striped bass, pickerel—it doesn't seem to matter," I answered through a chuckle. "He always manages to outfish the two of us, doesn't he?"

"Or anyone else for that matter," John shot back with an obvious jealous edge to his voice.

James was a gifted boy. There were times when he was the only person catching trout in the river. Fishing for James was a finely honed intuition—not just an acquired skill. He sensed where the fish were, what they were feeding on and the best way to approach them without spooking them, even if he had never fished in that stream before. It was as though God in his infinitely wise grace had bestowed on my son a special gift to make up for what he had taken away.

"Whatcha thinking about, Dad?" John interrupted.

"Nothing . . . nothing important," I said. But I knew that answer wouldn't satisfy a very perceptive sixteen-year-old, so I continued cautiously, not wanting to rub it in. "I was just thinking about what you said before about James being such a virtuoso on the trout stream—"

I was interrupted by the ratchet sound coming from James' reel again. But this time it wasn't the broken pattern produced by a person working out a cast. It was the very familiar song of a reel spool spinning backwards at a speed that meant only one thing.

"I don't believe it," John said, in a way that betrayed that only half of him was happy for his brother.

"C'mon, let's go see," I motioned, stepping off the deck into the clearing in front of the trailer. John followed behind me as we made our way through the short buffer of woods bordering the river.

James was standing in the middle of the stream, in a quiet eddy immediately below a huge boulder. With his rod held high, it was easy to follow the taught fluorescent orange fly line downstream to the point where what appeared to be a huge fish was giving him the battle of his life.

As the trout slowed its run, it exploded in a shower of spray from the head of the pool below us. James lowered his rod tip to cushion the shock of the trout's jump.

"Unbelievable," John said. "Dad, it never fails. Look at the size of that fish!"

James was walking downstream now, reeling in slack line as he deftly maneuvered over the algae-slicked rocks in the stream bed without once making you think he was going to slip and fall.

"Dad, I want to see this trout," John said excitedly, knowing his younger brother rarely lost a fish at this point in the contest.

As we quietly picked our way along the riverbank, the trout attempted one more half-hearted run, but this fight was over. Coaxing the exhausted fish into the shallows, James knelt in the slack water. Finally, leading the fish gently into his hands, he quickly backed out the barbless hook and began to help the trout gather its strength, pointing its nose into the current, forcing the cold water through its gills with a delicate rhythmic motion.

It was then that a stranger, who apparently had been watching from behind a tree concealing him from our view, walked up behind James.

"Nice fish, son," we heard the elderly man comment warmly as we drew closer.

James didn't turn to look.

"I said, nice fish, young man."

James's eyes were locked on to the trout as he made sure it was getting enough oxygen back into its bloodstream.

"Excuse me, son," the kind old man persisted, now with a slight edge to his voice, "I just wanted to compliment you on the way you handled that fish. I have never seen anybody take such command of a situation from beginning to end. It was just like you owned the river, I mean . . ."

But James ignored him.

As we drew closer to my son and the stranger, the chafing sound from our waders gave our approach away. It was only the stranger who turned to look in our direction.

Here we go again, I thought.

"He's deaf," I said matter-of-factly, having used this opening to initiate the same conversation a thousand times over with countless strangers.

"Aren't they all at that age!" the old man shot back now, his feelings obviously hurt. "Teenagers! No respect for their elders . . . !"

"No, no, you don't understand. I mean, he's deaf, profoundly deaf, as in he can't hear you—or anything else for that matter."

My words cut the old man like a knife. His body seemed to shudder with the realization. I was familiar with what was to follow.

"I'm . . . I'm . . . so sorry," he stammered. "Please forgive me . . . I . . . I . . . didn't know."

At that moment John and I came into James's field of view. He immediately looked up and, taking one hand off the trout, he quickly finger-spelled "enormous," then shook the same hand in a familiar motion, which simply meant, "Wow!"

I pointed to the stranger behind him, and James quickly shot a glance over his shoulder. Releasing the fish, he waded out to join us on the river bank and signed to me, "Who . . . what he want?"

"What did he say?" the old man asked, obviously feeling remorse and wanting to somehow make it up to my son by engaging him in conversation.

"He asked me who you are and what you wanted."

"My name's Ben," the stranger said to James. "That was some fishing, son. Why, I . . ."

"He's deaf," I interrupted. "He can't hear you; he can't even read your lips."

"Oh, right, how stupid of me."

"This is Ben," I signed to my son, "and he was watching you from behind that large maple over there. He had walked up behind you to pay you a compliment for the way you handled that fish and started getting a little irritated when you didn't answer him right away."

"I get it," James signed. "Old geezer, want respect, thought me rude, sorry."

"What did he say? What did he say?" Ben asked anxiously.

Avoiding all mention of "old geezer," I explained, "He said he is sorry that you thought he was being disrespectful to you."

"Poor kid—how'd he get that way?" Ben asked.

"Heredity," I explained, after interpreting Ben's question for my son then replying simultaneously in sign and voice so everyone could understand what was being said. "His maternal grandparents were both profoundly deaf. The doctors told us it usually skips generations and then occurs in twenty-five percent of the grandchildren. There are four grandsons, and only one's deaf. You're looking at him."

"But how does he fish?" the old man pressed, really bewildered now. "How does he fish so good? His casting was smooth, like a willow branch carried on a zephyr. He laid that fly on a patch of glass surrounded by cross currents with nary a hint of drag from what I could see. The strike was perfection."

"You don't have to hear to fish," I explained.

"James's deafness is actually a blessing when it comes to fishing," I continued. "When we fish together, we don't talk, we sign. I can be fifty yards away from him and carry on a normal conversation without making any noise. We never have to yell, 'What are they taking?' or 'How big was that one?'"

"Well, I'll be," the old man said, taking off his hat and scratching his head as he headed off.

"How big was that fish, son?"

"I don't know exactly," James motioned with his hand, shrugging his shoulders at the same time. "Big, really big, fat, tough fish."

"You know, I continue to be amazed at your prowess on the river. Most folks would've waded through the spot you dropped your fly on. How did you know that fish was there in the first place?"

James started laughing. He had one of those infectious laughs that got us all tickled, and pretty soon we were staggering through the shallows like three drunken sailors who had just spent the night at the local saloon. I finally had to sit down. John joined me on the riverbank.

"What is so funny?" I asked through a silly, boyish giggle.

James held up one hand the way an itinerant preacher would to command the quiet attention of his congregation. Satisfied that he had our "ear," he turned to us with as solemn an expression as he could muster.

"The secret," James signed, "simple—very simple. If you listen, you can hear them."

We pondered the irony of the thought for a brief moment in silence. Then, as if on cue, the three of us reverted to our giddy laughter and started walking back upstream to the faster water. As my two boys sloshed up ahead of me, they never realized that my laughter had turned to tears.

Gregory J. Rummo

"Reverend Smith always seems to know
where to catch the big ones."

Mother Duck's Miracle

Be kind to your web-footed friends, for that duck may be somebody's mother.

Mitch Miller

"Just a couple hours now," said Dad, "and we'll soon be at our campsite!"

The year was 1950, and we were on our family vacation, doing our family thing—camping. I settled down in my corner of the back seat to take a nap. The rhythm of the moving car soothed me into a deep sleep.

Wham! I woke with a start, my face on the floorboard of the back seat. Dad had braked sharply.

"What happened?" I asked. "Where are we?"

"Half an hour from our campsite," he answered, "and I don't know what the holdup is, but all the cars have stopped. I'll see what's going on."

Dad stepped out of the car. Mom, my little brother David and I waited.

"Bet there's been an accident!" David was excited.

Mom shook her head. "Probably a bear crossing the

road," she said. David bounced up and down in his seat. That was even better than an accident!

Dad came running back to the car. "Come on!" he said very excitedly. "Come on, kids! You've all got to see this!"

I jumped out of the car and ran to catch up with him. "What is it, Daddy?" I asked. He grinned and reached for my hand. "Come see, Carolyn," he said.

I knew that, whatever it was, it was nice because my father was happy about it. I grabbed his hand and skipped excitedly along beside him. We walked past a dozen parked cars. Ahead, a group of people stood "ooh-ing" and "aah-ing."

Looking in the same direction as everyone else, we saw a mother duck, sleek and proud, promenading up the middle of the road, nine little ducklings waddling after her. The babies were marching single file behind their mother, totally ignoring the people and automobiles.

No one from any of the stalled cars appeared to mind waiting on a fearless mother duck and her nine ducklings parading up the highway as if it were exclusively theirs.

We all followed Mrs. Duck and family a quarter of a mile up the hill. There Mrs. Duck led her children off the road, over a small embankment and into a little creek winding its way down the mountainside.

I walked back to the car with the adults and listened to their conversation with strangers.

"Oh, you're from Milwaukee? We lived there for four years!" They were discovering people and places they had in common.

I was quiet as we continued our journey, wondering about what we had just witnessed. Later in camp, I sat on a large rock next to my father, our feet dangling in the creek.

"Daddy?" I asked. "How did Mrs. Duck know that all those busy people would stop to let her walk along the road with her babies?"

Dad picked up a smooth stone, thoughtfully rubbed it between his thumb and forefinger, then skimmed it over the water.

"Well, honey," he said, watching the little stone skim the water, "that's one of God's miracles. God used that mother duck and her babies to slow everyone down so they could enjoy life a little bit more. He arranges opportunities like this, sort of as a reminder to make people think about what's important in life."

I sat there for a moment, smiling over Dad's words. Soon, Mom joined us, stuck her tired feet into the cool water and sighed, "Oh-h, that feels good!"

David wandered up and sat beside Mom, cuddling close. We all relaxed there by the creek as the mountain breeze played a soothing symphony in the trees above, just for us.

Yes, it truly was a miracle!

Carolyn Griffin

Reprinted by permission of George Crenshaw, Masters Agency.

Walking Passage

What do you suppose will satisfy the soul except to walk free?

Walt Whitman

John and I crawl on our bellies, the lights on our head-lamps glancing off the walls of the cave. The only sounds are the scraping of our tennis shoes as we push ourselves forward. Our knees ache from the sharp rocks lining the cave floor. We're shivering in our cheap coveralls. There is a good chance we're lost, and we couldn't be happier.

We have been exploring this unnamed cave for hours, far past the twilight zone—that place where surface light lingers, then ends. We have chimneyed up steep sloping walls, jockeyed around deep pits, and wriggled in and out of dead ends. The packs we carry with us hold the jumars and rope we will need for the ascent back to the entrance.

Ahead of me, John stops and manages, with a grunt, to sit upright.

"Two leads," he says.

Automatically we look behind us, the way we have come. Going out looks very different from going in, and it is easy to wander for hours, missing landmarks that seemed obvious heading in. John and I trade excited glances. The air seems charged with possibility.

"I'll check that one," he says. Under his hard hat, he is grinning fiercely, and the thrill of adventure is gleaming in his eye. His face is black with dirt and his blond beard more unruly than usual. He looks like a wild man.

With effort, he squeezes through an impossibly small passage. In order to fit, he must take off his hardhat and backpack and push them in front of him. Muffled curses trail in his wake.

Alone, I take off my work gloves, worn to protect the delicate formations from the oils on my hands. I drink some water and turn off my headlamp to conserve batteries. The darkness is total. The weight of tons of rock presses against my back. I feel as if the Earth is holding me in its arms.

John yells from below. "Hey, come down!"

I hesitate. "Is there something good down there? Does it go?"

"Walking passage!" he shouts.

I am electrified. When we dreamed, it was of walking passage—large tunnels, mysteriously carved by water and time, where we can walk, not crawl. In time, those passages might open to huge rooms, bigger than cathedrals.

John's lead is one of the tightest yet. In places, I have to move an arm, a leg, then twist my body in contorted positions to move forward, but hope of walking passage pushes me onward.

Finally, I spot John curled into an awkward position under a low-hanging ceiling. Ahead of him is more twisting, body-crunching passage.

I peer into the darkness, then at John. He is trying to contain himself, but bursts into loud guffaws. His laughter echoes through the tunnel. I have to smile. He has pulled this trick before, and I have fallen for it again.

"I knew you'd come down if I said it was walking passage," he smiled. "Now, let's check out this lead."

We never did find large rooms that day, or even any

walking passage. At midnight, John and I emerged from the cave, hungry, thirsty and bruised. We slung ropes over our shoulders and headed for the car under a bright ceiling of stars.

Many years have gone by since I last saw or spoke with John, although I hear he has married and still visits the caves in the gray cliffs. There have been other caves, other darkness that seemed so total, passages that seemed so difficult that I wanted to stay behind where it was safe, in my own little circle of light.

When that happens I stop and remember that day deep underground. If I close my eyes, I can still feel the damp rock against my back and my sore knees as I crawled. I can hear the sound of water dripping and the encouragement of a friend. I know then that I can make it through even if I have to crawl.

Mary Emerick

Donnie

Problems are only opportunities in work clothes.

Henry John Kaiser

The rap on the door was sharp, urgent, insistent—a fore-boding of crisis—rappity-rappity-rappity rap . . .

Me, rushing to the door, fumbling with the lock, pumping my adrenaline, preparing for emergency.

Small boy. Odd expression. Hands me a scrawled note on much-folded paper: "My name is Donnie. I will rake your leaves. $1 a yard. I am deaf. You can write to me. I can read. I rake good."

Across the back of our house is a row of middle-aged matronly maple trees, extravagantly dressed in season in a million leaf-sequins. And in season the sequins detach. Not much wind in our sheltered yard, so the leaves lie about the ladies' feet now like dressing gowns they've stepped out of in preparation for the bath of winter.

I like the way it looks. I like the way it looks very much. My wife does not. The gardening magazine does not like it, either. Leaves should be raked. There are rules. Leaves are not good for grass. Leaves are untidy. Leaves are moldy and slimy. But I like leaves so much. I once filled my classroom at school ankle-deep with them.

There is a reason for leaves. There is no reason for mowed grass. So say I.

My wife does not see it this way. There is an unspoken accusation of laziness in the air. We have been through this before. But this year a bargain has been struck in the name of the Scientific Method. Half the yard will be properly raked, and the other half will be left in the care of nature. Come summer, we shall see. And so her part is raked and mine is not. Let it be.

Like a pilot in a fog relying on limited instruments, the boy looks intently at my face for information. He knows I have leaves. He has seen them. Mine is the only yard in the neighborhood with leaves, in fact. He knows his price is right. Solemnly he holds out pencil and paper for my reply. How can I explain to him about the importance of the scientific experiment going on in my backyard?

In a way, the trees are there because of the leaves. With unbridled extravagance, zillions of seeds have helicoptered out of the sky to land like assault forces to green the earth. The leaves follow to cover, protect, warm and nourish the next generation of trees. Stony ground, rot, mold, bacteria, birds, squirrels, bugs and people—all intervene. But somehow, some make it. Some tenacious seeds take hold and hold on and hold on—for dear life. In the silence of winter's dark they prevail and plant themselves and survive to become the next generation of trees. It has been thus for eons, and we mess with the process at our peril, say I. This is important.

"My name is Donnie. I will rake your leaves. $1 a yard. I am deaf. You can write to me. I can read. I rake good."

He holds out the pencil and paper with patience and hope and goodwill.

There are times when the simplest of events call all of one's motives into question. What would I do if he wasn't deaf? What will it do for him if I say no? If I say yes? What difference? We stand in each other's long silence, inarticulate for different reasons.

In the same motion, he turns to go, and I reach for the

pencil and paper to write, solemnly: "Yes. Yes, I would like to have my leaves raked."

A grave nod from the attentive businessmanchild.

"Do you do it when they are wet?"

"Yes," he writes.

"Do you have your own rake?"

"No."

"This is a big yard—there are lots of leaves."

"Yes."

"I think I should give you two dollars."

A smile. "Three?" he writes.

A grin.

We have a contract. The rake is produced, and Donnie the deaf leaf-raker goes to work in the fast-falling November twilight. In silence he rakes. In silence I watch—through the window of the dark house. Are there any sounds at all in his mind? I wonder. Or only the hollow, empty sea-sound I get when I put my fingers in my ears as tightly as I can.

Carefully, he rakes the leaves into a large pile, as instructed.

Yes, I am thinking I will spread them out over the yard again after he is gone. I am stubborn about this.

Carefully he goes back over the yard, picking up missed leaves by hand and carrying them to the pile. He also is stubborn about his values. Raking leaves means *all* the leaves.

Signing that he must go because it is dark and he must go home to eat, he leaves the work unfinished. Having paid in advance, I wonder if he will return. At age forty-five, I am cynical.

Too cynical.

Come morning, he has returned to his task, first checking the previously raked yard for latecomers. He takes pride in his work. The yard is leaf-free. I note his picking up several of the brightest yellow leaves and putting them into the pocket of his sweatshirt, along with a whole handful of helicoptered seeds.

Rappity-rappity-rappity-rap! He reports to the door, signing that the work is done. As he walks away up the street, I see him tossing one helicoptered seed into the air at a time. Fringe benefits. I stand in my own door in my own silence, smiling at his grace. Fringe benefits.

Tomorrow I will go out and push the pile of leaves over the bank into the compost heap at the bottom of the ravine behind our house. I will do it in silence. The leaves and seeds will have to work out their destiny there this year. I could not feel right about undoing his work.

My experiment with science will have to stand aside for something more human. The leaves let go, the seeds let go, and I must let go sometimes, too, and cast my lot with another of nature's imperfect but tenacious survivors.

Hold on, Donnie, hold on.

Robert Fulghum

What a Difference a Walk Makes

Be part of the miraculous moment.

Thich Nhat Hanh

My father and I had walked together a lot, but after he underwent both heart bypass and back surgery, we faced the possibility that his long-distance hiking days were over at seventy. But miraculously, only one year after his set-backs, he was able to join me on a 180-mile coast-to-coast trek across Wales.

One late afternoon, while traversing a long, curving ridge, we came upon an elderly woman and her beagle hiking toward us. Teetering along on a walking stick, she wore a motoring cap and clutched a bunch of wildflowers.

I said hello, and after some discussion she told us that she was almost ninety. I studied her carefully and couldn't believe what great shape she was in. She seemed so fit and content.

"What's the secret to a long and happy life?" I asked.

She smiled and spoke softly, "Moments." There was a quiet pause before she carried on. "Moments are all we get. A true walker understands this."

She bid us good-bye and continued on her way, her dog

trotting a few steps in front. Just before she disappeared into the horizon, I looked back at her, plodding ahead with timeless poise and bearing, and sent a smile to my father.

She was right; that is all we get.

Bruce Northam

River Recipe

Ingredients

- Freshly melted snow from the spires of the Cascades
- Navy-blue blackberries as dark as the summer night's sky
- The stars and the planets mixed together in a puree
- Marshmallow clouds
- Wild mushrooms (can be found in any nearby heart of a forest; make sure they are finely pounded by the sleek hooves of neighboring elk)
- About 100,000 acres of lush, green farmland

Directions

1. Mix all ingredients together except for the clouds and the farmland.
2. After many moons, stop stirring and let it sit for five days. Then soak in the finest silks from India and sprinkle across a dry landscape in Washington.
3. Surround your river with the farmland and then wait until they connect.

4. Float the clouds up to the sky; wait until they have made themselves comfortable in heaven.
5. Take yourself on a walk in the misty morning and find a comfortable spot on the bank of the river. Gaze into the river until you've found your reflection. Learn something special about yourself.

Robin Andrews, age 11

Reprinted with permission of Kristin Sheldon.

More Chicken Soup?

Many of the stories and poems you have read in this book were submitted by readers like you who had read earlier *Chicken Soup for the Soul* books. We publish at least five or six *Chicken Soup for the Soul* books every year. We invite you to contribute a story to one of these future volumes.

Stories may be up to 1,200 words and must uplift or inspire. You may submit an original piece, something you have read or your favorite quotation on your refrigerator door.

To obtain a copy of our submission guidelines and a listing of upcoming *Chicken Soup* books, please write, fax or check our Web site.

Please send your submissions to:

Chicken Soup for the Soul
P.O. Box 30880
Santa Barbara, CA 93130
fax: 805-563-2945
Web site: *www.chickensoup.com*

Just send a copy of your stories and other pieces to the above address.

We will be sure that both you and the author are credited for your submission.

For information about speaking engagements, other books, audiotapes, workshops and training programs, please contact any of our authors directly.

What Is the National Audubon Society?

The Audubon mission is to conserve and restore natural ecosystems, focusing on birds, other wildlife, and their habitats for the benefit of humanity and the Earth's biological diversity.

Audubon is dedicated to protecting birds and other wildlife and the habitat that supports them. Our national network of community-based nature centers and chapters, scientific and educational programs, and advocacy on behalf of areas sustaining important bird populations, engage millions of people of all ages and backgrounds in positive conservation experiences.

Audubon's Centers, its sanctuaries and education programs are developing the next generation of conservation leaders by providing opportunities for families, students, teachers and others to learn about and enjoy the natural world. The science program is focused on connecting people with nature through projects like Audubon at Home and Great Backyard Bird Count. Audubon's volunteer Citizen Scientists participate in research and conservation action in a variety of ways, from monitoring bird populations and restoring critical wildlife habitat to implementing healthy habitat practices in their own backyards. Audubon's public policy programs are supported by a strong foundation of science, environmental education, and grassroots engagement. Working with a network of state offices, chapters and volunteers, Audubon works to protect and restore our natural heritage.

To learn more about Audubon:

Audubon
700 Broadway
New York, New York 10003
(800) 274-4201
www.audubon.org

Who Is Jack Canfield?

Jack Canfield is one of America's leading experts in the development of human potential and personal effectiveness. He is both a dynamic, entertaining speaker and a highly sought-after trainer. Jack has a wonderful ability to inform and inspire audiences toward increased levels of self-esteem and peak performance.

He is the author and narrator of several bestselling audio- and videocassette programs, including *Self-Esteem and Peak Performance, How to Build High Self-Esteem, Self-Esteem in the Classroom* and *Chicken Soup for the Soul—Live*. He is regularly seen on television shows such as *Good Morning America, 20/20* and *NBC Nightly News*. Jack has co-authored numerous books, including the *Chicken Soup for the Soul* series, *Dare to Win* and *The Aladdin Factor* (all with Mark Victor Hansen), *100 Ways to Build Self-Concept in the Classroom* (with Harold C. Wells), *Heart at Work* (with Jacqueline Miller) and *The Power of Focus* (with Les Hewitt and Mark Victor Hansen).

Jack is a regularly featured speaker for professional associations, school districts, government agencies, churches, hospitals, sales organizations and corporations. His clients have included the American Dental Association, the American Management Association, AT&T, Campbell's Soup, Clairol, Domino's Pizza, GE, ITT, Hartford Insurance, Johnson & Johnson, the Million Dollar Roundtable, NCR, New England Telephone, Re/Max, Scott Paper, TRW and Virgin Records. Jack has taught on the faculty of Income Builders International, a school for entrepreneurs.

Jack conducts an annual seven-day Training of Trainers program in the areas of self-esteem and peak performance. It attracts entrepreneurs, educators, counselors, parenting trainers, corporate trainers, professional speakers, ministers and others interested in developing their speaking and seminar-leading skills.

For further information about Jack's books, tapes and training programs, or to schedule him for a presentation, please contact:

Self-Esteem Seminars
P.O. Box 30880
Santa Barbara, CA 93130
phone: 805-563-2935 • fax: 805-563-2945
Web site: *www.jackcanfield.com*

Who Is Mark Victor Hansen?

In the area of human potential, no one is better known and more respected than Mark Victor Hansen. For more than thirty years, Mark has focused solely on helping people from all walks of life reshape their personal vision of what's possible. His powerful messages of possibility, opportunity and action have helped create startling and powerful change in thousands of organizations and millions of individuals worldwide.

He is a sought-after keynote speaker, bestselling author and marketing maven. Mark's credentials include a lifetime of entrepreneurial success, in addition to an extensive academic background. He is a prolific writer with many bestselling books such as *The One Minute Millionaire*, *The Power of Focus*, *The Aladdin Factor* and *Dare to Win*, in addition to the *Chicken Soup for the Soul* series. Mark has also made a profound influence through his extensive library of audio programs, video programs and enriching articles in the areas of big thinking, sales achievement, wealth building, publishing success, and personal and professional development.

Mark is also the founder of MEGA Book Marketing University and Building Your MEGA Speaking Empire. Both are annual conferences where Mark coaches and teaches new and aspiring authors, speakers and experts on building lucrative publishing and speaking careers.

His energy and exuberance travel still further through mediums such as television (*Oprah*, *CNN* and *The Today Show*), print (*Time*, *U.S. News & World Report*, *USA Today*, *New York Times* and *Entrepreneur*) and countless radio and newspaper interviews as he assures our planet's people that *"you can easily create the life you deserve."*

As a passionate philanthropist and humanitarian, he's been the recipient of numerous awards that honor his entrepreneurial spirit, philanthropic heart and business acumen, including the prestigious Horatio Alger Award for his extraordinary life achievements, which stand as a powerful example that the free enterprise system still offers opportunity to all.

Mark Victor Hansen is an enthusiastic crusader of what's possible and is driven to make the world a better place.

Mark Victor Hansen & Associates, Inc.
P.O. Box 7665 • Newport Beach, CA 92658
phone: 949-764-2640 • fax: 949-722-6912
FREE resources online at: *www.markvictorhansen.com*

Who Is Steve Zikman?

Steve Zikman is the author of the highly acclaimed book, *The Power of Travel: A Passport to Adventure, Discovery and Growth* and coauthor of *Chicken Soup for the Traveler's Soul*. Born and raised in Canada, Steve Zikman has ventured through more than fifty countries on six continents.

Steve is an avid nature lover and outdoor enthusiast, especially when it comes to hiking, camping, canoeing and sea kayaking.

A dynamic and captivating keynote speaker and certified workshop facilitator in the travel and outdoor adventure industries, Steve uses seasoned and successful practices to help audiences shift their perspective, conquer their fears and embrace life's challenges.

Steve is the founder of *GOscape.com*, providing powerful tools to enrich, enhance and expand the appreciation of travel, the outdoors and the adventure of life.

As a member of the American Society of Journalists and Authors, Steve is a contributor to a variety of online and print media, including *Interline Adventures, SoulfulLiving.com* and *Personal Journaling*. He has appeared on hundreds of national and international radio and television programs, including ABC, CBS, NBC and FOX.

When he's not speaking or writing, Steve can often be found exploring the majestic mountains near his home in Los Angeles.

For further information on Steve Zikman's inspirational speaking programs, consulting services and writings, or to schedule him for a presentation, please contact:

GOscape.com
P.O. Box 292581
Los Angeles, CA 90029
phone: 323-644-9064
fax: 323-644-6864
e-mail: *explore@GOscape.com*
Web site: *www.GOscape.com*

Contributors

Several stories were taken from previously published sources, such as books, magazines, newspapers and online publications. Most of the other pieces were sent in from readers of previous *Chicken Soup for the Soul* books and others who responded to our requests for submissions. To learn more about our contributors, please refer to the information provided below.

Linda Armstrong is a senior editor for *Exhibitor* magazine, as well as a freelance writer specializing in domestic and international travel guides, how-to books and short fiction. She welcomes inquiries, offers and comments at *larmstro@pressenter.com, larmstrong@exhibitormagazine.com* or 651-460-6589.

Norm Augustine is the retired chairman and CEO of Lockheed Martin Corporation, a former under secretary of the Army and a former member of the faculty of Princeton. He has served as the chairman of the American Red Cross, the Boy Scouts of America and the National Academy of Engineering. He lives in the Washington, D.C. area.

Linda Swartz Bakkar is from the Puget Sound region of the Pacific Northwest. She enjoys hiking and skiing with family and friends. Linda continues to publish written accounts of her backpacking adventures that inspire people—especially older women—to explore the backcountry. Please reach her at *lbakkar@hotmail.com.*

Linda Ballou lives on an island in southwest Florida where her favorite activity is mucking about in mangrove swamps. She works at a historical museum, does freelance writing and sells used books on the Internet. She escapes to tropical rainforests as often as possible. She can be contacted at *lindabai@aol.com.*

Nancy Blakey is the author of the Mudpies Activity Book Series: *Recipes for Invention: 101 Alternatives to Television; Lotions Potions and Slim;* and *Boredom Busters.* Her latest book is *Go Outside! Activities for Outdoor Adventures.* Nancy and her family continue to head up to Alaska every summer to work and play. She can be reached at *www.nancyblakey.com.*

Blaine Bonnar is an IT manager in Toronto, Canada, and currently lives on a farm just north of the city with his wife Sandra, sons Ryan and Matthew, and far too many family pets to list! Their daughter Cassie continues to be an integral part of their lives. Blaine's e-mail is *bbonnar@sympatico.ca.*

Dan Buettner has set three Guinness World Records for cycling across five continents. He created the Quest series of interactive expeditions, which he sold to Classroom Connect and is now used by hundreds of thousands of students annually. His award-winning books include *Africatrek, Sovietrek* and *MayaQuest*. Reach him at *dan@classroom.com* or see his net expedition at *www.classroom.com*.

William Canty's cartoons have appeared in many national magazines, including the *Saturday Evening Post, Good Housekeeping, Better Homes and Gardens, Woman's World, National Review* and *Medical Economics*. His syndicated feature *All About Town* runs in thirty-five newspapers. Bill can be reached at P.O. Box 1053, S. Wellfleet, MA 02663. Phone and fax: 508-349-7549. You can e-mail him at *wcanty@attbi.com*. His Web site is *www.reuben.org/Canty*.

Dave Carpenter has been a full-time cartoonist since 1981. His cartoons have appeared in such publications as *Harvard Business Review, Barron's, The Wall Street Journal, Better Homes and Gardens, Good Housekeeping, Reader's Digest*, as well as numerous other publications and *Chicken Soup for the Soul* books. Dave can be contacted at *davecarp@ncn.net*.

Lisa Cavanaugh is executive director of Camp Pacific Heartland, a Los Angeles–based nonprofit that provides summer camping opportunities for children and adolescents infected with and affected by HIV/AIDS.

Josh Cohen, C.H.T., founder of InnerQuest Adventures, offers eco-tours designed especially for wildlife enthusiasts, available in Costa Rica, Belize and other rainforest destinations. A renowned hypnotherapist and life coach, Josh also developed the nationally acclaimed HeroQuest Adventure, a spiritual journey that unleashes nature's power to transform lives. Learn more about both types of adventures at *www.innerquest.com* or 1-800-990-4376.

Diane Graff Cooney received her master's degree in counseling and guidance in 1980, and was the high-school counselor in Pagosa Springs, Colorado, for eight years after teaching business for two years. Diane has written an entire manuscript about Blair's young life and brave struggle in his fifteen-month battle with leukemia. Please reach her at *judd@juddcooney.com*.

Nancy Coulter-Parker is the editor-in-chief of *Hooked on the Outdoors* magazine. Growing up in Vancouver, British Columbia, helped nurture her love for the outdoors. She now spends time outside under the blue skies of Boulder, Colorado, where she resides with her husband and daughter.

Lynne Cox received her Bachelor of Arts degree from the University of California, Santa Barbara, in 1979. She writes, and gives seminars and motivational lectures. Her first book, *Swimming Beyond Borders*, will be published by Knopf. Lynne is working on a second book, as well as some children's stories, a major swim and a movie.

Charles Doersch received his MFA from Columbia University and is an art instructor at Front Range Community College in Boulder, Colorado, where he teaches art appreciation, humanities and writing. With his partner, Sean, he has trekked across Africa, Australia, North America, Polynesia, and parts of Asia and Europe on camels, elephants, horses, bamboo rafts, trucks, trains, ketches, tuktuks and matatus. Charles has produced three children's books with Sean, and has also published magazine articles, nature articles and poems. E-mail him at *Bergbock@aol.com*.

Lois Donahue is an eclectic writer who draws on a medical background and her love for travel. She has traveled to seven continents and sailed to many ports. A keen observer of people and places, her stories paint vivid and luring reflections of her experiences. Her work has been published in magazines and travel brochures. A love of sailing prompted this lifelong Buckeye to now make her home on the shores of the Chesapeake Bay. E-mail Lois at *Loisdonahue@dmv.com*.

Janice Duvall has won gold medals the past three years at the Water Skiers with Disabilities (WSDA) National Tournament, and was the Female Athlete of the Year in 2001. Her goal is to win the world record in all three events (slalom, trick and jump). She also hopes to bring other hemiplegics to the sport, and prays her success is an encouragement to other challenged athletes. She can be contacted at (318) 868-6069 or *jjduvall@earthlink.net*.

Mary Emerick has been a firefighter and wilderness ranger for the National Park Service and other federal agencies. Currently, she is the manager for the Steens Mountain Wilderness in Oregon and does most of her writing while camped in a tent in the mountains.

Suzanne English-Walker and her husband Bill were raised in Quincy, Illinois. They and their family moved to southern Missouri eighteen years ago to be closer to their beloved Roaring River State Park. They have retired and are traveling throughout the United States, as Jon would have liked to do.

Laura Evans founded Expedition Inspiration, the assault by seventeen breast-cancer survivors on the 23,000-foot Mt. Aconcagua, raising $2.3 million for cancer research. *The Climb of My Life*, published by Harper, is the story of her inspiring recovery from breast cancer. Laura passed away in 2000 of an unrelated brain tumor. More information is available at *www.expeditioninspiration.org*.

Virginia Frati is the executive director of the Wildlife Rescue Center of the Hamptons, Inc., a not-for-profit corporation dedicated to the rescue and rehabilitation of injured, orphaned or sick animals in order to return them to the wild. The Center may be contacted via e-mail at *wrwrch@aol.com*.

Stephen Geez holds bachelor's and master's degrees from the University of Michigan. A musician at heart, he spends too much of his time writing and not enough on scuba diving. Look for more at *www.StephenGeez.com*.

Garth Gilchrist's Cascade and Sierra Mountain boyhood inspired his work as an environmental educator, poet and storyteller. He visits hundreds of organizations and schools yearly, inspiring a deeper sense of our relatedness to land and to each other. Garth's recordings of nature adventures and children's stories are highly acclaimed. Contact Garth at *GarthTales@aol.com*.

Anne Goodrich is a Web designer at the Kalamazoo Regional Educational Service Agency in Kalamazoo, Michigan. This mother of three is the creator of *OhAngel!com* (*www.OhAngel.com*), an inspirational and angel e-card Web site. Ms. Goodrich can be contacted through her Web site or by e-mailing her at *webmaster@ohangel.com*.

Carolyn Griffin is a mother, wife, grandmother and freelance writer from Tucson, Arizona, who spends a half hour every week reading her own stories to fourth-graders. She enjoys working with plants, camping, doing handicrafts, crocheting and writing.

Linda M. Hasselstrom writes, ranches and conducts writing retreats for women on the ranch homesteaded by her grandfather in 1899. Her Web site, *www.windbreakhouse.com,* provides details about her published poetry and nonfiction. Contact her at *info@windbreakhouse.com.*

Sharon R. Haynes studied creative writing at Kent State University. During her study days, she received KSU's Virginia Perryman Award in writing. Sharon has written feature articles for local newspapers for over twenty years. Her stories have also appeared in several Christian magazines, such as Billy Graham's *Decisions* magazine, *Faith and Friends, Family Digest* and *Woman's Touch.* Sharon and her husband Richard have a grown son and daughter. They now enjoy traveling, staying at bed and breakfast inns, hiking, and photography. You may reach her at *emily@maplecom.com.*

Robert Hedderman promoted concerts through the '70s, received a Bachelor of Science in marine biology in 1984, and then founded a restaurant in 1986. He now lives in northern New Mexico where he is attempting to develop a career as a screenwriter and actor. He may be contacted at *Bhedd48@hotmail.com.*

James Hert is a business systems project manager. He and his wife Amy live and work in the Lansing, Michigan, area where they enjoy many outdoor activities such as fishing, cross-country skiing and mushroom hunting. Many a winter evening will find Jim writing while Amy creates watercolor paintings. Contact Jim at *jamyeshert@cablespeed.com.*

Kristin Hostetter was *Backpacker's* gear editor for seven years. Aside from full-time momhood (two boys, Charlie and Joe), she currently writes a monthly column for *Backpacker* called "The Answer Chick" and a bimonthly column for the *Seattle Post-Intelligencer* called "Gearing Up." Her new book, *Don't Forget the Duct Tape: Tips and Tricks for Repairing Outdoor Gear,* comes out this summer.

Norm Houze is a doctor of natural medicine and chiropractic, practicing in Bloomington, Indiana. He is the director of deCyclesIndiana, a unique youth-development program offering long-distance summer bicycle trips designed to challenge the body, mind and spirit. You can reach Norm at *nhouze@kiva.net.* For information about the deCycles, please visit the Web site at *www. geocities.com/decyclesindiana.*

In his book, *Blind Courage,* **Bill Irwin** is portrayed as the only blind person to complete the Appalachian Trail. His historic hike began in Georgia and ended nine months later in Maine—an inspiring example of overcoming the odds! Purchase his books and products by contacting: Irwin Associates, Inc., 207-564-6922, *www.billirwin.com, info@billirwin.com.*

Joyce Johnson is a homemaker, mother of four children and grandmother of four grandchildren. She is an out-of-doors enthusiast and enjoys camping, hiking and backpacking. Joyce has hiked the Grand Canyon and completed the 2,116-mile-long Appalachian Trail. Please reach her at 210 Johnson Lane, Anna, IL 62906.

Stan R. Kid is a police sergeant and freelance writer who lives on Long Island, New York, with his wife and three children. Born in the Bronx, he learned a love of fishing while watching his father during summers on Long Island's South Shore. He is not as easily charmed by seagulls. He can be reached at *Writerman@onebox.com.*

Wendy Knight is a freelance writer and climber living in Vermont. She received her bachelor of science degree from Cornell University in 1987. Ms. Knight's latest book is *Making Connections: Mother-Daughter Travel Adventures.* For further information, go to *www.wendyknight.com.*

Charles Kuralt's job for twenty-eight years was to drive the back roads of America in a CBS camper. More than 600 episodes of *On the Road with Charles Kuralt* were filed from every state in America. Audiences will long remember the rich, slow, mahogany tones of his voice on *Sunday Morning with Charles Kuralt.* He leaves us seven bestselling books, so many stories and so many memories.

Mel Lees spent about twenty years as a mountain climber. Next he became a racewalker, competing internationally. He is a retired life-insurance salesman whose second career is writing. He can be reached at 805-543-3457 or *Lemseel@aol.com.*

Stephen Leggatt received his undergraduate degree from Brown University, master's degrees from the University of Pennsylvania and the University of California, San Diego, and juris doctor from the University of Michigan. Stephen and Paul (the subject of Stephen's essay) have helped to found USAccessible, a nonprofit corporation organized to help disabled persons. Information on how you can help is available at *www.usaccessible.org.*

June Lemen is a freelance writer in southern New Hampshire, where she lives with her husband and daughter. She writes a newspaper column for the *Nashua Telegraph* that appears every Tuesday. Please reach her at *june.lemen@verizon.net.*

Patricia Lorenz, who enjoys all the nature she can cram into her busy writing/ speaking life, is one of the top contributors to the *Chicken Soup* books, with stories in seventeen of them. She's the author of over 400 articles, a contributing writer for fifteen *Daily Guideposts*, an award-winning newspaper columnist, and the author of four books. Her two latest, *Life's Too Short to Fold Your Underwear* and *Grab the Extinguisher, My Birthday Cake's on Fire* can be ordered through *Guideposts Books* at *www.dailyguideposts.com/store*. To contact Patricia for speaking opportunities, e-mail her at *patricialorenz@juno.com.*

Donald B. Louria, M.D., is a professor in the Department of Preventive Medicine at the University of Medicine and Dentistry of New Jersey-New Jersey Medical School. He is a graduate of Harvard College and Harvard Medical School. His major focus currently is developing programs to help people live longer, healthier lives. Contact him at 973-972-0125, fax 973-972-0025 or *louriado@umdnj.edu*. Visit his Web site at *www.healthfullife.umdnj.edu.*

Derek Lundy is the author of *Godforsaken Sea: The True Story of a Race Through the World's Most Dangerous Waters*. His next book, about an ancestor's square-rigger voyage around Cape Horn in the last days of sail, was published in September 2002. Derek discovered his outdoor soul at sea.

Tom Lusk, a lifelong outdoorsman, is a Parks Canada employee, amateur naturalist and outdoor writer. "Goose Island" is from a work-in-progress entitled, *Super Natural Encounters*, a collection of photographs and essays dealing with Tom's firsthand experiences in the natural world. Contact Tom at *tomlusk@ hotmail.com.*

Born in Seymour, Indiana, in 1935, Guy Lustig attended Seymour schools, Butler University, (BA, 1963), Indiana University Law School and University of Indianapolis. Married with a son and a daughter, he now lives in Indianapolis and enjoys golf, photography and his granddaughter, Annabel.

Bruce Masterman is a writer and photographer from High River, Alberta, Canada. He is the author of *Heading Out: A Celebration of the Great Outdoors in Calgary and Southern Alberta* and *Paradise Preserved: The Ann and Sandy Cross Conservation Area*. Bruce can be reached via his Web site at *www.brucemasterman.com.*

Willa Mavis is an innkeeper, cookbook author and TV cooking show host. She has worked as a secretary, nursery school teacher, CBC Radio freelancer, media buyer for her own advertising company and a fashion consultant. Willa doesn't know what she wants to be when she "grows up." Please reach her at *spa@innonthecove.com*.

Linda Mihatov has cared for animals for over twenty years as a licensed wildlife rehabilitator and veterinary technician. Her husband and sons have shared their help and home with many wild and domestic critters. A published author, Linda's writing centers on animals and family. She can be reached at *wildlife@tellurian.net*.

T. Edward Nickens is a freelance writer based in Raleigh, North Carolina. More examples of his writing can be found at *www.tedwardnickens.com*.

A member of the famed 1996 IMAX expedition, **Jamling Tenzing Norgay** was able to follow in the footsteps of his legendary father, Tenzing Norgay Sherpa, who with Sir Edmund Hillary was the first to summit Mount Everest in 1953. He runs Tenzing Norgay Adventures and is based in Darjeeling, India.

Bruce Northam's books include *Globetrotter Dogma: 100 Canons for Escaping the Rat Race and Exploring the World; In Search of Adventure: A Wild Travel Anthology* and *The Frugal Globetrotter*. His multimedia presentations, held at universities and seminar centers nationwide, celebrate the spirit of circling the globe many times *freestyle*. His next project is American Detour. Details on his books and world travel presentations are on *AmericanDetour.com*.

Sally Wendkos Olds has written extensively about child and adult development and relationships. She is an award-winning author or coauthor of ten books and more than 200 articles. Her most recent book is *A Balcony in Nepal: Glimpses of a Himalayan Village*. Reach her through her Web site at *www.sallywendkosolds.com*.

Jennifer Olsson, author of *Cast Again: Tales of a Fly-Fishing Guide*, resides with her husband in Sweden during the summer months, teaching and guiding fly-fishers. She can be reached at *www.scandiwestflyfishing.com*. She wishes to thank Tim and Lena Conlan of *www.crossinglatitudes.com* for providing the opportunity to sea kayak in Norway.

Delia Owens, with her husband Mark, studied wildlife in Africa for twenty-three years. They wrote the international bestsellers, *Cry of the Kalahari* and *The Eye of the Elephant,* and have published in *Natural History, Nature* and *International Wildlife*. Delia received her Ph.D. at the University of California, Davis. They continue their work through the Owens Foundation for Wildlife Conservation at *www.owens-foundation.org*.

Jewel Palovak is the program director for Grizzly People, a nonprofit organization dedicated to preservation of wilderness and endangered species. A USC graduate, she is coauthor of *Among Grizzlies* (HarperCollins, 1997) and currently lives in Malibu, California.

Gil Parker is a Canadian writer and engineer with experience in Arabia, India and Russia. A life member of Alpine Club and a certified yoga teacher, he has written *Aware of the Mountain,* a book combining mountaineering and yoga. His book about modern Russian is at the publisher's. See *www.telus.net/ascent.*

Penny Porter is the wife of a retired rancher, Bill, mother of six, grandmother of eight, and has always been in love with life and family. She is "one of the most successful freelancers ever to hit *Reader's Digest,*" and has published in a wide range of national magazines, including *Arizona Highways, Catholic Digest* and *Guideposts.* She is the current president of The Society of Southwestern Authors, and her work has appeared in seven of the *Chicken Soup for the Soul* books. Signed copies of her fourth book, *Heartstrings and Tail-Tuggers,* are available through *wporter202@aol.com.*

Lisa Price graduated from Shippensburg State College in Pennsylvania (B.A., English, 1980). In 1990, when her company was sold, she used the severance pay to hike the Appalachian Trail. Shortly after completing her hike, she moved to Maine, where she is a registered guide and writer. Reach her at *lisalprice@hotmail.com.*

Heather Trexler Remoff, a freelance writer and anthropologist, lives in Eagles Mere, Pennsylvania. Her published work has been featured in periodicals in the United States and Canada. She is the author of *Sexual Choice* (E.P. Dutton, 1985) and *February Light* (St. Martin's Press, 1997). Please contact her through *www.theomnibus.org.*

Doug Rennie taught advanced placement classes in American and European history before moving to Portland, Oregon, in 1991 to become a full-time writer. He writes a monthly travel column, "On the Road," for *Runner's World* magazine, and Creative Arts Books recently published a collection of his short fiction, *Badlands.* Reach him at *rainguy@earthlink.net.*

River of Words was founded in 1995 to promote literacy, the arts and environmental awareness. This nonprofit organization, in affiliation with The Library of Congress, conducts a free annual international poetry and art contest for children in kindergarten through twelfth grade on the theme of "watersheds." Robin Andrews was a finalist. Visit *www.riverofwords.org.*

Ferris Robinson is the mother of three boys and lives in Lookout Mountain, Georgia. She and her husband are co-owners of Walden 19th Century Antique Log Homes (*www.waldenloghomes.com*). She is also the author of *The Gorgeless Gourmet's Cookbook,* a collection of easy, low-fat recipes she published after her husband's heart surgery at age thirty-four. Contact her at *Ferrisrobinson@cs.com.*

Leigh Rubin took his first steps on the path to cartoon success by creating a publishing company and distributing his own greeting cards. His two most recent collections include *Rubes Bible Cartoons* and the award-winning collection *Rubes—Then and Now*. As one of the most popular single-panel cartoons, *Rubes* is now distributed by Creators Syndicate to more than 400 newspapers worldwide. Rubin is married and has three sons.

Gregory J. Rummo writes columns for several New Jersey newspapers. His book, *The View from the Grass Roots*, an anthology of these commentaries, is available at a discount from Publishers Direct Bookstore at *www.pdbookstore.com*. Contact Rummo at *GregoryJRummo@aol.com*.

Hope Saxton is an author from Ontario, Canada. Her work has appeared in *A 6th Bowl of Chicken Soup for the Soul* and *Chicken Soup for the Preteen Soul*. She was featured in a "Remembering Your Spirit" segment of the *Oprah* show. Her motivational speaking has taken her to schools and churches, where she speaks out on child abuse prevention and school violence. Contact Hope at *Hopewrites@yahoo.com*.

Germaine W. Shames, an itinerant adventurer, has written from six continents—soon to be seven—on topics ranging from environmental politics to the plight of street children. Winner of the Literary Fellowship from her home state of Arizona, Shames is author of *Transcultural Odysseys: The Evolving Global Consciousness*, available from Intercultural Press (1-800-370-2665/ *www.interculturalpress.com*).

John Soennichsen is a writer who lives in the Pacific Northwest and has published more than 100 articles, essays, interviews and human-interest pieces for regional and national magazines. This story is an excerpt from a chapter of his forthcoming nonfiction book, *Death Valley Diary*.

Lin Sutherland writes humor and travel from her horse ranch in Austin, Texas. She is published in numerous national magazines and anthologies. She still travels with Mama (age ninety) and still admires Abraham Lincoln. You may reach her at *linsuth@juno.com*.

Since 1967, **Nancy Sweetland** has published over 250 feature articles, fifty-five short stories for adults, fifty-five short stories and poems for children, and six picture books. She's won forty-seven regional and national writing awards. You can reach her at *nsweetland@prodigy.net*.

Marie Sylvester studied graphic design before realizing that writing is her true passion. She is a freelance writer and borough historian for the tiny little community of Interlaken at the New Jersey Shore. She enjoys walking, reading and collecting anything old, for both preservation and aesthetic purposes. She is currently working on a second novel while attempting to publish the first. Feel free to drop her a line regarding her work at *mmsylvest@aol.com*.

Allegra Taylor is the author of several books including the bestselling *I Fly Out with Bright Feathers* and *Ladder to the Moon*. She teaches creative-writing workshops in London and abroad and also has a private healing practice. She has raised six children and has eleven grandchildren. Check out *www.allegrataylor.com*.

Barbara Earl Thomas is a Seattle-based painter and writer. She has artwork in collections throughout the United States. In 1998–2000, she received The Seattle Arts Commission award for new creative nonfiction. Her essays have appeared in numerous publications and anthologies. *Storm Watch: The Art of Barbara Earl Thomas* was published in spring 1998 by the University of Washington Press.

Brenda Timpson received her B.A., B.Ed., from Queen's University in Kingston, Ontario. She teaches primary and junior grades in Frankford, Ontario. Brenda enjoys camping, canoeing and playing her guitar.

Carol Troesch received her Bachelor of Arts in communications from the University of Evansville in 1989. She is owner of The Write Stuff, a freelance writing company, writes columns for several newspapers, and produces *inkspots*, a quarterly "fun and free" newsletter for the entire family. Please reach her at *writstuf@psci.net.*

Jon Turk is an adventure writer who has kayaked and climbed in the Arctic, bicycled through the Gobi Desert, and skied in Central Asia. Jon's recent book, *Cold Oceans*, explores expedition success and failure. He speaks on outdoor adventure and our daily lives. Contact Jon at *jonturk@montana.com* or see *www.coldoceans.com*.

Carolyn and **Norman Vaughan** live in Alaska in a one-room log cabin near Mt. McKinley. Carolyn plans trips for groups and families visiting Alaska. Norman has written two books about his life, which can be ordered online at *www adventurequestinc.com*. They can be reached at *Cvaughan@adventurequestinc.com*.

Zach Wahl received his Bachelor of Arts summa cum laude, from Dickinson College in 1998. He is a government consultant in the Washington, D.C. area.

Christine Watt was born and educated in England and has worked throughout Europe and North America as an editor, nonfiction writer and animal-rights advocate. Currently, she is writing fiction in Oregon. For a list of her other publications, please e-mail *cwalt50@hotmail.com*. Her passions include opera, tennis, painting and languages.

Star Weiss is a freelance writer, enthusiastic hiker, cookbook editor and nature lover living in Victoria, British Columbia, Canada. She also teaches journalism at Victoria's Western Academy of Photography. A former New Yorker, Star enjoys introducing readers to Canada's West Coast. She can be reached at 250-478-9565 or *starweiss@shaw.ca*.

Jim Whittaker, the first American to reach the summit of Mt. Everest, was born in Seattle in 1929 to a family that revered the natural world and never put bounds on what he could accomplish. Today, Jim shares his enthusiasm for adventure—on land and sea—with his wife and sons.

Karen Lynn Williams has lived in Malawi, Africa and Haiti. She is the author of a number of picture books and chapter books for children, several of which are based on her experiences living abroad. They include *Galimoto* (Lothrop), *Baseball and Butterflies* (Lothrop), *First Grade King* (Clarion), *Applebaum's Garage* (Clarion), *When Africa Was Home* (Orchard), *Tap-Tap* (Clarion), *Painted Dreams* (Lothrop), *A Real Christmas This Year* (Clarion) and *One Thing I'm Good At* (Lothrop).

Doersch. First published in *Colleen Sutherland's Nature Notes* column in the *Seymour Times-Press Syndicate,* Wisconsin.

On Top of the World. Reprinted by permission of Diane Graff Cooney. ©2001 Diane Graff Cooney.

The Emily Tree. Reprinted by permission of Carol J. Troesch. ©1999 Carol J. Troesch.

Paddling Down North. Reprinted by permission of Gilbert M. Parker. ©2002 Gilbert M. Parker.

Mosquitoes. Reprinted by permission of Guy Edward Lustig. ©2000 Guy Edward Lustig.

Cassie. Reprinted by permission of Blaine Bonnar. ©2001 Blaine Bonnar.

Picking Marshmallows. Reprinted by permission of Nancy Sweetland. ©1980 Nancy Sweetland.

Climbing with the Kennedys. ©1999 by Jim Whittaker. Text from the book, *Jim Whittaker: A Life on the Edge* included with permission of the publisher, The Mountaineers, Seattle, WA.

In the Hills of Africa. Reprinted by permission of Dan Buettner. ©1998 Dan Buettner.

Maps. Reprinted by permission of Norman R. Augustine. ©1985 Norman R. Augustine

Wild Turkeys and Cat Calls. Reprinted by permission of Delia Owens, Ph.D. ©2000 Delia Owens, Ph.D.

Snow Days. Reprinted by permission of Marie Sylvester. ©1999 Marie Sylvester.

Trouble on the Rips. Reprinted by permission of Bill Irwin. ©1998 Bill Irwin.

Fishing with Robby. Reprinted by permission of Ferris Kelly Robinson. ©2000 Ferris Kelly Robinson.

Bypass. Reprinted by permission of Lisa Price. ©1999 Lisa Price.